D0947052

Voices from the Warsaw Ghetto

Voices from the Warsaw Ghetto

Writing Our History

Edited and with an Introduction by
DAVID G. ROSKIES

Foreword by
SAMUEL D. KASSOW

A companion volume to the Posen Library of Jewish Culture and Civilization

Yale UNIVERSITY PRESS
New Haven and London

Published with assistance from the foundation established in memory of Amasa Stone Mather of the Class of 1907, Yale College.

Yale University Press books may be purchased in quantity for educational, business, or promotional use. For information, please e-mail sales.press@yale.edu (U.S. office) or sales@yaleup.co.uk (U.K. office).

Set in Minion type by IDS Infotech Ltd.
Printed in the United States of America.

Library of Congress Control Number: 2018958129
ISBN 978-0-300-23672-9 (hardcover : alk. paper)

A catalogue record for this book is available from the British Library.

This paper meets the requirements of ANSI/NISO Z39.48-1992 (Permanence of Paper).

10 9 8 7 6 5 4 3 2 1

To the memory of
Leyb and Esther Rochman,
two of the surviving remnant

Contents

Foreword

Samuel D. Kassow

The members of Oyneg Shabes had few illusions about their survival, but they believed in their mission. Theirs was a battle for memory, and their weapons were pen and paper. In Majdanek, Ringelblum's teacher, the historian Isaac Schipper, told a fellow inmate that what was usually known about murdered peoples was what their killers chose to say about them. The members of Oyneg Shabes did all they could to make sure that the Germans would not have the last word.

In the last weeks and months of their lives they consoled themselves with the belief that when their time capsules surfaced, they would make a difference. They would shock the world's conscience and make it a better place. Gustawa Jarecka, asked by Ringelblum to describe the roundups on the streets of Warsaw in the summer of 1942, hoped that her words would hurl "a stone under history's wheel,"[1] that the horrors she saw

1. [Gustawa Jarecka], "The Last Stage of Resettlement Is Death," in *To Live with Honor and Die with Honor: Selected Documents from the Warsaw Ghetto Underground Archives "O.S." (Oneg Shabbath)*, ed. Joseph Kermish (Jerusalem: Yad Vashem, 1986), p. 704.

would never happen again. The seventeen-year-old David Graber wrote in his final testament, written as he buried the first cache of the archive in August 1942, "What we were unable to cry and shriek out to the world we buried in the ground. . . . I would love to see the moment in which the great treasure will be dug up and scream the truth at the world. So the world may know all. So the ones who did not live through it may be glad, and we may feel like veterans with medals on our chest. We would be the fathers, the teachers and educators of the future."[2]

But it would be safe to say that David Graber's hopes went unfulfilled. The tight-knit band of comrades forged by Ringelblum did not become the "teachers and educators" of the future. Even as interest in the Holocaust increased in the 1970s and '80s, few people paid much attention to the archive. Much time passed before the writings of Oyneg Shabes finally found an audience of interested scholars and readers. Very little appeared at all until the late 1980s. Even today the story of Oyneg Shabes is largely unknown.

Why was this so?

One major reason was that the Germans murdered the archive's natural readership, the millions of Polish Jews who would have best understood the ethos and aspirations of Oyneg Shabes—a multilingual readership that was very much at home in Yiddish, Polish, and Hebrew. Even in defeat, Hitler still won his war against these eastern European Jews, whom the Nazis especially loathed as the biological and cultural core of world Jewry. No Jewish communities in the world before the war had been as nationally conscious or as culturally creative as Polish

2. Samuel D. Kassow, *Who Will Write Our History? Emanuel Ringelblum, the Warsaw Ghetto, and the Oyneg Shabes Archive* (Bloomington: Indiana University Press, 2007), p. 3.

(and Lithuanian) Jewry, despite, or perhaps because of, escalating economic and political difficulties. And Oyneg Shabes was a direct product of that prewar cultural milieu, where Jewish historians held a special place of honor as fighters who used their craft to defend Jewish honor and protect Jewish rights.

Ringelblum and Oyneg Shabes drew their inspiration from the ethos of the prewar YIVO, the Yiddish Scientific Institute founded in Berlin in 1925. The YIVO sought to convince Jews to know themselves and to collect the documents and build the archives that would make that possible. A stateless people without an army needed self-knowledge and self-respect. The YIVO wanted to study the Jews as a living community and to do so in Yiddish, the language of the Jewish masses. Everything that concerned Jews was important: their history, their folklore, their food, their jokes, how they raised their children, the songs they sang. Unbound by the constraints of conventional academia, the YIVO brought different disciplines together: psychology, history, folklore, philology, literary studies—all in an effort to study Jewish life "from the ground up" and not just as a record of intellectual and rabbinic elites. The YIVO brought scholars and ordinary Jews together. History by the people and for the people used the study of past and present to lay the groundwork for a better future.

Until 1942, when chilling rumors of mass murder turned into horrible reality, Oyneg Shabes to a large extent continued the YIVO's mission in the Warsaw Ghetto: collecting (*zamlen* in Yiddish) as a national mission and as a collective endeavor. Ringelblum, as he pointed out in his essay on the archive, wanted to study every possible aspect of Polish Jewish life during the war. No detail was too small, nothing was unimportant. And that meant everything, the good as well as the bad: corruption and demoralization along with self-sacrifice and decency, favoritism and class conflict alongside nobility and solidarity. The knowledge that Jews gained about themselves would help them rebuild after the war, identify leaders who failed, respect their own national resilience, and gain more insight into their fraught but critical relationship with their Polish neighbors.

It was even more important, Ringelblum believed, for the archive to collect as much as possible in real time. In the ghetto, life changed rapidly, and almost invariably for the worse. What seemed important today could well be entirely forgotten tomorrow. Ringelblum considered it crucial that the archive focus on the here and now, to "work badly" and to write "as if the war was already over."[3]

Ringelblum wanted the archive to penetrate the microcosms of ghetto life, to enter the communities of the courtyards and the house committees. He wanted writing that recorded the pulse of Jewish life and the flow of Jewish time.

What the archive collected in its early days would have been irretrievably forgotten had it waited even half a year. "Real time" meant recording a community that was not yet destroyed, voices that were not yet stilled, folk humor that was not yet blunted. Shimon Huberband's collection of Jewish folklore from the early days of the occupation—jokes, messianic hopes, stories—was a key example of the YIVO method at work. So was Peretz Opoczynski's study of one courtyard where simple Jews, who could have been characters in a prewar Yiddish novel, gossiped, bickered, traded rumors, and tried to figure out how to survive. The brilliant young Polish-language poet Władysław Szlengel in his poem "Telephone" described the deep feelings of alienation and abandonment that he felt in the ghetto,

3. See his "Oyneg Shabes," in this volume.

sharing no common language with the Yiddish-speaking Jewish masses and yet finding little friendship and support from the Poles whose culture he shared.

By mid-1941 the tribulations of 1939 and 1940 seemed like a picnic. Life in the ghetto became more dire, and for those without money to buy food, their access to soup kitchens only prolonged a drawn-out process of slow starvation. Leyb Goldin's Arke traces this process minute by minute, hour by hour, in a tug-of-war between total obsession with hunger and a lingering sense of humanity still contained in the written word. While Goldin and Opoczynski were writing before zero hour—the beginning of mass murder—the writings of Chaim Kaplan and Rabbi Kalonymus Shapira reflect the slow transition from rumor to horror that gripped more and more Jews in the spring of 1942. Kaplan struggles with the devastating news from Lublin, while Shapira tells his disciples that they were not to blame for their suffering. God was not punishing them for their sins but weeping with them. Would the Piaseczner Rebbe have said this in 1939? Probably not. But by July 1942 he had grasped that what he was seeing had never happened before in Jewish history.

When the mass murder began in 1942, Oyneg Shabes reached a breaking point. Most of its members perished, and those who survived often returned home to find their loved ones taken away. In the summer of 1942 Ringelblum could barely finish a sentence, much less an essay. But somehow the archive kept on going. Harried and hunted, the dwindling number of comrades grouped around Ringelblum described the deportations, took down accounts of the death camps, sent information to London, and even studied the traumatized and shattered Jewish community that was left in the ghetto after the first phase of the deportations ended in September 1942. Ringelblum himself recovered his emotional balance, in the fall of

1942, and now searched for answers to painful questions. Were the Jewish police and Gestapo agents marginal outliers, or did they reflect a moral rot that had begun in Jewish society long before the war? And how, Ringelblum asked, had the Germans managed to deport close to three hundred thousand Jews with hardly any physical resistance?

Now the surviving writers of Oyneg Shabes looked into the abyss and searched for words to somehow convey what they saw and what they felt. Szlengel's "Things" traced the steady tightening of the noose, the narrowing of space, the steady impoverishment of previously wealthy Jews, and the final journey in the cattle car. After 275,000 Jews have been sent to Treblinka, Yehoshue Perle is one of the "lucky ones" who received a number, 4580. No more names, just a number. Bitter irony, self-blame, vicious anger at the Judenrat, outrage at the conduct of his fellow Jews all come together in a searing essay written by someone who knows that he is sitting in a trap and sees no way out. Auerbach's "Yizkor, 1943" searches for the right words to describe not only murdered Jews but an entire murdered city. Ultimately, she can only turn to the liturgy of her childhood memories.

Perle. Auerbach. Opoczynski. Szlengel. Why did so many years have to pass before they were translated and read?

One reason was that postwar Jewish communal memory of the Holocaust was more interested in stirring narratives of armed resistance or mournful narratives of mass martyrdom than it was in accurate history. It was far from easy to face the nuanced and complex legacy of an archive that tried to convey Jewish life as it really was and in all of its complexity. So much of the material collected by Oyneg Shabes seemed in retrospect to be too prosaic or too controversial or too painful. The YIVO concern with the Jewish everyday had little resonance in postwar Israel or America. Who really cared about soup kitchens, jokes, or courtyards in the Warsaw Ghetto? Who wanted to confront Jewish rage against other Jews or the sordid story of the Jewish police in the Warsaw Ghetto?

If wartime Jewish writing registered Jewish anger and fury leveled against other Jews, after the war Jews preferred to forget this and think about the fighters. In Israel the new Jewish state heralded the saga of armed resistance in the ghettos and forests as a salvation of Jewish honor and as a fundamental link in a historical chain that led from exile to sovereignty.

It would be wrong to say that the men and women of Oyneg Shabes rejected armed resistance. They did not. The pride in those first shots fired at the Germans in January 1943, so dramatically described in Szlengel's "Counterattack," was real. Indeed, between September 1942 and April 1943 the psychology of Warsaw's surviving Jews underwent a fundamental change in favor of resistance, and Ringelblum wrote about this. The Warsaw Ghetto was the only major ghetto where ordinary Jews supported the fighters. This was not the case in Vilna or Bialystok. And without the more than 750 bunkers built by "ordinary" Jews in the Warsaw Ghetto, so well described in "The Ghetto in Flames," the armed uprising would have been crushed in a day. In the last months of Ringelblum's life he paid ample tribute to Mordecai Anielewicz, the fallen commander of the Jewish Combat Organization, even as he made the case for the courage and heroism of his political arch enemies, the Revisionist fighters of the Jewish Military Union.

But the theme of resistance was only a very small part of the Oyneg Shabes legacy. Had the missing third cache of the archive, buried in April 1943, been found, it no doubt would have contained a priceless trove of material on the mood of Warsaw Jews as they prepared for the final showdown. But even so, Ringelblum and Oyneg Shabes put armed resistance in its proper proportions. For all its heroism, it was never a viable choice for most Jews, nor should Polish Jews be judged by whether they fought in battle. A key message of the archive was that Polish Jews indeed resisted but in many other ways: through self-help, in the soup kitchens, in the clandestine schools, through the archive itself. To make armed resistance the touchstone of memory would do them a great disservice.

When Rachel Auerbach wrote "Yizkor, 1943" some months after the ghetto uprising, she did not mention resistance. Instead she began her essay with an image of a destructive flood in the mountains that carried off confused victims in an irresistible torrent, and she ended with the words of the prayer for the dead. In between she described a great community with empathy and respect. Decades later that message is finally ready to be heard.

Timeline

September 1, 1939	Germany attacks Poland; the Second World War breaks out.
October 1, 1939	The Wehrmacht enters Warsaw.
October 7, 1939	Adam Czerniakow is officially appointed chairman of the Warsaw Judenrat.
October 26, 1939	The General-Government, the area of Poland under German civilian administration, is established.
October 28, 1939	The official census conducted by the Judenrat counts 359,827 Jews in Warsaw.
November 14–19, 1939	The Hebrew-Yiddish poet and playwright Yitzhak Katzenelson arrives in Warsaw from his native Łódź.
December 1939	Jews in Warsaw over twelve years old must wear a white band with a blue Star of David on the right arm.

January 26, 1940	Jews in the General-Government are forbidden to travel by rail.
April 1, 1940	On the orders of the occupation authorities, the Warsaw Judenrat begins building walls around the "area threatened with an epidemic."
May 1940	Emanuel Ringelblum begins to handpick the staff of his underground archive.
June 14, 1940	Paris falls; the German army enters the city without resistance; the camp at Auschwitz is established to hold Polish political prisoners.
July 23, 1940	In Kraków appears the first issue of *Gazeta Żydowska*, the official paper for all the ghettos in the General-Government.
End of September 1940	Trams only for Jews appear in the streets of Warsaw, painted yellow with a Star of David on both sides and the inscription "Nur für Juden."
October 1940	Jews in Warsaw are forbidden to leave their homes between seven p.m. and eight a.m.
November 16, 1940	The ghetto in Warsaw is sealed off; almost 400,000 Jewish residents are crammed into 1,483 houses.
November 1940	The Oyneg Shabes archive begins its work.

December 6, 1940	*In redl* (In the circle), a Yiddish theatrical revue, premieres at the Eldorado Theater at 1 Dzielna Street.
January 15, 1941	The Warsaw Judenrat takes over the delivery of mail from the German post office.
March 1941	The Warsaw Ghetto population reaches 460,000 Jews.
April 14 and 19, 1941	Commemorative evenings are held to mark the twenty-sixth anniversary of I. L. Peretz's death.
May 1941	A celebration marking the one hundredth anniversary of the birth of Abraham Goldfaden, founder of the Yiddish theater, is held.
May 15, 1941	Heinz Auerswald is appointed the German commissioner for the Warsaw Ghetto.
June 22, 1941	Germany launches Operation Barbarossa, the attack on the Soviet Union; the *Einzatzgruppen*, or "special units," moving behind the army, begin the systematic murder of Jews; Yitzhak Katzenelson's *Job: A Biblical Tragedy in Three Acts* is published by the Zionist youth movement Dror in about 150 copies.
July 26, 1941	A commemorative gathering is held to mark the sixth anniversary of the death of the Hebrew

	national poet Chaim Nachman Bialik.
July–August 1941	The typhus epidemic in the Warsaw Ghetto reaches its height; about five thousand people die a month.
September 1941	The first "Month of the Child" organized by Centos (the Central Organization for Orphan Care) opens with great fanfare at the Femina Theater; its motto is "The child is our holy of holies."
September 13, 1941	A commemorative gathering is held to mark the third anniversary of the death of the Polish-Yiddish novelist I. M. Weissenberg.
October 4, 1941	The first of many meetings is held to commemorate the twenty-fifth anniversary of the death of Sholem Aleichem.
October 23–December 21, 1941	The Warsaw Ghetto is reduced in size, and seventy-five thousand Jews are forced to relocate.
November 17, 1941	Eight Jews are publicly executed in the Warsaw Ghetto for illegally crossing over to the so-called Aryan Side.
December 1941	The mass murder of Jews in gas vans begins at Chełmno; the United States enters the war.
January 1942	Oyneg Shabes begins carrying out its "Two-and-a-Half-Year Plan" under the directorship of Emanuel

	Ringelblum, Menachem Linder, and Lipe Bloch.
February 1942	Szlamek Fajner reaches the Warsaw Ghetto after escaping from the Chełmno extermination center, and the Oyneg Shabes staff records his testimony.
March 1942	*Live News*, a Polish satirical revue, begins performing at the Stzuka café, with Władysław Szlengel as the master of ceremonies; the underground Antifascist Bloc is formed in the Warsaw Ghetto, later to become the Jewish Combat Organization.
March 22, 1942	Chaim Kaplan records the first rumors about the mass deportations of Jews from the Lublin Ghetto; on April 17, he mentions rumors that all were "burned to death by electricity," marking the beginning of Operation Reinhardt.
Night of April 17–18, 1942	In the first act of collective terror in the Warsaw Ghetto, the Germans shoot dead fifty-two specific people in the streets, among them the economist Menachem Linder.
May 1, 1942	A German film crew arrives in the Warsaw Ghetto to shoot an anti-Jewish propaganda film.

May 30, 1942	There are gala performances in the Femina Theater by children from all the centers in the ghetto; members of the Oyneg Shabes staff hear testimony from a lawyer from Lwów about the extermination of the Jews of Lwów and the whole of eastern Galicia.
June 26, 1942	BBC Radio broadcasts a program on the extermination of Polish Jewry on the basis of materials from Oyneg Shabes.
July 18, 1942	The children of Janusz Korczak's Orphans' Home stage Rabindranath Tagore's *Post Office*.
July 21, 1942	The Great Deportation begins in the Warsaw Ghetto; the last transport leaves the Umschlagplatz bound for Treblinka on September 24; Leyb Goldin, Shimon Huberband, and Chaim Kaplan are among the deported.
July 22, 1942	The scheduled opening of *Droga do szczęścia* (The road to happiness), a three-act comedy starring Diana Blumenfeld, never happens; there are no more theatrical performances in the Warsaw Ghetto.
July 23, 1942	Adam Czerniakow, the chairman of the Warsaw Judenrat, commits

	suicide; he is succeeded by the engineer Marek Lichtenbaum.
July 28, 1942	The Jewish Combat Organization (Żydowska Organizacja Bojowa, ŻOB) is formed in the Warsaw Ghetto.
August 3, 1942	Israel Lichtenstein, aided by two helpers, buries the first part of the Oyneg Shabes archive in the cellars of the school at 68 Nowolipki Street, where he was a teacher; the archive includes over three hundred art works by his wife, Gela Seksztajn.
August 28, 1942	Members of Oyneg Shabes record the testimony of Dowid Nowodworski about the Treblinka death camp.
September 6–10, 1942	*Dos kesl* (the cauldron), the most terrible days of the Great Deportation, takes place.
October 1942	The Jewish Combat Organization (ŻOB) is reconstituted to include members from most of the youth movements in the ghetto.
January 18, 1943	The second deportation Aktion begins in the Warsaw Ghetto, triggering the first armed resistance; Abraham Lewin is killed during the fighting; Peretz Opoczynski is among the five thousand Jews deported to Treblinka.

February 2, 1943	The German army is defeated at Stalingrad.
February 1943	Emanuel Ringelblum goes into hiding with his family on the Aryan Side but returns to the ghetto on the eve of the uprising.
End of February 1943	The second part of the Oyneg Shabes archive is buried in two large milk canisters in the cellar of a house at 68 Nowolipki Street.
March 9, 1943	Rachel Auerbach leaves the Warsaw Ghetto for the Aryan Side.
April 19, 1943	The Germans enter the Warsaw Ghetto and are met with armed resistance from the Jewish Combat Organization; the Warsaw Ghetto Uprising begins.
April 1943	A third part of the Oyneg Shabes archive is buried near the brush makers' "shop" at 34 Świętojerska Street; Israel Lichtenstein, Gela Seksztajn, and Władysław Szlengel perish during the uprising.
May 16, 1943	SS General Jürgen Stroop sends a 125-page report to Himmler, with the title *Es gibt keinen jüdischen Wohnbezirk in Warschau mehr!* (The Jewish Quarter of Warsaw is no more!); the Germans blow up the Great Synagogue on Tłomackie Street to signal their victory.

October 1, 1943	Yehoshue Perle and his son Lolek are among eighteen hundred Polish Jews who arrive in Auschwitz in a sealed train from Bergen-Belsen; they are sent to the gas chambers the same day.
November 3, 1943	Rabbi Kalonymus Kalman Shapira is killed during the liquidation of the Trawniki concentration camp, and Josef Kirman is killed in the liquidation of the Poniatowa concentration camp; the Germans call this day *Aktion Erntefest*, Operation Harvest Festival.
March 7, 1944	The bunker where Ringelblum and his family are in hiding is discovered; all its inhabitants are shot on the ruins of the ghetto three days later.
April 30, 1944	The transport carrying Yitzhak Katzenelson and his surviving son, Zvi, arrives in Auschwitz from the Drancy internment camp in France; they perish the same day in the gas chambers.
September 18, 1946	A search team led by Hersh Wasser recovers the first part of the Oyneg Shabes archive.
December 1, 1950	As part of urban renewal, two milk canisters containing the second part of the Oyneg Shabes archive are unearthed on the grounds of the former ghetto; the third part is never found.

Voices from the Warsaw Ghetto

Introduction

David G. Roskies

On New Year's Day 1915, as the war sweeping across Europe engulfed one country after another, three prominent Jewish writers—I. L. Peretz and Jacob Dinezon from Warsaw and S. An-ski from Petrograd—issued this dire warning to their fellow Jews:

> Woe to the people whose history is written by strange hands and whose own writers have nothing left but to compose songs of lament, prayers and dirges after the fact.
>
> Therefore, we turn to our people that is now and evermore being dragged into the global maelstrom, to all members of our people, men and women, young and old, who live and suffer and see and hear, with the following appeal:
>
> BECOME HISTORIANS YOURSELVES! DON'T DEPEND ON THE HANDS OF STRANGERS!
>
> Record, take it down, and collect![1]

1. D[ina] A[bramowicz], "Oyfruf," *YIVO-bleter* 26 (1952): 351. Petrograd was the new name for St. Petersburg. I. L. Peretz (1852–1915), Jacob (Yankev) Dinezon (1856?–1919), and S. An-ski (Shloyme-Zaynvl Rapoport, 1863–1920) were leaders of the Jewish cultural renaissance in Yiddish, Hebrew, and Russian.

All relevant documents and photographs were to be mailed—C.O.D., if necessary—to the Jewish Ethnographic Society in Petrograd.

The Jews of eastern Europe were now triply vulnerable. Concentrated in towns and cities that lay exposed along the Eastern Front, they had, in addition, been split into warring camps—quite literally, for the men in uniform. The local populations, moreover, viewed them with hatred and suspicion. To whom should they turn in this hour of need? Not to their rabbis and liturgists, whose hermetic response to crisis was to plead with the God of Israel. Rather, Jews should heed the call of their secular writers, who for the past half century or so had been trying to guide them in a measured transition from a traditional religious folk into a modern people.

Peretz, Dinezon, and An-ski were urging a paradigm shift, a revolution in historical consciousness that had been gaining momentum since the beginning of the prior century. Once upon a time, it was enough for Jews to recycle memories, to encounter the present through the lens of the mythic, hallowed past. But since the rise of a Jewish press, Jewish scholarship, modern Jewish schools, societies for the advancement of Jewish music and ethnography, Jewish political parties of the right, left, and center, and especially a vibrant secular literature of prose, poetry, and drama, the writing of history had become a way of redefining the nature of Jewish existence. To become an actor in history, one had to know history. A bold new narrative of the model person, the model place, and the model time could help redirect the destiny of the Jewish body politic, especially when it was under siege.

More than to Jewish writers, therefore, Jews should turn to themselves: ordinary men and women, young and old, who as members of an embattled minority must understand the pressing need to chronicle the catastrophe in real time. Whatever else, they must not depend on the hands of strangers, that is, the enemies of Israel, who were working overtime to vilify the Jews and would most certainly produce "a factory of lies and fabrications" against them.[2] Absent a record of Jewish pain, suffering, and sacrifice in wartime, warned the three signatories, there would be no place for the Jews at the table of postwar restitution and nothing to prevent a new wave of discrimination and persecution.

Although it was still early in the First World War, it was already too late to adequately chronicle the unfolding catastrophe. Jewish Warsaw was strained to the limit trying to provide relief for the thousands of refugees flooding into the city from villages and towns, and Peretz, who had stood at the center of this relief work, supervising the expansion of soup kitchens, orphanages, and schooling facilities for children, died of a heart attack in April, at age sixty-four. In July, the tsarist government closed down the entire Jewish-language press, imposed strict censorship on all news from the war front, and banned the use of the Hebrew alphabet in the mails. The following month, the Germans occupied Warsaw.

When, on November 2, 1917, British Foreign Secretary Arthur James Balfour wrote to Baron Rothschild that "His Majesty's Government view with favour the establishment in Palestine of a national home for the Jewish people," the clock of history was reset. There was an Old-New Land (to borrow Theodor Herzl's phrase) under the Middle Eastern sun that actually could be rescued from the mythic past. Five days later, the Bolsheviks seized power in Petrograd, heralding

2. Ibid.

the long-awaited Russian Revolution, auguring similar upheavals elsewhere. And when the world war finally ground to a halt, the concept of minority rights, protecting the national and cultural autonomy of Jews and other ethnic minorities, was adopted at the Versailles Peace Conference. In 1919, Jews were not only granted a place at the table of postwar restitution. They were now set free to reinvent the past and to reimagine the future.

Among the nation-states that were signatories at Versailles was the reconstituted Republic of Poland. These were heady years both for Poland, recently freed from tsarist domination, and for its Jews, newly liberated from the shtetl, the medieval market towns that they had called home for centuries. By the end of the war, Warsaw had become the new center of Jewish cultural activity; even before Armistice Day in November 1918, the Union of Yiddish Writers and Journalists in Warsaw had moved into permanent quarters on Tłomackie 13, next door to the Great Synagogue. There, the Yiddish prose writer Yehoshue Perle was in his element. Jovial and ebullient, salt of the Jewish earth, he spoke his broad, superidiomatic Polish Yiddish for all the world to hear. Many still remembered his public readings presided over by the Olympian Peretz, for Perle had moved to Warsaw in 1905, when he was all of seventeen. It was Peretz, at a rehearsal of the Yiddish Drama Circle, who had introduced Perle to the beautiful and talented Sarah, the gravedigger's daughter, the love of his life.

A more recent arrival was the twenty-three-year-old doctoral student in the history faculty of Warsaw University named Emanuel Ringelblum. Already displaying his innate organizational abilities, Ringelblum helped found the Young Historians Circle, a group that eventually grew to forty members. Published jointly and severally, their research redefined the scope, language, and purpose of history. Instead of focusing on the glories of Ancient Israel or the "Golden Age" of Spanish Jewry, following the lead of the dean of Russian-Jewish historians, Simon Dubnow, they placed the Jews of eastern Europe center stage. Ringelblum wrote his dissertation on "the Jews of Warsaw until 1527" and later published original research on the active role of Jews in the failed Kościuszko uprising of 1794. Although completely bicultural and the product of Polish universities, this group chose Yiddish, the spoken vernacular of eastern European Jewry, as their language of preference for disseminating knowledge of the past, consistent with its belief in "history of the people and by the people." They had no hope anyway of making academic careers in a Polish university. Nor was this three-pronged program theirs alone, for in 1925, the Yiddish Scientific Institute, YIVO for short, was called into being, as an autonomous institutional base for Yiddish scholarship, first in Berlin, then in Vilna and Warsaw. Four academic sections were soon up and running: the Philological Section for the study of language, literature, and folklore; the Economic-Statistical Section; the Historical Section; and the Psychological-Pedagogical Section. Ringelblum joined the YIVO in the year of its founding and quickly became a mainstay of its Historical Section.[3]

A decade before, the writers Peretz, Dinezon, and An-ski had issued their fervent appeal for a grassroots, communal memory bank. How slapdash and amateur the idea appeared once that socioeconomic, demographic, ethnographic, linguistic, literary, historical, and social-psychological research had become possible on a global scale, with the YIVO operating an

3. Samuel D. Kassow, "Ringelblum, Emanuel," *YIVO Encyclopedia*, accessed January 1, 2017, www.yivoencyclopedia.org/article.aspx/Ringelblum_Emanuel.

American Section as well. The rise of the YIVO and the *Landkentenish* movement in Poland, which stressed the age-old link of Jews to the Polish landscape through "engaged tourism," made the preservation of the specificity and individuality of Polish Jewry into a social mandate. In 1931, Max Weinreich, the YIVO's leading scholar and theoretician, called on Polish Jews "tsu derkenen dem haynt"—to systematically study everyday life. Soon thereafter, he founded the Division of Youth Research to study the problems of contemporary Jewish children and adolescents from an interdisciplinary perspective. Since Yiddish lacked a term for "adolescence," Weinreich made one up. Since no documentation existed on the inner lives of Jewish youth, they were invited to commit their own experiences to writing in three autobiography contests that generated more than six hundred submissions.[4] The memory clock was fully wound and ticking away, keeping Jewish time in time with the latest scholarly trends and most pressing social concerns.

Then, on September 1, 1939, the Blitzkrieg began, ushering in another time of world war. In addition to curfews and endless waits on bread lines and in offices of internal security, in the ghettos there was the Judenrat's strategy of buying time, which was inadequate to alleviate starvation time and ultimately did nor forestall deportation time. In hiding, there was fugitive time; there was, for some, resistance time, and for most of Europe's Jews, either in some nearby forest or in a camp with an unheard-of name, killing time—the end of time.[5] SS

4. See *Awakening Lives: Autobiographies of Jewish Youth in Poland before the Holocaust*, ed. Jeffrey Shandler, with an introduction by Barbara Kirshenblatt-Gimblett, Marcus Moseley, and Michael Stanislawski (New Haven, CT: Yale University Press, 2002).

5. Michael Robert Marrus, "Killing Time: Jewish Perceptions during the

General Jürgen Stroop, to mark his victory in the multipronged war against the Jews, sent Himmler a 125-page, leather-bound, and richly illustrated report, emblazoned calligraphically with the title *Es gibt keinen jüdischen Wohnbezirk in Warschau mehr!* (The Jewish Quarter of Warsaw is no more!). Stroop's blow-by-blow account of how his forces crushed the Jewish armed bandits, flushed the Jewish fighters and surviving citizens out of their underground bunkers, and burned the Warsaw Ghetto to the ground was designed to be the final word, the word of an implacable enemy such as the Jews had never known. And it would have been the final word, were it not for the memorial mandate, so well rehearsed by now, which was carried out against all odds. Assembling a team of chroniclers, statisticians, economists, social scientists and activists, medical doctors, reporters, poets, photographers, and graphic artists, the thirty-nine-year-old Emanuel Ringelblum ensured that the victims would be able to tell their own stories in their own voices in real time, against time and for all time.

This book, then, draws its literary and documentary material from a vast encyclopedic project, the likes of which had never been attempted before: the collective record of a civilization responding to its own destruction. Already schooled in catastrophe, the Jews of Europe were singled out for methodical, incremental, and total annihilation, something without precedent or name. Yet throughout the time span that would come to be known and classified as "Holocaust, Jewish (1939–1945)," there were many Jews who heeded the call of Dubnow,

---

Holocaust," in *Hasho'ah: Historyah vezikaron: Kovets ma'amarim shai leYisrael Gutman*, ed. Shmuel Almog, Daniel Blatman, David Bankier, and Dalia Ofer (Jerusalem: Yad Vashem and the Institute for Contemporary Jewry, 2001), pp. 10–38.

Peretz, and Ringelblum. They recorded, took it down, and collected. They congregated, collaborated, composed, contested, protested, debated, conspired, concealed, performed, lamented, rejoiced, declaimed, proclaimed, educated their young, and protected their writers and intellectuals, insofar as possible. Of all these people, only a few survived. Of all the documentation, however, 1,693 items comprising 35,000 pages were recovered from the Ringelblum Archive alone. So it is through paper that today one can conjure up the people anew—through all manner of minutes, memoranda, diaries, memoirs, last letters, essays, poems, songs, jokes, novels, stories, plays, questionnaires, charts, scholarly treatises, sermons, classroom compositions, diplomas, proclamations, posters, photographs, drawings, and paintings. Out of that profusion and confusion of voices, seventeen have been chosen to narrate the story of their murdered city as seen through their eyes and as spoken in their words.

A Multiplicity of Voices

The code name of the underground archive in the Warsaw Ghetto was Oyneg Shabes (pleasure of the Sabbath), for reasons that the reader will learn from its chief architect and major historian, Emanuel Ringelblum, whose synoptic overview opens this volume. Ringelblum recruited the staff of Oyneg Shabes from among the most Jewishly and socially committed members of Polish Jewry, young and old, men and women, Marxists and Zionists, believers and skeptics, to chronicle the entirety of their experience and to preserve the record in multiple copies. "We tried to have the same events described by as many people as possible," he writes in the opening selection of our volume. "By comparing the different accounts, the historian will not find it difficult to reach the kernel of historical truth."

But what if it is not the kernel of historical truth that we seek but, rather, to the contrary, the multiplicity of truths, the screaming contradictions, the polyphony of voices? To have the same events described by different eyewitnesses, each representing a different age group, generation, social class, or ideology, can yield the kind of truth that only great literature provides.

As the storied center of the Jewish underworld, Warsaw had a robust class of Jewish smugglers. No sooner were the ghetto walls erected than they began to ply their trade. Yet there was fierce division among ghetto chroniclers about their place in Jewish collective memory. For Chaim Kaplan, the Hebrew pedagogue and former instructor of Bible, the ghetto smugglers were scum of the earth. "Two leeches suck our marrow," he wrote in his diary, *Scroll of Agony*, on January 7, 1942, "the Nazi leech, the elite of the elites and the *primum mobile*, the first 'father' in setting up the machinery to make us perish and suck our blood, and its spawn: the Jewish leech, born of contraband and price gouging. Despite draconian measures, smuggling does not cease. Even the danger of death does not restrain it." "That is human nature," Kaplan concludes, citing the prophet Isaiah. "In a crisis the urge grows stronger: *Eat and drink, for tomorrow we die!*" Nothing can be further from this sweeping condemnation than the position of Ringelblum and his staff, who saw in smuggling proof of Jewish vitality and adaptability. "During the whole period of the ghetto's existence it saved the four hundred thousand members of the Jewish community from dying of starvation," is Ringelblum's judgment. "If the Jews of Warsaw had had to live on the official ration of 180 grams of bread a day, all trace of Jewish Warsaw would long since have vanished." As for the future, "in the liberated Poland of the future a monument should be set up to smuggling, which, by the way, also saved the Polish population of the cities from dying of hunger." With even greater pathos, looking back to a city of Jews that no longer exists, Rachel Auerbach writes in "Yizkor, 1943," "Ah, the ways of Warsaw—the black soil of Jewish Warsaw," and among its incalculable losses includes the "ghetto peddlers, ghetto smugglers supporting their families, loyal and courageous to the end."

Most visible were the children. As of January 1942, there were close to fifty thousand school-age children incarcerated in the Warsaw Ghetto, almost evenly divided among boys and girls, including about ten thousand children of refugees and deportees. Orphaned, helpless, sick, and abandoned children were a ubiquitous sight on the horribly crowded ghetto streets, so much so that in February 1941, Centos, the Central Organization for Orphan Care, decided to set up day-care centers specifically for street children—the child beggars and young criminals.[6] Children forced to fend for themselves, children whose anguished faces and emaciated bodies made them look elderly, and children small enough to smuggle food through sewers and gutters became a fraught and fearful subject. In song, poetry, and reportorial fiction, they stand for two opposite positions: an indictment of the community at large, proof that Jewish solidarity has collapsed and that Jewish agency is impotent; or evidence of Jewish loyalty, resilience, and boundless courage.

From the moment the young Warsaw-born artist Gela Seksztajn took up painting, she made children a primary focus, and *Portrait of a Jewish Child* would have been the title of her first solo exhibition had it not been for the outbreak of the war. All the works are indoors, formally posed and costumed por-

6. Barbara Engelking and Jacek Leociak, *The Warsaw Ghetto: A Guide to the Vanished City*, trans. Emma Harris (New Haven, CT: Yale University Press, 2009), pp. 317, 326, 344. Hereafter cited as *Guide*.

traits of pensive, intelligent, secular Jewish boys and girls, the girls often holding a doll or wearing a ribbon. Most of these children do not look ethnically Jewish. Seksztajn continued doing portraits in the ghetto, including her newborn daughter, Margolit, whom she captures while she sleeps, and now she also draws children who are bandaged, bruised, and starving. In her last will and testament, buried along with her entire portfolio, she bequeaths her work "to the Jewish Museum that will be established in the future in order to re-create prewar Jewish cultural life up to the year 1939 and study the terrible tragedy of the Jewish community in Poland during the war."

However well known Henryka Łazowert was before the war as a member of the Polish new wave, it was as a ghetto poet that she gained enduring fame, thanks to a single poem. "The Little Smuggler" was translated into Yiddish, set to music, and sung throughout the ghetto. Orphan songs were a staple of the Yiddish stage. And outside the poet's window in the ghetto, she could hear beggars singing for a handout, but this poem captures something else: a child smuggler full of spunk and street smarts who each day risks his life to feed his starving mother. He begins full of bravado and ends with forebodings of death.

Stefania Grodzieńska wrote a rhymed requiem for the children of the ghetto—for Yankl, Jurek, Hershek, Abramek, Adzia, Józio, Dawid, Zosia, Rutka, Jola—describing how each of them perished. Twelve-year-old Hershek, for example, another child smuggler who is his family's sole means of support, is terrified each time he takes off his armband and steals over to the so-called Aryan Side, uttering the same prayer as he leaves and as he makes his way back. Alas, finally his luck runs out. "In war, the Lord has bigger things to do— / The ghetto has no direct line to God."

The heroism of the ghetto is the heroism of mostly small deeds, acts of selflessness, bonding, loyalty, love. The tragedy of the ghetto, as seen through the same lens, is the complete powerlessness of mothers and fathers, including one's Father in Heaven, to fulfill their essential roles. As for the children, they are trapped in a ghetto that is the perversion of childhood.

No less desperate is the nuclear family, as seen from the fathers' perspective. "Come on, get out of the house!" shouts the husband to his wife in Yitzhak Katzenelson's "Song of Hunger." "I'm ashamed to say / It's empty anyway." The youngest child might just as well stay home, for "when he's a grownup Jew / He'll die on the street of hunger for sure." Old enough to remember the outbreak of the war, the son whom the father addresses in Josef Kirman's prose poems saw "the steel birds" hail down death as the family fled to the woods. Since then, however, the child's only exposure to nature is the sight of doves on the barbed-wire fences, and these doves may prove to be morally lethal, because they fail to distinguish between victim and persecutor ("I Speak to You Openly, Child"). Each poem is a desperate attempt to wrest positive meaning, some portent of hope, from within this terrible, imploding time—and beyond.

And there was ghetto humor. "God forbid that the war last as long as the Jews are able to endure it," is one of the many Yiddish examples that Shimon Huberband recorded on behalf of the archive (see "Ghetto Folklore"). What will prevail: the monomaniacal, implacable German quest to render Europe *Judenrein*, Jew-free, or the stubbornness of Jewish survival?[7] There is another, even darker version: "How long will the hardships last? God forbid that the hardships last as long as the Jews

7. Ruth R. Wisse, *No Joke: Making Jewish Humor* (Princeton, NJ: Princeton University Press, 2013), pp. 17, 154.

can endure. Because if the hardships last that long, who knows if they will really endure them?"

There were three "communities" in the Warsaw Ghetto: the official community, also known as the Judenrat, forced to carry out the German orders; the alternative community, with its parallel social service networks; and the countercommunity, where the political underground and the youth movements found their home.[8] Each community kept a different set of records; each had a different stake in the future. In the ghetto of Łódź-Litzmannstadt, the archive operated aboveground as an arm of the Bureau of Statistics and almost immediately began to compile an official daily chronicle of events in the ghetto: first in Polish, then in both Polish and German, and as of January 1943, exclusively in German.[9] The Oyneg Shabes archive represented a completely different model. It was an arm of the Jewish Self-Help, the alternative network of social service agencies in the ghetto and a sworn enemy of the Judenrat, that "bastion of the Jewish bourgeoisie," which since time immemorial, Ringelblum maintained, had exploited the poor and the downtrodden.[10] Almost all the ghetto writers, even those who like Peretz Opoczynski and Yehoshue Perle found employment in some branch of the Judenrat, were relentless in their criticism. Even as they referred to it by its traditional, prewar name—not *Judenrat*, a German coinage, but *kehillah*, Jewish

8. Lucy S. Dawidowicz, *The War against the Jews, 1933–1945* (New York: Holt, Rinehart and Winston, 1975), pp. 223–78.

9. *The Chronicle of the Łódź Ghetto, 1941–1944*, ed. Lucjan Dobroszycki, trans. Richard Lourie, Joachim Neugroschel, et al. (New Haven, CT: Yale University Press, 1984).

10. Samuel D. Kassow, *Who Will Write Our History? Emanuel Ringelblum, the Warsaw Ghetto, and the Oyneg Shabes Archive* (Bloomington: Indiana University Press, 2007), pp. 94–95, 135–36.

community council, from the Hebrew—they were expressing a moral judgment.

"At the first opportunity, not one stone will remain upon another of the building at 26 Grzybowska Street," raged Chaim Kaplan on December 2, 1941, referring to the office of the Judenrat,

> which has become the headquarters of injustice and tyranny, a den of robbers and evildoers. And if a prophet lived among us to reprimand us, he would raise his voice against them:
>
> —*Why do you oppress My people?!* [Isa. 3:15]
>
> And his voice would be heard from one end of the earth to the other. From the depths of our troubles we would be consoled at once: "Their day shall come too!" They will not be immune forever. Together with the Nazi they will be undone, and the property of strangers that they have swallowed—they will vomit it forth.

How do we reconcile Kaplan's prophetic denunciation with the cameo appearance that Adam Czerniakow makes in Leyb Goldin's "Chronicle of a Single Day"? This brilliant anatomy of one day in the life of Arke, Goldin's fictional stand-in, centers on the daily bowl of soup he receives at precisely the same hour at a soup kitchen, most probably the soup kitchen for writers at 40 Leszno Street run by Rachel Auerbach on behalf of the Jewish Self-Help.[11] On his way there, Arke happens upon a scrap of an official proclamation signed by Adam Czerniakow, who was appointed chairman of the Warsaw Judenrat on October 7, 1939,

11. *Guide*, pp. 309–10.

the very personification of Jewish power for the utterly powerless ghetto population. Seeing Czerniakow's name jolts Arke into yet another food-related reverie, this one addressed directly to Czerniakow: "Therefore, I request of you, Mr. Chairman, that you see to it that I receive a piece of bread every day. I know, much honored sir, that you have a thousand other things to do. What importance at all can it have for you that such a wreck of a person as I am should kick the bucket. All the same, Mr. Chairman of the Judenrat . . ." Kaplan's prophetic rage is here replaced by a theater of the absurd. Behold a ghetto intellectual reduced, in his feverish dream state, to petitioning the head of the Judenrat for a daily piece of bread.

Contributing to the extraordinary range of voices was the unique status of Warsaw as a city of refugees—and of refuge. The Warsaw Ghetto was home, albeit a typhus-ridden home, to 150,000 refugees, most of them expelled from hundreds of surrounding towns, a cross-section of the Yiddish-speaking heartland, who Ringelblum hoped would provide him with the laboratory conditions to chronicle the diversity and vitality of Jewish communal life in Poland. He came to view this shtetl project as the single greatest achievement of Oyneg Shabes.[12]

There were any number of individuals who also traveled circuitous routes before their work found its way to the Oyneg Shabes archive. A native of Łódź, the Hebrew-Yiddish poet and playwright Yitzhak Katzenelson found refuge in Warsaw between November 14 and 19, 1939. Even before he was welcomed by the commune of the Zionist youth movements Dror-Hechalutz, Katzenelson adopted the children of the ghetto, the orphans in particular, for whom he adapted stories and composed original

12. Kassow, *Who Will Write Our History?*, pp. 268–78.

works. Virtually everything that he wrote in the ghetto—one-act and full-length plays, epic and lyric poems, literary criticism—he declaimed before a live audience. Private readings of his most ambitious works he reserved either for such authority figures as Ringelblum and the philosopher-mystic Hillel Zeitlin or for the members of the Zionist underground.[13]

Yehoshue Perle never dreamed that he would end up back in Warsaw after joining tens of thousands of refugees fleeing eastward to the Polish territories annexed by the Soviet Union as part of the Ribbentrop-Molotov Pact. Sometime in November 1939, along with his son, Lolek, and new daughter-in-law, Judyta, he reached Lwów-Lemberg, where the newlyweds found work as engineers, and Perle senior was admitted into the newly established Soviet Writers Union, embracing Ukrainians, Poles, and Jews. The Soviet regime showered Perle with all the usual rewards—public readings before factory workers, translation into Russian, a trip to Kiev as an honored guest, and lucrative book contracts—provided that he submit his work to censorship, which he willingly did. But no sooner did the Germans conquer eastern Poland than Lwów and environs became the site of a massive pogrom carried out by local Ukrainians, followed by the more systematic mobile killing units of the Germans. The Warsaw Ghetto was a haven by comparison, so the Perle family returned to its old haunts, on Nowolipie Street, and Perle found immediate employment in the Judenrat under the patronage of the munificent Shmuel Winter. After hours, Perle set out to write a comic-satiric novel about ghetto life, a

13. Yechiel Szeintuch, "Yitskhok Katsenelsons literarishe shriftn fun Varshe in zeyer historishn kontekst," in *Yidishe geto-ksovim Varshe 1940–1943*, by Yitzhak Katzenelson, ed. Yechiel Szeintuch (Tel Aviv: Ghetto Fighters' House and Hakibbutz Hameuchad, 1984), pp. 35, 71–73.

lost work titled *Our Bread of Affliction*, featuring such real people as Rubinshteyn, the ghetto comedian. Perle was also commissioned by Ringelblum to produce a detailed report on the Soviet occupation of Lwów.[14] Comprehensiveness was not an empty claim of the Oyneg Shabes archive. The ghetto writ large and its underground archive writ small were a veritable *kibbutz galuyot*, an Ingathering of the Exiles of Israel on the eve of their destruction.

Ghetto Time

Ringelblum encouraged members of Oyneg Shabes to describe what they saw immediately and not to wait. "Every month brought profound changes that radically altered Jewish life. . . . What a quantum leap from the pre-Deportation 'shop' to that which came after!" he wrote in his retrospective essay. "The same is true of smuggling and of social and cultural life; even the clothes Jews wore were different in the different periods. O[yneg] S[habes] therefore tried to grasp an event at the moment it happened, since each day was like decades in an earlier time." It was such eyewitness, contemporaneous accounts that would give future historians some understanding of "ghetto time."

14. Emanuel Ringelblum, "Vi azoy zaynen umgekumen di yidishe shrayber," in *Ksovim fun geto, 2: Notitsn un ophandlungen (1942–1943)*, 2nd, photo-offset ed. (Tel Aviv: Y. L. Perets, 1985), pp. 180–81; Rachel Auerbach, *Varshever tsavoes: Bagegenishn, aktivitetn, goyroles 1933–1943* (Tel Aviv: Yisroel-bukh, 1974), chap. 35; Jonas Turkow, *Azoy iz geven . . . (Khurbn Varshe)* (Buenos Aires: Dos poylishe yidntum, 1948), pp. 92, 124; "Answers to a Questionnaire by Yehoshue Perle" (Ringelblum Archive, I/86), in *To Live with Honor and Die with Honor: Selected Documents from the Warsaw Ghetto Underground Archives "O.S." (Oneg Shabbath)*, ed. Joseph Kermish (Jerusalem: Yad Vashem, 1986), pp. 755–56.

No one was better equipped than Peretz Opoczynski to capture events as they happened. A seasoned reporter before the war, Opoczynski was well known to readers as the scribe of urban poverty and neglect in Warsaw. In the ghetto, he worked by day as a letter carrier. A thoroughly enervating and thankless job, it exposed him to the speech, slang, behavior, hypocrisy, apathy, and boundless tragedy of every kind of ghetto inmate. Opoczynski produced memorable vignettes of ghetto life by locating each in time and place. One reportage describes a twenty-four-hour cycle in the lives of ghetto smugglers, their wives, customers, and cronies. Another, his most ambitious work by far, is "House No. 21," which traces the changing fortunes and misfortunes of a single tenement courtyard over the first year of the German occupation.

Time in this tenement is both centripetal and centrifugal. On the one hand, the tenement is a shtetl-in-miniature, and its tenement committee is a latter-day Jewish Community Council. As Opoczynski was a member of its tenement committee himself, he believed that for all the corruption, self-interest, and fractiousness, the self-governing committees would weather the Nazi storm. Thus, no matter how cruel the delousing brigades, the victims still emerge from the baths with a self-deprecating joke. The fast-talking, aggressively self-confident Pearl, who dominates Opoczynski's narrative as she does the entire courtyard, is a close cousin of the garrulous women in Sholem Aleichem's fiction. Pearl and her archrival, the landlady, can be said to represent the ingenuity and staying power of the Polish-Jewish collective. Savvy Jewish women are for Opoczynski what they are for Sholem Aleichem: though powerless to stem the rapid pace of change, they will fight tooth and nail to preserve and protect what is theirs.

Not so the men, restless, chafing at the bit, ready to try anything, no matter how impractical, so long as it promises a fresh start. "The army tailor and the Zelechower," we read, "both waiting for their apartments to be made ready, spend entire days dreaming like schoolboys about going to Russia, making it to the big cities—Moscow, Leningrad, Kharkov, where you can get huge loaves of white bread and bowls filled with rice, fish, and meat." Later on, they draw one more male tenant into their circle: "The cane maker, the Zelechower, and even the army tailor, although they too can eke out livings, are drawn to the world beyond the border. They don't have the patience to wait for the Russians; they want to be free." So with wonderful economy, learned from the master comedian of dissolution, Sholem Aleichem, Opoczynski has the women personify the centripetal pull and the men personify the centrifugal push of wartime. At story's end, it is Pearl's husband, the army tailor, who has the last word. Despite all the setbacks and dangers, he is absolutely determined to leave for Russia—by himself.[15]

How is it possible to resist the centrifugal force of ghetto time? How can one hope "rightly to number our days," as the Psalmist says (Ps. 90:12) and as Jews rehearse in their Sabbath morning liturgy, "that we may gain a heart of wisdom," when, to quote Ringelblum, images succeed one another "with cinematic speed," when the very words that one uses are subject to radical shifts in meaning? When Opoczynski speaks of the "Other Side" in his description of life in House No. 21, he means crossing over the Polish border into the putative freedom of the Soviet Union. After the establishment of the ghetto, in November 1940, it will mean escaping to the Aryan Side of the city,

15. For a representative sampling, see *In Those Nightmarish Days: The Ghetto Reportage of Peretz Opoczynski and Josef Zelkowicz*, ed. Samuel D. Kassow and David Suchoff, trans. David Suchoff (New Haven, CT: Yale University Press, 2015).

where one can survive only with forged papers, a flawless Polish accent, an "Aryan" appearance, and lots of money.

The meaning of the ghetto itself also changes. In the folk imagination (to judge from the legends that Huberband recorded), "ghetto" signifies a safer place to be than among the Poles, but when the first eight Jews are publicly executed for illegally crossing over to the Other Side (on November 17, 1941), Kaplan records the shock and despair of the entire population. In 1940, the worst indignities that the Jews of Warsaw experience are the hated *paruvkes*, or delousing, of their apartments, with forced baths in the middle of winter (as described by Opoczynski). Two years later, in March 1942, Kaplan describes the mass graves of the emaciated dead in the Gęsia cemetery.[16] Then, within a few months, a whole new vocabulary comes into being: the *Umschlagplatz*, or roundup point for the *Great Deportation* of close to three hundred thousand Jews in the course of six weeks to the *Treblinka* death camp; the *blockades* set up to trap the inhabitants of various streets; the German-owned *shops*, where the survivors of the Great Deportation are set to work; the *number* that each has to be assigned; the *wild-cat houses* abandoned by the deportees, where thirty-five thousand "illegal" or unregistered Jews seek refuge; and, finally, the underground *bunkers* used during the *Uprising* and the *Final Liquidation* of the ghetto.

There *is* a way to keep centrifugal time at bay. It is by trying—consistently, collectively, and stubbornly—to live by a different reckoning, by keeping a separate and culturally autonomous calendar.[17] Ghetto diarists, even those who call

16. Gęsia is pronounced GENsha.

17. See Alan Rosen, "Tracking Jewish Time in Auschwitz," *Yad Vashem Studies* 42, no. 2 (2014): 11–46.

themselves secular, routinely log in the relevant Jewish holidays; they keep Jewish calendrical time, along with the vast majority of the ghetto population, who continue to observe the major holidays and to keep the Sabbath holy as best they can, whether inside the home or courtyard or at clandestine and officially sanctioned services.[18] The Germans, for their part, also keep time with the Jewish calendar, choosing the holiest days for days of destruction, desecration, and slaughter.[19]

During five of the most terrible days of the Great Deportation, known as *dos kesl* (the cauldron), from September 6 to 10, 1942, Abraham Lewin does not open his notebook. All Jews left in the ghetto are forced to leave their homes and assemble in the streets adjacent to the Umschlagplatz. Those not assigned to recognized workplaces are deported by cattle car to Treblinka. Lewin resumes writing on Friday, September 11, the eve of Rosh Hashanah, returning to the coincidence of sacred and apocalyptic time. "Today is the eve of Rosh Hashanah," he writes at the end of his entry. "May the coming year bring salvation for those who have survived. Today is the fifty-second day in the greatest and most terrible slaughter in history. We are the tiny remnants of the greatest Jewish community in the world."

In addition to the calendar of Sabbaths and festivals, secular Jews also marked the more recent cultural achievements of the Jews of eastern Europe in Yiddish, Hebrew, and Polish. The roster of cultural events, concerts, and cabaret and theatrical performances held in the Warsaw Ghetto[20] is studded with gatherings to commemorate the passing of such classic writers as I. L. Peretz (observed in April 1941), Abraham Goldfaden, the

18. *Guide*, pp. 640–57.
19. *Guide*, p. 642.
20. *Guide*, pp. 594–640.

founder of the Yiddish theater (May 1941), the Hebrew national poet Chaim Nachman Bialik (July 1941), the Polish-Yiddish novelist Itshe Meyer Weissenberg (September 1941), and the Polish-language poet Mieczysław Braun, who had just perished in the ghetto (February 1942), as well as to celebrate such living writers as the Yiddish poet and prose writer Avrom Reisen (March 1942) and, one of their own, the Polish actor and playwright Władysław Lin (July 1942)—these in addition to numerous benefit concerts billed as "jubilees" to celebrate a quarter century of work on the Yiddish, Polish, or musical stage. So on September 13, 1941, marking the third anniversary of the death of I. M. Weissenberg, Abraham Lewin uses the occasion to express two conflicting, even mutually exclusive, ideas. One is to protest the life-crushing impact of the ghetto, where "death rules in all its majesty, while life hardly glows under a thick layer of ashes," where "the very soul, both in the individual and in the community, seems to have starved and perished, to have dulled and atrophied. There remain only the needs of the body; it leads merely an organic-physiological existence." The other is to celebrate "one of those creative artists who come to us as though by themselves, who grow like a flower in an untilled field." Turning to the young people in the audience, Lewin draws out the analogy of nature-in-bloom to conjure up a Jewish cultural renaissance even in a prison such as this, which will "spring up like a hidden source from under the earth."[21] In the ghetto, commemoration was not a mere exercise in nostalgia, the lost heritage recalled at a safe remove. Each lecture, performance, or

21. Abraham Lewin, *A Cup of Tears: A Diary of the Warsaw Ghetto*, ed. Antony Polonsky, trans. Christopher Hutton (Oxford, UK: Basil Blackwell in association with the Institute for Polish-Jewish Studies, Oxford, 1988), pp. 243–44.

religious rite was happening in the present, and so long as there was a present, it forged a living, defiant link to the past and expressed the hope of a collective future, a life in the first-person plural. "Our aim," wrote Ringelblum, "was that the sequence of events in each town, the experiences of each Jew—and during the current war each Jew is a world unto himself—should be conveyed as simply and faithfully as possible."

By collecting personal diaries, therefore, while keeping a historical diary of his own, Ringelblum accomplished several goals at once. He upheld the inviolability of the individual, subjective experience: each Jew a world unto himself. So doing, he also preserved the sequential, durational aspect of ghetto time, a highly individuated sense of time, of the day-to-day response to despair, deprivation, disease, and starvation—something, one might add, rarely captured by postwar testimony. Ringelblum singled out the Hebrew diary of Chaim Kaplan for special praise and deeply regretted that the writer refused to deposit the original manuscript in the archive. For Ringelblum, it was precisely Kaplan's ordinariness and his relative isolation from the world around him that made the ghetto portion of his diary so valuable. For Kaplan, the journal, which he began in 1933, was his life, his companion and confidant. "Without it I would be lost," he starts his entry for November 13, 1941. "In it I pour out all my heart's feelings, until I feel somewhat relieved." More than that, it is the source and object of his creativity, and "in the future let them evaluate it as they may."

Most difficult to render, because it is most difficult to withstand, is the enervating, debilitating, relentless regimen of starvation time. Arguably the most accomplished literary work preserved in the Oyneg Shabes archive is Leyb Goldin's "Chronicle of a Single Day," whose entire plot is this: Before the daily bowl of Soup, During the Soup, and After the Soup. Acknowledging that he is not the first writer to render the malleable and evanescent quality of time, with Thomas Mann's *The Magic Mountain* as the towering precedent, Goldin's narrator protests his own predicament: "The war has been going on for a full two years, and you've eaten nothing but soup for some four months, and those few months are thousands and thousands of times longer for you than the whole of the previous twenty months—no, longer than your whole life until now." Everything hinges on the bowl of soup that Arke is to receive at twenty minutes to one.

To provide the full flavor of that bowl of soup, Goldin draws numerous analogies between time present and time past. Pre-ghetto time was so rich with possibilities: it was a time of love and great literature, of struggling for the betterment of the masses, even of suicide (which seems like such a luxury today, in 1941), whereas in ghetto time, there lies the terrible split between Arke the Intellectual and his Stomach.

> Who is talking to you in this way? You are two people, Arke. It's a lie. A pose. Don't be so conceited. That kind of a split was all right at one time when one was full. *Then* one could say, "Two people are battling in me," and one could make a dramatic, martyred face.
>
> Yes, this kind of thing can be found quite often in literature. But today? Don't talk nonsense—it's you and your stomach. It's your stomach and you. It's 90 percent your stomach and a little bit you.

Having marshaled the literary and ideological evidence at his disposal, Arke denies that culture or politics can in any way mitigate even one minute's worth of hunger. Arke decides that the only proper analogy for the starving ghetto is to a zoo. "Each day the profiles of our children, of our wives, acquire the mourning look of foxes, dingoes, kangaroos. Our howls are like the cry of jackals." Yet before the day is done, he witnesses an operation to save the life of a ghetto child and is forced to admit that this is something that animals will never do.

But even this is not the final word, because Arke's self-consuming monologue is cyclical; it ends where it began, with the same bits and snippets of information from the official news service (most probably the *Gazeta Żydowska*, the *Jewish Gazette*, published in Kraków under German auspices) and with the constant, gnawing hunger. The date is only August 1941, and the worst is yet to come.

Not for the likes of Arke was the trendiest news source in the Warsaw Ghetto: the popular and prestigious Sztuka (Art) café on 2 Leszno Street.[22] The runaway hit of the 1942 season was *Live News*, a Polish satirical revue, presided over by the all-time-favorite master of ceremonies, Władysław Szlengel, who both wrote and performed his topical material. Szlengel's prodigious output can itself provide an accurate measure of ghetto time. "Telephone" dates from the early months of the ghetto, but the poet's reportorial eye is already very much in evidence. The speaker is on telephone duty; that is, there is a single working telephone in his building, manned by a rotation of tenants, who take all incoming calls. Eyeing the silent telephone, he is reminded of his many acquaintances living outside the ghetto walls: those Christian Poles, once so close, who would most certainly refuse to take his call. In the next twenty stanzas of the poem, not reproduced here,[23] he picks up the receiver anyway and dials

22. *Guide*, pp. 585–90.

23. See Władysław Szlengel, "Telephone," trans. John and Bogdana Carpenter, *Manhattan Review* 15, no. 2 (2012–13), www.themanhattanreview.com/archive/15_2_telephone.html.

"Miss Clock," the female voice of an automated recording, and launches into an animated dialogue with her about his favorite prewar haunts. From 10:53 to 11:55 p.m., in fifty-two minutes of real time, he rehearses out loud the sights, sounds, and culinary delights of nightlife in his beloved part of town, so hopelessly remote from this dismal, loveless night inside the walled ghetto of Warsaw.

"Things" is something else again. Written in the immediate wake of the Great Deportation, Szlengel includes this among the "poem-documents" that he wrote not for the living but for the dead.[24] He may have first recited the poem in a private apartment on Świętojerska Street, where he continued to perform weekly installments of *Live News* before a much diminished—and sadder—audience. In six syncopated stanzas, the poem recapitulates the methodical murder of Polish Jewry. Each stanza represents, metonymically, another station of the cross: neither of one exemplary martyr nor of the people entire but of their "furniture, tables and chairs, / suitcases, bundles," as the owners are dispossessed and moved to ever more desolate and restricted quarters; forced by Station Four to move "along a Jewish road / with no big bundles or little bundles, / no furniture or chairs"; reduced to carrying "A small suitcase and a knapsack, / no need for anything else," as they are marched off in even rows of five to the Blockhouses reserved for slave labor and, finally, to their deaths, leaving behind their "abandoned apartments, / abandoned bundles, / suits and down covers, / and plates and chairs." Aryans then inherit the spoils in the first of two endings. In the Second Coming of the "Jewish things," however, they return in a grand and vengeful procession

24. Kassow, *Who Will Write Our History?*, pp. 316–17.

of *materia mnemonica*, retracing the Via Dolorosa of a martyred people.

When, on January 18, 1943, the Germans resumed the deportations from the ghetto, expecting to follow the same plan as before, the self-defense units of the Jewish Combat Organization, made up of members of the Zionist and the Bundist underground, took up arms and fought back, claiming their first German casualties. The author of *Live News* also sprang into action and produced his manifesto of armed resistance, the poem "Counterattack," which was copied and widely circulated in the ghetto.[25] Read in sequential order, then, Szlengel's poems provide an accurate measurement of ghetto time: from segregation to annihilation to resistance. Read metaphorically, they present the most tragic chapter of Polish Jewry as a sequence of precise metonymies: from a useless telephone to vast processions of ownerless property to the blood-spattered boxes of Junos, the German-army-issue cigarettes.

A few blocks away, but at the farthest remove from Szlengel's worldview and poetics, was Rabbi Kalonymus Kalman Shapira, the Rebbe of Piaseczno, a Talmudic scholar and the scion of two Hasidic dynasties. Once his home on 5 Dzielna Street was incorporated into the ghetto, he turned it into a combination synagogue and soup kitchen for his hundreds of followers. There he delivered sermons on the weekly and festival Torah readings throughout the war, from Rosh Hashanah 1940 until July 18, 1942, four days before the Great Deportation began—sermons that he himself translated from Yiddish into Hebrew and edited for posterity.[26] Menakhem Mendel Kon, one

25. *Guide*, pp. 547, 763–66.

26. See Rabbi Kalonymus Kalman Shapira, *Sermons from the Years of Rage: The Sermons of the Piaseczno Rebbe from the Warsaw Ghetto, 1939–1942: A*

of Ringelblum's closest associates, was probably responsible for depositing the manuscript in the Oyneg Shabes archive, along with Shapira's other unpublished writings, early in 1943.[27]

The weekly Torah sermon is an exercise in cosmic time travel, an existential dialogue with the eternal past, an exploration of God, providence, and the trajectory of Jewish fate. As Rabbi Shapira came to appreciate the unprecedented nature of the trials and tribulations of the People Israel, he began to explore a parallel universe, the mostly uncharted territory of divine suffering. Rabbinic sources going back almost two millennia had spoken of God's suffering with Israel and God's participation in Israel's exile. By February 1942, it was time to contemplate a new notion of the infinite magnitude of God's suffering. Rabbi Shapira pictures the world poised on the brink of destruction—one divine spark of pain could destroy the universe were it to pierce its boundaries. This sermon enunciates a kind of "mysticism of catastrophe."[28] It is precisely from the ruins, Rabbi Shapira intimates, that a revelation may emerge; external destruction is internalized, so that the boundaries of one's ego dissolve, allowing one to hear the heavenly voice . . . weeping.

In the sermon for March 14, 1942, Rabbi Shapira pushes the idea of a human-divine partnership in suffering one step further. Turning to the concept of *hester panim* (divine hiddenness, or what the German-Jewish philosopher and theologian Martin Buber called "the eclipse of God"), Rabbi Shapira

---

Critical Edition According to the Author's Manuscript, with an Introduction, Notes and References [in Hebrew], ed. Daniel Reiser, 2 vols. (Jerusalem: Herzog Academic College, Yad Vashem, and the World Union of Jewish Studies, 2017).

27. Ibid., 1:31–32.

28. Nehemia Polen, *The Holy Fire: The Teachings of Rabbi Kalonymus Kalman Shapira, the Rebbe of the Warsaw Ghetto* (Northvale, NJ: J. Aronson, 1994), pp. 106–21.

explains this hiddenness as God's desire to weep in seclusion. In situations of extreme suffering, he preaches, a person can burst into God's hidden chamber, so to speak, and join God in His sorrow. The weeping that man does with God can then be a source of renewed strength. From this mystical communion *in extremis* can come a renewed commitment to action—the study of Torah and the observance of God's commandments.

The final and most radical move comes on July 11, 1942, in Rabbi Shapira's penultimate sermon. Here he redefines the traditional theology of suffering by reformulating the Jewish concept of martyrdom, Kiddush Hashem. Kiddush Hashem is not to be understood as the consequence of martyrdom, the surrender of one's life in a trial of faith that testifies to the glory of God, but rather its origin. In the present war, God is the primary object of attack. Because Israel identifies with the divine cause, it has to share in God's suffering. Jews suffer on God's account. The war against the Jews, therefore, is perceived by Rabbi Shapira to be a war against God, and in this war, Jews are God's soldiers. Hence, Jewish suffering, no matter how great, is but ancillary to the Lord's. Say not that the catastrophe is punishment for any sin, whether large or small, committed by Israel. Say rather that the catastrophe is a manifestation of Israel's identification with God.

So in the Warsaw Ghetto, time was managed in two completely different ways. According to the newer system of keeping time, all members of the Jewish people, "men and women, young and old, who live and suffer and see and hear," were expected to become historians themselves, to write down what was happening today so that it would not be forgotten tomorrow. It was their job precisely to render the duration of time, the recapitulation of time, the push and pull of centrifugal and centripetal time. Then there was the Jewish faith community, schooled in the ancient memorial calendar, whose members sought direction from its spiritual masters. One of the most revered preachers, perceiving that the End Time was approaching, linked their suffering with the pathos of God. In such times of great catastrophe, he assured them, God, who was beyond time, could be moved, as it were, to weep, and God's tears were the surest sign of an ongoing, heroic covenant.

Time Before / Time After

One night the Germans appeared in Yehoshue Perle's courtyard and shouted for everyone to come down. Perle ignored the order, stayed put, and survived. As one of the still living, he continued to write for the underground archive, producing, among other things, his ferocious satire on what he calls the "Chosen-Peoplish" Jews, those thirty thousand who survived the Great Deportation, just long enough to work as slave labor. "4580"—the title of Perle's last-known work—is Perle himself, a once-proud Polish Jew transformed into a faceless, historyless set of digits. His number was "chosen" and issued a dog tag, in a diabolical perversion of the biblical promise and in a vicious caricature of statistical efficiency.

"4580" is part meditation on the meaning of a person's name, part last will and testament, part summation of its author's life and literary career, and part self-indictment. Here Perle recalls his beloved Sarah, who committed suicide in 1926. Here he alludes to the rescue of his good name by his abandoning pulp fiction and writing *Everyday Jews*, a singular achievement of modern Yiddish prose.[29] Here he admits, "In order to

29. See Yehoshue Perle, *Everyday Jews: Scenes from a Vanished Life*, ed. David G. Roskies, trans. Maier Deshell and Margaret Birstein (New Haven, CT: Yale University Press, 2007).

become a number, my fifty-three years had to be jabbed at until they bled. Jabbed at, mocked, raped." That which sustains him in his darkest hour, the one Jewish text that still speaks to the present moment, is none other than *Motl, the Cantor's Son*, Sholem Aleichem's tale of the lively and lovable orphan boy. Playing on Motl's tragicomic slogan, "Lucky me, I'm an orphan," familiar to every reader of Yiddish, Perle signs off with the bitter words, "Lucky me, I'm a number!"

Another way to signal the point of no analogy, of time split in two—Time Before / Time After—was by switching languages. In the first days of the Great Deportation, Abraham Lewin abruptly switched from keeping his ghetto diary in Yiddish to Hebrew. Saturday, the thirtieth of May 1942, which he describes as "among the most difficult, the most nightmarish of all days that we are now living through," when the staff of Oyneg Shabes transcribes a tale of horrors from a lawyer from Lwów, Lewin is still writing in Yiddish. A mere three months later, on August 28, when once again the staff is taking testimony, from the first eyewitness of the Treblinka death camp, Lewin has already begun to write in Hebrew. Why switch from one Jewish language to another? Did writing in Hebrew transform one's private testimony onto a metahistorical plane? Ensure the document's eternality? Render it more conspiratorial? Create a psychological buffer zone? Or all four? Whatever the reasons, the confusion of languages signaled an attendant confusion of addressee. Who was this document intended to reach? Who would be left to decipher its contents?

There were two poles of response. Some people saw the destruction of European Jewry as the dark culmination of all previous ordeals; others saw it as a terrible new beginning, as an archetype that as yet lacked its own name. For Rachel Auerbach, looking back from the Aryan Side of Warsaw, the turning point was the Great Deportation in the summer of 1942. What unlocks the memory of those weeks of unsurpassed terror is an incident that happened to her while riding the Warsaw streetcar. Sitting opposite her on the streetcar was a Polish Catholic woman, whose son had been shot, her head thrown back, talking to herself. Seeing and hearing that bereaved mother crying, like one mad or drunk, reminds the Jewish passenger of another woman who seemed drunk or mad with personal grief, the biblical Hannah in Shiloh, crying her heart out before God because she is childless (1 Sam. 1). But as a Jew living on Aryan papers, it is too dangerous for her to cry in public. What can the passenger do? She can sit down and write this chronicle. She can return to the ancient rite of Jewish mourning, to the recitation of Yizkor, the Memorial Prayer for the Dead.

For "Maor," also in hiding on the Aryan Side, the turning point came not with the uprising, in which he seems to have fought, but with the systematic, wholesale destruction of the entire ghetto for the sake of killing its few thousand underground Jews. At one moment, he is reminded of a Chaplin film, but upon seeing the whole ghetto in flames, he knows that no cinematic imagination, no matter how extravagant, has ever encompassed a Holocaust.

When a bright, sunny day dawned, it revealed to the last survivors "the incinerated houses of the ghetto of the murdered city."

"And let this," he writes, "remain for a memory."

Reading in Time

Some monuments to the severed past are more legible than others. Proceeding along the Honor Row that leads directly from the brick-and-stonework entrance to the Warsaw Jewish

Cemetery on Okopowa Street, now fully restored, it is easy to find the semicircular marble tomb that marks the grave of I. L. Peretz. Home to over two hundred thousand marked graves, the cemetery miraculously escaped the German destruction that reduced 98 percent of Warsaw to rubble. In death, Peretz is reunited with Jacob Dinezon and S. An-ski, as the three of them were united in their appeal to the Jews of eastern Europe to become their own historians during catastrophic times. The magnificent tomb, sculpted by Abraham Ostrzega, whose work appears in twenty-six other tombstones, stands today as it did when first unveiled with pomp and ceremony during Passover 1925, on the tenth anniversary of Peretz's death, a backstory that makes for fascinating reading.[30] It is still possible to decipher the Yiddish inscription, taken from Peretz's verse drama *Di goldene keyt*, which, true to its name (The golden chain), portrays four successive generations of Hasidic leaders. "Singing and dancing," it reads, "we go to greet Him. / We, Jews of grandeur and glory, / Jews of Sabbath rejoicing, / Our souls aflame!" A visit to the Warsaw Jewish Cemetery, in short, offers an embarrassment of riches, and this tomb in particular can serve as an emblem of remarkable, indeed miraculous, endurance.

A milk canister that contained the second part of the Oyneg Shabes archive, now on permanent loan to the United States Holocaust Memorial Museum in Washington, DC, makes a very different impression. It seems like a time capsule dropped from another planet, all of whose inhabitants have perished. A primitive relic, it is surrounded by scattered papers written in remote languages. But now that the Oyneg Shabes archive has been painstakingly preserved and reassembled, thoroughly

30. Ruth R. Wisse, "A Monument to Messianism," *Commentary*, March 1991, pp. 38–42.

accessioned and catalogued, and as the publication and translation of its contents continues apace, and as its story inspires historians and filmmakers, it is finally possible to take its measure as literature, as works of historical engagement that will endure for generations to come. It is a memory site put together in real time by people who were trained to write in time and against time. Jewish writings from the Warsaw Ghetto represent an unbearably restricted and drastically shrinking civilization-in-miniature. Rendered through a multiplicity of competing and contentious voices—the voices of refugees and locals, smugglers and tailors, teachers and preachers, artists and artisans, beggars and merchants, policemen and mailmen, mothers and fathers, husbands and wives, optimists and pessimists, fighters and mourners, and the voice of one official historian—they are specifically designed to be read in time. Once these voices have been heard and have been restored to a living time line, they can never be silenced again.

EMANUEL RINGELBLUM

Oyneg Shabes

During three and a half years of war the ghetto archive was run by the group called Oyneg Shabes.[1] This curious name originated from the planning sessions of the group, which took place on the Sabbath; the whole institution was dubbed Oyneg Shabes for reasons of secrecy. I was the one who initiated the archive in October 1939. At that time the atmosphere in Warsaw was very oppressive. Every day brought new ordinances against the Jews. People were afraid of political reprisals; they dreaded politically motivated searches. They feared the files of the Regierungs-Kommissariat and the Defensywa.[2]

The scare dragged on for months but proved groundless. The Germans were not looking for individual "criminals." Their aim, which they achieved, was the collective. They aimed at whole groups and professionals, not individuals. In the first months of occupation, especially in January of 1940, mass arrests occurred, and there were probably also mass executions of the intelligentsia. The arrests were made according to a roster of the groups concerned (the doctors' association, the engineers'

1. Literally: Enjoyment of the Sabbath; here, a recreational gathering in honor of the Sabbath.

2. The Defensywa (Polish Political Secret Police) kept a file on left-wing party activists that fell into the Germans' hands.

union, etc.). They were not linked with any particular searches. In general, the Germans did not carry out any investigations at all but took the easiest course and shot all who fell into their hands.

The frequent and thorough searches that were actually carried out were aimed at something altogether different: finding foreign currency, gold, diamonds, valuables, merchandise, and the like. Such searches have been going on during the entire three and a half years of war and continue to this day.

We have dwelt on the nature of the searches because it greatly affected the survival of written documents from the war period. During the earliest months the population was terror stricken and in dread of the searches. Everything was burned, down to innocent books that even Hitler did not regard as *treyf* [unkosher]. Most of the socialist literature in libraries and private dwellings was destroyed. The exiled German writers, such as Thomas and Heinrich Mann, [Lion] Feuchtwanger,[3] and [Emil] Ludwig,[4] also suffered. Anticipating searches, people were afraid to write.

The terror kept mounting, but as we have said, the targets were whole groups and classes. The Germans did not care what the Jews did in their own homes. So the Jews began to write. Everyone wrote: journalists, writers, teachers, community activists, young people, even children. The majority wrote diaries, in which daily events were illumined through the prism of personal experiences. A great deal was written, but the largest part by far was destroyed along with the end of Warsaw Jewry

3. Author (1884–1958) of *The Jew Suess* and other historical novels.
4. Author (1881–1948) of many historical biographies, e.g., of Napoleon.

in the Deportation. All that remained was the material preserved in O[yneg] S[habes].

I began collecting contemporary materials as early as October 1939. As director of the Jewish Self-Help (at that time it was the coordinating committee of the welfare organizations), I was in active daily contact with the life around me. News reached me about everything that was happening in Warsaw and its suburbs, because the coordinating committee was an outgrowth of the Joint,[5] where delegations came from the provinces almost every day and told about the harsh experiences of the Jewish population in their areas. In the evenings I recorded the mass of information I had heard during the day and supplied footnotes of my own. As time went on, these records grew into a sizeable book, several hundred densely written pages, which provide an overview of that period. After a while I replaced these daily recordings with weekly and monthly reports. I did this when the staff of Oyneg Shabes had grown into a large body.

Already in the first months of my work with O[yneg] S[habes] I chose several people to assist, but no great advantage came of this. It was not until I enlisted the cooperation of the young historian Rabbi Shimon Huberband[6] that Oyneg Shabes acquired one of its best workers. Unfortunately, however, Rabbi Huberband kept his records in the form of marginal notations inside various religious books so that they should pass for textual emendations. Not until later did he let himself

5. The American Jewish Joint Distribution Committee was founded in 1914. Isaac Gitterman, who headed the Polish office, was a close friend of Ringelblum's.

6. See "Ghetto Folklore," in this volume.

be convinced that no danger accrued in his recording everything rather than using the cryptic method he had first employed.

In May 1940 I felt that the time had come to give this very important work a broad social base. Because I had made a good choice of personnel, the work started off in the right direction and was carried on with appropriate scope. The staff of O[yneg] S[habes] then elected as its secretary Hersh W[asser], who continues in this post up to the present.[7] Through his political activities, Comrade W., himself a refugee from Łódź, had acquired the experience necessary for this kind of work. His daily contact with hundreds of refugee delegates from every part of the country made it possible to produce the hundreds of monographs on cities, which are the most important treasure in the O[yneg] S[habes] project.

Our congenial comrade, Menakhem [Mendel Kon, a social and cultural activist] brought the finances up to the required standard. A rich cultural life began developing in Warsaw. Benefit public readings, special forums, and concerts were given. This provided a basis for extending and deepening the work of O[yneg] S[habes].

The creation of the ghetto, the confinement of the Jews within walls, gave the archival work still greater opportunities. We became convinced that the Germans cared very little what the Jews did among themselves. Meetings were held in an atmosphere and on subjects that would not have been possible before the war. In every house committee, soup kitchen, and meeting place of a social institution, people could say anything that came into their heads without the slightest interference. The Jewish informers for the Gestapo were busy searching for rich Jews, warehouses full of

7. A Left Labor Zionist who survived and helped retrieve the Archive after the war.

goods, smuggling, etc. They took little interest in politics. We reached the point where illegal editions of work of all political leanings were published with almost complete freedom. People read them openly in cafés, collected money for the press fund, debated with rival publications; in short, they behaved almost as they had before the war. It is not surprising that in this "freedom" that prevailed among the prisoners of the ghetto, the work of O[yneg] S[habes] had favorable opportunity for development. The project branched out. Dozens of people joined the staff of O[yneg] S[habes], some full-time, others part-time. The project extended its range but remained conspiratorial.

In order to give our work a legal sanction, we announced to some dozens of writers, teachers, and intellectuals that we were holding a contest and offering money prizes. These prizes, which were funded by the Joint with a single cash payment, enriched the archive with a series of valuable works, such as the work on the Yiddish theater in wartime by Jonas T[urko]w, [the well-known writer, stage director, and actor]; the monograph on Jewish life in Lemberg under Soviet rule, by [the Zionist activist] Esther M[angel] and her husband, Sh[vayge]r; the history of a Jewish family during the war by the poetess Henryka Łazowert;[8] and the monograph on the Kampinos labor camp by Rabbi Huberband.

O[yneg] S[habes] branched out so widely, and so much valuable material was assembled, that it seemed to all of us that the time had come to make, if not a synthesis, at least a summing up of various problems and important phenomena in Jewish life. If this plan had been realized, it would have been a highly important contribution to the history of the Jews in the days of

8. See her poem "The Little Smuggler," in this volume.

Hitler. It is to be greatly regretted that only part of the projected work was carried out. We lacked the peace and quiet necessary for a project of such scope and size. The authors who undertook to work on one chapter or another did not have the opportunity to bring their work to a conclusion. More than one writer went to [his or her death at] the Umschlagplatz (Mrs. [Cecylia] Słapak, Rabbi Huberband, [Helena] Szereszewska[9]); more than one was killed by a bullet (Menakhem Linder, Shmuel Breslav, Josef Kaplan[10]); more than one crossed to the Other [Aryan] Side.

The plan was familiarly known as "The Two-and-a-Half-Year Plan" because it was intended to provide a survey and summing up of Jewish life in Warsaw during two and a half years of war. The plan was divided into three [in fact four] parts: a general section, an economic section, a cultural-scientific-literary-theatrical section, and one dedicated to social welfare. The work, which was started at the beginning of 1942, was directed by an editorial board consisting of the present writer, along with Menakhem Linder and Lipe B[lo]ch.[11]

The present writer took on [the task of writing] the first and third sections; Linder, the economic section; and Lipe B., social welfare. The work was intended to have a semilegal character. New forces joined the project, professionals from various walks of life. The work was designed to be more than sixteen hundred printed pages long and one of the most important

9. Szereszewska (1891–1978) actually survived, on the Aryan Side.

10. Breslav and Kaplan, active in the left-wing Zionist youth movement Hashomer Hatsair, were shot by the Gestapo in September 1942.

11 The economist Linder (b. 1911) was shot in the Aktion of April 18, 1942. Bloch (b. 1889) was active in the democratic wing of the General Zionists and headed the Keren Kayemet in Poland. He died in Mauthausen.

documents of the war. We wanted to hold our coworkers' attention to certain guidelines and set the direction for them to follow. By this we did not mean to impose any particular approach on the writers of the articles. Articles were written on the Jewish Police, on corruption and demoralization in the ghetto, about social activities, the school system; there was a questionnaire on the life and work of Jewish artists during the war, Jewish-Polish relations, smuggling; a questionnaire on the state of the different artisan groups, youth, women, etc.

Seeing that it was difficult to elicit the work that had been assigned to the various authors, we introduced the principle that each author was obliged to submit the source material that he collected in connection with his work, for example, the biographical data on the adolescents who were to have formed the basis of his monograph on ghetto youth. In this way interesting material was amassed on various aspects of our wartime situation.

In the course of our work, our experience as to how such a project should be carried out was greatly enriched. Many authors had already made much progress in their assignment, but just when the two and a half years [of the "plan"] was about to turn into three, a new disaster descended on the heads of all the Warsaw Jews, a disaster that cost us three hundred thousand victims—the [Great] Deportation.

The work of O[yneg] S[habes], along with the whole of our social and economic life, was disrupted. Only a very few comrades kept pen in hand during those tragic days and continued to write about what was happening in Warsaw. But the work was too sacred and too deeply cherished in the hearts of the O[yneg] S[habes] coworkers, the social function of O[yneg] S[habes] too important, for the project to be discontinued. We began to reconstruct the period of the Deportation and to collect material on the slaughterhouse of European

Jewry—Treblinka. On the basis of reports made by those who returned from various camps in the province, we tried to form a picture of the experiences of Jews in the provincial cities during the time of the Deportation. At the moment of writing, the work is proceeding full force. If we only get some breathing space, we will be able to ensure that no important fact about Jewish life in wartime will remain hidden from the world.

There were two classes of coworkers in O[yneg] S[habes]: full-time, who dedicated themselves entirely to the project, and part-time, who wrote on a one-time basis about their personal experiences in their city or town and then ended their connection with O[yneg] S[habes]. Everyone appreciated the importance of the work that was being done. They understood how important it was for future generations that a record remain of the tragedy of Polish Jewry. Some realized that the collection of writings would also serve to inform the world about the atrocities perpetrated against the Jewish population. There were several part-time coworkers who became so involved in the project that they stayed on full-time.

Of the several dozen full-time staff, the great majority were self-educated intellectuals, mostly from proletarian parties. We deliberately refrained from drawing professional journalists into our work, because we did not want it to be sensationalized. Our aim was that the sequence of events in each town, the experiences of each Jew—and during the current war each Jew is a world unto himself—should be conveyed as simply and faithfully as possible. Every redundant word, every literary gilding or ornamentation grated on our ears and provoked our anger. Jewish life in wartime is so full of tragedy that it is unnecessary to embellish it with one superfluous line. Second, there was the matter of keeping a secret, and, as is well known, one of the chief failings of journalists is that they reveal secrets. A few able journalists might have been enlisted as time went on, had they not sought contact with the Gestapo informer [Abraham] Gancwajch,[12] and although this relationship was not of a "professional" nature, it nonetheless made it impossible for us to associate with the journalists in any way.

Those who helped us with a single piece of work were ordinary people who had lived the whole of their daily lives in their hometowns. Upon arrival in Warsaw with the horde of 150,000 refugees, they continued to lead their [fellow] townspeople in the so-called *landsmanshaftn*[13] organized by the refugee center of the Jewish Self-Help. After a day of hard work at the committee, distributing bread or performing other kinds of assistance, these delegates of the landsmanshaftn spent the evening writing, according to our plan, the history of their town; or they related it to our coworkers, who later wrote it up. This was very arduous work. In the terrible overcrowding of the ghetto, the refugees lived in [housing] conditions that simply cannot be described. To preserve secrecy under such conditions was a difficult task. It was cold in the winter nights; last winter most of the Jewish houses did not have electricity. Writing necessarily has attendant risks and indescribable difficulties, and to obtain the chronicle of a town required long weeks and months of exertion. It demanded much effort to encourage my coworkers not to be distracted by all these obstacles and to do their work. Let me complete the picture by adding that at the

12. Gancwajch headed the Office to Combat Usury and Profiteering in the ghetto, popularly referred to as the "thirteen," which was subject directly to the Germans. He vied with the Judenrat for control of the ghetto and fell from power in July 1941.

13. Hometown associations.

beginning there was a fear of being discovered by the Gestapo informers. More than one manuscript destined for O[yneg] S[habes] was destroyed as the result of a search in a tenement.

As we have mentioned, our coworkers were mostly [just] ordinary people. Among them were talented individuals whom we spurred on to literary creativity. Had these people not died of hunger or disease, or in the Deportation, we would have been enriched with their new writing talent. And new literary energy would have been infused into a field that was so neglected among us [eastern European Jews]—the writing of memoirs. Because most of our coworkers were suffering great hunger in Warsaw, that city of pitiless Jews, O[yneg] S[habes] had to provide for them. We lobbied the social institutions to supply them with food parcels.

O[yneg] S[habes] strove to give a comprehensive picture of Jewish life in wartime—a photographic view of what the masses of the Jewish people had experienced, thought, and suffered. We did our best to arrange for specific events—in the history of a Jewish community, for example—to be described by an adult and by a youngster, by a pious Jew—who was naturally concerned with the rabbi, the synagogue, the Jewish cemetery, and other religious institutions—and by a secular Jew, whose narrative emphasized other, no less important factors.

Typhus, which claimed thousands of victims among the Jewish population of Warsaw, was rampant among our coworkers. This was not surprising. Our people worked among thousands of refugees, who constituted the largest contingent of its victims. Our people came into contact with returnees from the labor camps, who were the principal carriers of typhus among the population. No one was immunized against typhus because no one could afford a five-hundred- to six-hundred-zloty injection.

Rabbi Huberband, Hersh W., and Peretz O[poczynski] recovered from typhus. A whole group of our coworkers died of it. [. . .]

Comprehensiveness was the chief principle of our work. Objectivity was the second. We aspired to present the whole truth, however painful it might be. Our depictions are faithful, not retouched.

The atrocities of the Germans against the Jewish population predominate in our work. However, quite a lot of material reveals humanity on the part of Germans. There are constant indications, both in the completed essays and in the oral reports, that we must be objective even in the case of our deadly enemies and give an objective picture of the relationship of Germans and Jews.

The same can be said of Polish-Jewish relations.[14] Opinions prevail among us that anti-Semitism grew significantly during the war, that the majority of Poles were glad of the misfortunes that befell the Jews in the Polish towns and cities. The attentive reader of our material will find hundreds of documents that prove the opposite. He will read, in more than one report on a town, how generously the Polish population behaved toward the Jewish refugees. He will encounter hundreds of examples of peasants who, for months on end, concealed and fed Jewish refugees from the surrounding towns.

In order to ensure the greatest possible objectivity and to obtain the most exact, comprehensive view of the events of the war as they affected the Jews, we tried to have the same events

14. Ringelblum's monograph on this subject has been published separately as *Polish-Jewish Relations during the Second World War* (Jerusalem: Yad Vashem, 1992).

described by as many people as possible. By comparing the different accounts, the historian will not find it difficult to reach the kernel of historical truth, the actual course of an event.

Our coworkers wrote the truth; and they had an additional reason for doing so. We assured everyone that the material, insofar as it concerned living people, would not be exploited for immediate use. Therefore, everyone should write as if the war were already over. He should fear neither the Germans nor those *kehillah*[15] members who were attacked in a report on a given city. Because of this, the material of O[yneg] S[habes] is of great importance for the future tribunal, which, after the war, will bring to justice offenders among the Jews, the Poles, and even the Germans.

The war changed Jewish life in the Polish cities very quickly. No day was like the preceding. Images succeeded one another with cinematic speed. For the Jews of Warsaw, now closed in within the narrow confines of a [large German factory called a] "shop," the ghetto period seems like a paradise and the pre-ghetto period an unreal dream. Every month brought profound changes that radically altered Jewish life. It was therefore important to capture at once every event in Jewish life in its pristine freshness. What a quantum leap from the pre-Deportation "shop" to that which came after! The same is true of smuggling and of social and cultural life; even the clothes Jews wore were different in the different periods. O[yneg] S[habes] therefore tried to grasp an event at the moment it happened, since each day was like decades in an earlier time. We succeeded in doing this with many of the events. What greatly aided us in this task was that some of our own coworkers kept

15. Literally (traditional Jewish) community or council; used by Ringelblum as a synonym for the Judenrat. See also Perle's "4580," in this volume.

diaries in which they not only recorded the facts and happenings of day-to-day life but also evaluated noteworthy events in the ghetto.

As we have already said, the work of O[yneg] S[habes] was secret. We had to find ways of hiding the collected materials. In establishing contact with the hundreds of refugees from the province, we were afraid of falling afoul of one of the several hundred agents of the "thirteen," which was then at the height of its "glory." Fortunately, this danger was averted as a result of the extreme cautiousness of O[yneg] S[habes] operations. We had a principle: before entering into relations with anyone, we found out first about his character, social and political past, etc. Not until we had this information would we sit down and talk with the person to obtain the news we needed. Very few people knew the real purpose of the conversations we conducted with them. Very often, especially in the last months before the Deportation, our coworkers did not record the facts they had heard in the presence of the informant but did so afterward. This method of recording lessened the authenticity of the material, but there was no other way to keep the work as secret as it had to be.

In writing the monographs, we duped people into thinking we were collecting data on their native towns for use by the landsmanshaftn. Most people played innocent and pretended not to understand what our work was for.

Because of the secrecy that had to be employed in the O[yneg] S[habes] work, however far-reaching that work might be, it was still narrow in comparison with the vast treasury of news and facts that could and should have been assembled during the war. "We have to work badly" was the watchword of O[yneg] S[habes]. We had to do all we could to prevent the precious treasure of O[yneg] S[habes] from becoming an open secret.

For this reason we avoided all contact with people from the kehillah, even those among them who were honest. An atmosphere of Gestapo seeped from the walls of the Judenrat. We were afraid to have any dealings with it: that is why we are so poor in its official materials.

What sort of material is preserved in the O[yneg] S[habes] archive? The most important treasures are the monographs on cities and towns. They contain the experience of a given town from the outbreak of war to the deportation and liquidation of its Jewish community. The monographs, which were written according to our outline, encompassed all aspects of life: economic life; the relationship of Germans and Poles to the Jewish population; the kehillah and its activities; social welfare; important episodes in the life of the community, such as the arrival of the Germans, pogroms, expulsions, and acts of atrocity perpetrated during Jewish holidays; religious life; work and matters connected with it (labor camps, the obligation to work, impressment of labor, the Labor Department of the kehillah, relationship of Germans to Jews at work); etc.

Such was the appearance of a monograph in its general outline. Few monographs, however, conformed to the preceding outline in reality. The authors wrote in various ways. But all the monographs express the tragic sufferings of the Jews in the Polish cities. The monographs were written with a sense of compassion. It is often remarkable with what epic stoicism the authors relate the most tragic facts about their [own] towns. This is the stoicism of the graveyard, the stoicism born of painful ordeals and of the resignation that follows these ordeals. This is the stoicism of people who know that anything can be expected from the Germans, that there is no cause for surprise at the indescribable savageries that have been perpetrated.

The greatest number of monographs comes from former Congress Poland. The other regions of prewar Poland are meagerly represented. This is because all the monographs were written in Warsaw, and most of the refugees there had come from former Congress Poland. From Galicia, in particular from Lemberg, we began to receive news only after the outbreak of the Russo-German war, when people who had left in September 1939 or in the following months began returning to the capital. The same applies to Vilna, Slonim, Grodno, Rowno, etc., cities in the occupied eastern territories. From those areas, too, we received news from returnees. An especially large amount of information was brought by the wave of people returning from Białystok and the Białystok region.

Because of the conditions of conspiratorial work with people who had never before engaged in historical research, there is no complete record of what exists in the materials of O[yneg] S[habes]. Therefore, it is hard for me to tell how many monographs on cities we possess. It is certain at any rate that they can be numbered in the hundreds. On some cities there are several monographs or even several dozen.

Apart from comprehensive monographs, we sought accounts of single, significant episodes in the various cities. We elicited the accounts from those who were involved in the episode in question directly or indirectly, as participants, witnesses, or people associated with the episode in some other way. For example, to this category belong the account of the execution of fifty-two Jews from 9 Nalewki after a Jewish underground hero had killed a Polish policeman, the account of the Savoy Restaurant execution of seven dozen Łódź Jews,[16] etc.

16. On November 1, 1939, the Germans arrested fifteen Jewish social activists at the Astoria café in Łódź. All of them were shot.

We always endeavored to give the description of each happening the stamp of directness, of true experience. That is why the materials of O[yneg] S[habes] are so deeply imbued with subjective elements and why the narratives are often highly dramatic. The monographs on the cities are not free from this subjective approach.

In order to elicit the most direct report possible of a writer's or narrator's experiences, we dispensed with a set protocol in many cases and told him to relate what had happened in whatever order he thought best. Most of these narratives have the character of tales of wandering. A hair-raising example of this genre relates the death march of eight hundred Jewish POWs, of whom half were murdered on the way from Lublin to Biala.

Another narrative of a journey, by a Jewish Red Army soldier who originally came from Warsaw, has its beginnings as far away as Orshe. This route is marked everywhere by rivers of Jewish blood, spilt on the fields of White Russia, the Ukraine, Podolia, and Galicia. Another account of the mass slaughters of Jews in the southern parts of Russia is to be found in the wandering narrative of a young man from Warsaw, who strayed to Mariumpol in the Crimea.

"Blood-red Highways"—this is the name we can give to all the tales of wandering of Jewish men and women, young people and children, who roamed constantly from the time the Germans approached their homes until they found a place of rest and settled in a spot from which they could wander no farther. All the highways are stained, like Jewish history, with drops of blood shed by the Gestapo murderers or the Wehrmacht.

An important section of the O[yneg] S[habes] project is about the labor camps where thousands of young Jews died.

Except for the ghettos, the labor camps are one of the most effective instruments to destroy the Jewish population, robbing it of its best elements: the young people and men of working age. This is not the place to describe the labor camps, but one thing may be said: with a few minor exceptions, the labor camps were designed not for labor but to bring about the death of their inmates. Of those who did not succumb to the dreadful working conditions and inadequate nourishment, those who were not shot or tortured to death by the notoriously inhumane camp guards, most perished after their return home. A great portion of the blame rests on the Judenrats, who did very little to provide for the camp inmates or to keep alive those who returned. Of all the Jewish councils, the Warsaw kehillah was the worst in its relationship to the camp inmates. O[yneg] S[habes] succeeded in collecting a rich supply of material on almost all the labor camps, at least the major ones. Among the most important and comprehensive is the exhaustive description of the labor camp at Kampinos, where, on the notorious "Hill of the Dead," over fifty young Jews were buried alive, shot, or tortured to death by the camp guards. This account, compiled by Rabbi Huberband, is one of the most important documents on Nazi brutality toward Jewish laborers.[17]

The section of narratives under the heading "Experiences in Prisons and Concentration Camps" is a meager one, not because few Jews spent time in these places but for the simple reason that from the very outset, as a rule a Jew did not come out alive. Thousands of Jews were sent to Auschwitz, but not a single one returned. The one document relating to these

17. Published in *Kiddush Hashem: Jewish Religious and Cultural Life in Poland during the Holocaust* (Hoboken, NJ, and New York: KTAV and Yeshiva University Press, 1987).

victims is the telegram to their families, bearing the standard form message that the "guilty party" is dead and his property can be picked up at a specified place. I knew two people who had returned from Dachau. One of them was afraid to relate the slightest thing; the other—incidentally, a very interesting personality described by Rachel Auerbach in her diary—died of hunger.

Those who returned from the prison were [also] so intimidated that they were afraid to tell us the smallest detail. I was able to convince two former prisoners to relate their experiences. One of them was Meylekh Shteynberg, an activist of the Left Labor Zionists. A printer by occupation, he had earned a large income before the war managing the Left Labor Zionist newspaper *Arbeter-tsaytung*, on account of which he had been imprisoned in Polish jails more than once. Now too, in wartime, he was imprisoned in the Pawiak[18] for his previous crimes. By playing the role of a simpleton, he succeeded, with great good fortune, in being released from jail. Comrade Shteynberg, together with his family, died during the Deportation.

O[yneg] S[habes] also preserved materials from the Polish-German war of 1939. The Jewish population remembered well the sufferings of Jews in Germany and other occupied countries. They had a clear presentiment of what Hitler had in store for the Polish Jews. For this reason, the Jewish soldiers fought with extraordinary heroism. This is acknowledged by many leaders of the Polish Army. It was very important for future history, and for the mutual relations of Jews and Poles, to collect the account of experiences of Jewish soldiers in the German-Polish war. The collected materials illustrate a crisis

18. A tsarist-built prison situated in the ghetto and used by the Germans to imprison Polish political prisoners and Jews.

in the mood of the Polish population, and for a short time it liberated itself from the plague of anti-Semitism. Defeats on the battlefield and the need to find a scapegoat led to the resurgence of anti-Semitism; for example, in Warsaw it gave rise to the emergence of a new Jablonna,[19] i.e., the segregation of Jews from the common military divisions and setting up of unarmed Jewish battalions, detailed to work on fortifications.

This mood of anti-Semitism, which was already manifest in the dying days of the Polish Republic, was roused to full activity in the POW camps, where Jewish soldiers suffered far more from their Polish comrades [in arms] than from the German guards. A host of such facts is recounted in the personal narratives of the Jewish POWs in Germany. The best is by Daniel Fligelman; it is entitled *Die Waren in Deutschland gefangen*.

These narratives inform us of the highly gratifying fact that the Jewish POWs won themselves a reputation in Germany as a diligent and desirable element. "You came to Germany as damned Jews, and you are returning home as blessed children of Israel." Such were the words of praise with which a German characterized the changed attitude toward the Jewish POWs. This may well be the main reason why the Jewish soldiers were freed from captivity, whereas the Poles remain imprisoned up to this day.

It is impossible to list all the topics covered by the work of O[yneg] S[habes]. They are as numerous and variegated as our life. We attempted many subjects but did not find suitable staff to cover all of them. It can, however, be asserted with

19. Town near Warsaw where, in 1920, an internment camp was set up for Jewish soldiers and officers of the Polish Army who were accused of disloyalty during the Polish-Soviet war.

confidence that there is no important phenomenon of Jewish life in wartime that was not mirrored in the materials of O[yneg] S[habes]. A subject such as smuggling, which is always extremely important in wartime, is represented in O[yneg] S[habes] by the work of Comrade T[itelman]. In this work we see the tremendous scope of smuggling in Warsaw: during the whole period of the ghetto's existence it saved the four hundred thousand members of the Jewish community from dying of starvation. If the Jews of Warsaw had had to live on the official ration of 180 grams of bread a day, all trace of Jewish Warsaw would long since have vanished. Smuggling caused the loss of several Jewish lives every day and, on the eve of the Deportation, a dozen or dozens of lives a day. In the liberated Poland of the future a monument should be set up to smuggling, which, by the way, also saved the Polish population of the cities from dying of hunger.

Comrade T[itelman]'s work on smuggling portrays its folkloric aspects—argot, customs, etc.—rather than its economic significance.

O[yneg] S[habes] was in general somewhat unsuccessful in the economic field. Good plans were set up on various economic topics, with detailed outlines, but very few of these were carried out, owing to a lack of suitable coworkers. Economic problems [also] require a tranquil mind. They require time and the right materials, based on comprehensive investigations; we had neither time nor the proper working conditions. Nonetheless, we did manage to elicit a few valuable articles. One of these, by Comrade W[inkle]r, deals with the ability of a society in wartime to adapt itself to altered economic conditions. The author shows how the Jews, in the intolerable conditions of the ghetto, built up a whole series of branches of production to serve the so-called Aryan Side. The astonishing skill that the Jews displayed in obtaining raw materials and creative ersatz materials testifies to the tremendous ingenuity of the Jews in finding a way out of the most difficult situations. It is proof of the vitality of the Jewish population, which not only created this production but developed smuggling to a level at which the total production could get "abroad" [i.e., to the Aryan Side, the consumer].

Of the fragmentary projects in the economics section, we should mention the work of Comrade G[utkowski] on the foreign currency trade—another wartime phenomenon of great importance.[20] Comrade G[utkowski] succeeded in fathoming the deepest secrets of the foreign currency trade. He describes not only its economic aspect but also its folkways, the argot of the money changers and their customs. He gives highly important tables, which illustrate the fluctuating rates of exchange throughout almost the entire period of the war. It will be an interesting project for the future researcher to find in the events of world politics, in the occurrences in the surrounding Jewish and Polish life, and in yet other factors, the key to these fluctuating rates of exchange. Incidentally, we learn from the work of Comrade G[utkowski] the "secret" that a foreign currency factory existed on Pawia Street, where "hard ones" (gold dollars) and "pigs" (gold rubles) were forged. After the war, the national banks of the countries in question will no doubt be kept busy dealing with the currency "Made in the Ghetto."[21]

Among fragmentary articles on the subject of the kehillah, we find one on the Jewish mail, which was resurrected after a hiatus of more than a hundred years. One of the "mailmen" was

20. Eliyohu Gutkowski (1900–1943) was an active Labor Zionist in prewar Łódź and edited the information bulletin of Oyneg Shabes together with Hersh Wasser.

21. In English in the original.

the Yiddish journalist Peretz O[poczynski], who describes for us the hard work of a Jewish mailman and the relationship of the Jewish population to the mailmen, who often had to collect the tax from their neighbors, which the kehillah had decreed as an extra payment to be made on correspondence and also on parcels.

There are a few articles on the topic of sanitation; one of them, by the journalist Peretz O[poczynski], is dedicated to one of the ten plagues of the ghetto, the plague of Fumigation Brigades. The writer depicts a *paruvke* [delousing] in a poverty-stricken Jewish tenement.[22] The second article, by a member of the Fumigation Brigade, is like a final confession. The author admits and proves, with concrete facts, that the Fumigation Brigades were disseminators of typhus, as a result of the corruption and demoralization that prevailed among them. Peretz O[poczynsk]i reaches the same conclusion.

The same Peretz O[poczynsk]i conducted an interesting experiment, which, unfortunately, has not yet been concluded. He wrote "The History of a Warsaw Tenement during the War."[23] The starting point was the story of the House Committee, set against a background of the general condition of the tenement and its residents. The work, originally quite restricted in scope, grew into the history of a whole tenement courtyard and its inhabitants, beginning on the eve of the war and continuing through the bombing of Warsaw, the entry of the Germans, the flight [and wanderings on the way] to Russia, and so forth. This microcosm may serve as an introduction to the history of Warsaw, the macrocosm.

22. Also described in his "House No. 21," in this volume.
23. See "House No. 21."

"The History of the House Committee at 23 Nalewki" described the establishment and activities of one of the most interesting institutions in wartime Poland.[24] The house committees were transformed from social welfare organizations into institutions of a public nature, which fulfilled many different administrative functions. Apart from this, the house committees played a cultural and social role in introducing various cultural events and entertainment. There was no aspect of Jewish life in wartime that was not associated with the house committees. They provided for refugees who had returned from the camps, supported various children's institutions, took care of domestic sanitation, procured practical assistance for neighbors, solved various disputes between neighbors, and, most important, took responsibility for the fate of impoverished neighbors, for whom the house committee was the address to turn to in case of need.

Dr. Celina Lewin has portrayed one of the oldest and best organized house committees, which for many months ran its own kitchen and, during the bombing, even bought its own generator for a sum of seven thousand zlotys.

The writer Peretz O[poczynsk]i describes the activities of another house committee at 24 Leszno Street.

In the social welfare section, we should mention the work of the writer Rachel A[uerba]ch on the public kitchen at 40 Leszno. Describing the establishment of this kitchen and depicting its patrons, she comes to the melancholy conclusion that the Jewish Public Kitchen, which at times served up to a hundred thousand diners, i.e., a quarter of the Jews of Warsaw, did not save a single person from dying of hunger.[25] And that

24. Ringelblum himself was instrumental in setting them up.
25. See "Chronicle of a Single Day," in this volume.

is why there was such a rapid turnover of diners in the kitchens. While one group took its place in the mass graves of the Warsaw cemetery, the kitchen was filled with a new wave of diners from among the newly returned refugees or the pauperized, whose only food from then on was the thin soup of the People's Kitchen. Among the characters at the public kitchen at 40 Leszno Street, the most memorable was the man from [?], a refugee from Germany, whose health was ruined in the notorious Dachau camp. He was not helped by the five or six helpings of soup that the head of the kitchen, the writer Rachel A[uerba]ch, forced into him every day. Deprived of fats and other life-giving nourishment, his organs refused to go on working. Despite all the efforts of Rachel A[uerba]ch, he died of hunger.

This death proved clearly that social welfare can exist only when it has vast financial means at its disposal and can substantially help the needy; social welfare activities of minimal scope are a wasted effort.

A rich area of O[yneg] S[habes] was the diaries. We have already mentioned that during the present war everyone has been writing something, particularly diaries. Some wrote their diaries in a finished form, while others contented themselves with brief notes that could be written up after the war. Most of these diaries were destroyed during the Deportation or because their writers were dragged off to the Umschlagplatz and the writings they left behind were destroyed along with the rest of their property. Other diary writers also, because of the continual blockades and need to relocate from one street to another, often lost the greater part of their manuscripts. It is safe to estimate that dozens, if not hundreds, of diaries were lost, for it should be remembered that only a small fraction of those who wrote diaries admitted to it. Most of them kept it a secret.

The diary of the Hebrew writer and teacher [Chaim Aaron] Kaplan, written in Hebrew, amounted to thousands of pages and contained a mass of information about what happened each day in Warsaw.[26] Kaplan was not a man of broad interests, but the experiences of every ordinary Warsaw Jew, his sufferings and feelings, his thirst for revenge, etc., are all faithfully conveyed in Kaplan's diary. It is precisely the ordinariness of the writer that makes the diary important. I asked Kaplan more than once to give his manuscript to the archive, on the guarantee that it would be returned to him after the war. Most reluctantly he was persuaded to let us copy the manuscript. But this was very difficult. A part remains in the O[yneg] S[habes] archive. The complete manuscript was lost during the Deportation, together with the author, who was taken to the Umschlagplatz. [...]

The head of the Warsaw Jewish Council, the unfortunate [Adam] Czerniakow, kept a logbook on everything that happened in the ghetto during his tenure.[27] The diary or, more correctly, logbook is undoubtedly very interesting, for Czerniakow was in daily contact with the German authorities and also with the Polish municipal authorities, and, as chairman of the kehillah, he held the reins of Jewish daily life in his hands.

Professor Majer Balaban began writing his memoirs during the war, starting with his early childhood. His son, Alexander Balaban, informs me that his father's memoirs reached the war years, on which he wrote a considerable amount. The diary is on the Aryan Side.[28]

26. See "from *Scroll of Agony*," in this volume.

27. See *The Warsaw Diary of Adam Czerniakow: Prelude to Doom* (New York: Stein and Day, 1978).

28. Balaban was a major historian of Polish Jewry. He died in the Warsaw ghetto on December 26, 1942. His diary was lost.

The famous Polish-Jewish writer for children, and no less a famous pedagogue, Dr. Janusz Korczak (Dr. Goldschmidt) kept a diary, which is on the Other Side.[29] In this diary, Dr. Korczak, who was a master writer in Polish, has unquestionably left a monument to the tragedy of the Jewish children, whom the German occupation deprived of air, sun, school, and bread. Many materials for a diary were collected by the well-known singer and journalist [Menakhem] Kipnis. After Kipnis's death we endeavored to obtain these materials for O[yneg] S[habes]. However, his widow would not give her consent. She was taken to the Umschlagplatz, and no trace of the materials remains. The same thing happened to the diary of the journalist Krimski, who was taken during the Deportation.

My daily—later, weekly and monthly—recordings survive. Later these were especially important for the first year of the war, when others did not keep diaries. The weekly and monthly reports supply not only data on the most important events of this period but also an evaluation of them. Because of my social activities, these evaluations are important documents, as they express what the surviving remnant of Jewish society thought about the current questions of its life.

An important document is the diary of A[braham] L[ewi]n.[30] The author has kept his diary for the past year and a half and poured his entire literary creativity into it. Each sentence in the diary is planned. Comrade Lewin puts into it everything that is reported, not only about Warsaw but about the harsh sufferings of Jews in the provinces. Even in the period of the Deportation, when he suffered the terrible loss of his wife, Luba,

29. Published as *Ghetto Diary* (New Haven, CT: Yale University Press, 2003).

30. See the selections from Lewin's diary that are included in this volume.

he kept his diary daily, in conditions that seemed impossible either for work or for creativity. Because of the purity and conciseness of style, the exact rendering of facts and its profound content, the diary can qualify as an important literary document that should certainly be published after the war. It was written in Yiddish until the Deportation and in Hebrew thereafter.

The Deportation, which began on July 22, 1942, marked the start of a new era in the history of the Warsaw Jews. The work of O[yneg] S[habes] also changed in character. There was an interruption of several months in our activities. At a time when one was in constant danger of being caught [and sent off] to Treblinka, there could be no question of the systematic work of collection. Only a few coworkers continued to keep their diaries during the Deportation and note down their daily experiences. As soon as things settled down a bit, we started our work afresh. But it was not possible to write monographs on cities that[31]

The staff of O[yneg] S[habes] made up and continue to make a coherent group, inspired by a united spirit, guided by a single idea. O[yneg] S[habes] is not an association of scholars who compete and struggle among each other but a coherent group, a brotherhood in which each helps the others and strives toward the common goal. For months on end the pious Rabbi Huberband sat next to the Left Labor Zionist Hersh W[asser] and the General Zionist Abraham L[ewin] at one table. And yet we worked together, in harmony. O[yneg] S[habes] did not forget its coworkers. The faithful father and provider was the ailing Menakhem K[on], who saved both Hersh W[asser] and Rabbi Huberband from dying of typhus, who cared about the

31. Unfinished sentence in the original.

sick child of Comrade G[utkow]ski, and who greatly aided the writer and the journalist Peretz O[poczyn]ski, who was always suffering from hunger. The quiet dove, Daniel Fligelman, would have died long since had it not been for the constant and affectionate help of our dear Comrade Menakhem. There were countless occasions on which he pressed me to leave Warsaw after the bloody night of April [18], 1942.[32] Every coworker of O[yneg] S[habes] knew that his effort and pain, his difficult toil and tribulations, the risk he ran twenty-four hours a day in the clandestine work, carrying materials from one place to another—that all this was for the sake of a noble ideal and that, in the days of freedom, society will correctly evaluate and award it the highest honor of free Europe. O[yneg] S[habes] was a brotherhood, an order of brothers, who wrote on their banner, "Readiness for Sacrifice; Loyalty of One to Another; Service to Society."

End of January 1943
Ringelblum Archive II:263[33]
Translated from the Yiddish by Elinor Robinson

EMANUEL RINGELBLUM was a Polish Jewish historian, relief worker, political activist, and organizer of the underground Oyneg Shabes archive in the Warsaw Ghetto. Born in Buczacz, eastern Galicia, in 1900, Ringelblum moved to Warsaw in 1920, entering the history faculty of Warsaw University. In 1927, he completed his doctoral dis-

32. See Abraham Lewin's diary entry for May 30, 1942, in this volume.

33. The call numbers refer to *The Warsaw Ghetto Oyneg Shabes–Ringelblum Archive: Catalog and Guide*, ed. Robert Moses Shapira and Tadeusz Epsztein (Bloomington: Indiana University Press, 2009).

sertation, "The Jews of Warsaw until 1527," which was published in 1932. That year, he began to work for the American Jewish Joint Distribution Committee (JDC), where he learned how "self-help" could provide both economic assistance and moral support to Polish Jews fighting discrimination and pogroms. When World War II broke out, Ringelblum became a leader of the Aleynhilf (Jewish Social Self-Help), the key relief organization in the Warsaw Ghetto, as well as the Yidishe kultur-organizatsye (IKOR), a Yiddish culture organization. Ringelblum used the Aleynhilf to employ and support the Jewish intelligentsia and cultural elite. Ringelblum and his wife and son were murdered by the Nazis in March 1944, along with thirty-four other Jews who had been hiding in an underground bunker.

WŁADYSŁAW SZLENGEL

Telephone

With my heart broken, and sick,
with my thoughts on the other side
I was sitting one evening
next to the telephone—

And I think: let me ring
someone on the other side
when I am on telephone duty[1]
in the evening—

And suddenly I realize: my God there
is actually no one to call,
in nineteen thirty-nine
I went on a different road,

Our ways have parted,
friendships sunk to the bottom
and now, well . . . there is no one
I can telephone.

1. A building with a working telephone was manned by a rotation of tenants who took all incoming calls.

ca. 1940
Ringelblum Archive II:400
Translated from the Polish by John and Bogdana Carpenter

The poet, journalist, and actor Władysław Szlengel was born in Warsaw in 1914. In the 1930s, he emerged as an up-and-coming poet and songwriter who wrote, exclusively in Polish, on Jewish themes, anti-Semitism, and the worsening political situation. Szlengel played a major role in the cultural life of the Warsaw Ghetto. His poetry was widely copied and declaimed. Szlengel's "The Living Newspaper," parodies and satires of ghetto life, became a mainstay of the nightly shows at the Sztuka café, which also featured the best singers, actors, and pianists. Szlengel was killed during the Warsaw Ghetto Uprising in May 1943.

JOSEF KIRMAN

I Speak to You Openly, Child

(Short Poems in Prose)

Doves on Wires

. . . My child, on a cold and frosty day, with an evil wind blowing and shaking man and earth, your father dragged himself along, tired, in search of himself. He wandered through the streets, past buildings and people.

Instead of himself, he found wires—barbed wires that cut through the street and cut it to pieces. On both sides of the wire people walked up and down. Poverty and hunger drove them toward the fence through which one could see what went on on the other side. Jews, the badge of shame on their arms, walked on one side and Christian boys and girls on the other. When from the other side a loaf of bread was thrown over the fence, boys on this side tried to catch it. Police in jackboots, armed with rubber truncheons, beat up a child. The child cried, and German soldiers, looking on, shook with laughter. When a Jewish girl sang a song, begging, pleading, "I am hungry and cold," policemen drove her away, and the soldiers smiled when they saw the loaf of bread rolling on the ground.

People walked up and down. And your father stood there and looked over the fence. Suddenly a flight of doves came down, driven from somewhere out of the blue. Silently they settled on the wires and began quietly to coo. I felt the pain of their sadness and sorrow, I listened to their weeping hearts and understood the anguish of the freezing doves.

And yet, my child, how greedy man is! With his heart he feels sympathy, while his eyes are filled with envy. The doves have wings, and if they want to, they can fly, onto wires or up to rooftops, off and away!

Your father stood there, dreaming. And a policeman came and knocked him on the head. Ashamed, he began to move on, but he wanted to look once more at the doves. And, then, my child, your father saw something terrible:

The doves were still there, on the barbed wires, but . . . they were eating the crumbs, out of the hands of the soldiers! . . .

My child, your father grew very sad, and sad he still is: not about the doves on freezing wires, and not because they have wings and he has not, but because now he hates the doves, too, and he warns you: keep away from them, as long as innocence allows itself to be fed by murderous hands. . . .

Flames over Warsaw

My child, when the steel birds hailed down death, we all fled to the woods. You remember how terrified we were when the woods along our tracks caught fire and we went on in our flight without hope and without thought that we would ever reach our goal? Now it is different. . . . Come, come out into the street. Though a biting frost cuts the ears and it is late in the evening. My dear, beloved son, come, I will show you a fire that lights up the skies over Warsaw. I don't know where it comes from and what it is for. Maybe they are fliers from Russian fields, or maybe the birds came from the other side of the Channel, or maybe it is the work of hidden hands at home;[1] perhaps this, perhaps that. . . . But look, how the sky grows red. How beautiful the red is over the snow-covered town; it is evening and it's light and where the Vistula is frozen to ice, there rise up higher, and higher, and almost as high as the sky: giant tongues of fire and of smoke. Wherever we turn we see wide-open spaces lit up by the flames. It smells of sulfur, of white heat, though the frost is grim and the snow lies dense on roofs and walls. How beautiful is this wintry evening! Something great and unexpected is coming from over there, from the Vistula, where the fires are burning.

My child, you regret that you cannot put out the fire, that you are not a Polish fireman with a little trumpet: *tu-tu-tu!* . . .

Don't be a silly child! You'll be a fireman one day. But not yet, not yet. It's too early yet to extinguish the fires. Let them burn, let them burn, let them burn, my child!

Come children, let's form a ring and dance and clap our hands: *tra-la, tra-la-la!*

A pity the fire grows smaller . . . Someone asks me:

"What was on fire, Mister Jew, perhaps you know? What was it?"

"The wickedness of the world was on fire, I thought. . . ."

"Really?"—The woman who asked nods knowingly.

It Will Be as in Our Dream . . .

My son! You should not regret it that you have been with me in the locked-up streets of the ghetto—Dzika, Stawki, and Miła.

1. A reference to the partisans.

My son, you should not regret your crying today. It does not matter that, when you look up to the sun, tears come into your eyes.

For you will see, my child, you will see: where today there is wailing and sadness hovers in homes; and the Angel of Death reigns supreme like a drunken madman; and people in rags, heaps of shattered hopes, cower along old, dark, and smoky walls; and bodies of old men rot away in doorways or on bare floors, covered with newspapers or pieces of stone; and children shiver and whisper, "We are starving," and like rats stir in piles of refuse; and worn-out women hold up their hands, thin as ribbons in their last barren consumptive prayers; and frost and disease close in on dying eyes that, in their last agony, crave for a crust of bread—

There, my dear, my sunny child,
there will yet come
that great,
that greatest of days,
that last, the very last day—
and it will be as in our dream . . .

Warsaw Ghetto, February–March 1942
Published in the Bundist *Yugnt-shtime* (Voice of youth), no. 2/3
Translated from the Yiddish by Jacob Sonntag

JOSEF KIRMAN was born in Warsaw in 1896. A laborer who had been arrested for his leftist views, Kirman lived in poverty. His poems and stories, written in Yiddish, addressed the needs of the poor. Some of his most memorable works, dealing with his anguish on being separated from his family, were written in the Warsaw Ghetto, where they were published in the underground press. He was murdered in the liquidation of the Poniatowa concentration camp on November 3, 1943.

SHIMON HUBERBAND

Ghetto Folklore

I. Signs of the Messiah

As soon as the war broke out, on the seventeenth of Elul 5699 / September 1, 1939, all the Jews were confident that the Messiah and his redemption would come in the year 5700, because there were numerous allusions to that effect in holy books printed hundreds of years ago. There were, in addition, other such signs in holy books published a few decades ago, as well as popularly construed signs that were transmitted orally.

1. The earliest source stating that the redemption would come in 5700 is found in the commentary of R. Joseph Yahya on the book of Daniel. This work is no longer extant.

2. In R. Gedalia Ibn Yahya's *Shalshelet Hakabbalah* [The chain of tradition], reprinted in scores of editions during the past three hundred years, the following appears in the Warsaw edition of 1899 on page 64, under the entry "Maimonides": "My father and teacher in his commentary on the Book of Daniel proves that the end of days will be in the year 5700." This is the year 1939–40 according to the common calendar.

3. The *Otsar Yisrael* [Jewish encyclopedia], edited by J. D. Eisentadt,[1] presents the following under the entry "End of Days": "The kabbalists agree that the period in which we live is

1. Should be: Eisenstein.

suited for the redemption of Israel, for the ten supernal spheres[2] reach perfection every one thousand years. And if one subtracts three spheres, which are the broken vessels, from the year 6000, this gives the year of redemption 5700."

4. Since these holy books merely state that the redemption will come in the year 5700, the masses began to look for allusions to the specific date of the redemption. The strongest hint that emerged was that the redemption would be on the day after Passover, 5700.

5. When the day after Passover came and went without the arrival of the Messiah, people began to search for another date during the same year. Since the war began on the seventeenth of Elul, the date exactly nine months later fell on the Sabbath of the weekly reading: "When you enter the land . . ." [Deut. 26:1–29:8].[3] When the Sabbath morning service ended, Jews began to hope for Mincha-time, the late-afternoon prayer; when Mincha-time came, they hoped for the conclusion of the Sabbath. When three stars began to shine in the sky, the lights were lit, Havdalah was recited, and the Messiah still did not come, the mood turned despondent. But not for long. Soon a new sign was found that the redemption must occur in the year 5700.

6. The sign consisted of the final letters of the word in the verse "Timhe et zekher Amalek" (You shall blot out the memory of Amalek; Deut. 25:19). The *taf* of the first word refers to five thousand years. The *taf* of the second word, the *resh* of the third word, and the *kuf* of the fourth word add up to seven hundred. This was taken to mean that the memory of Amalek

2. *Sephirot*, divine emanations.

3. Ki Tavo: Read out of context, the opening words could mean "When it [the redemption] will come."

will be blotted out in the year 5700, and, as is well known, Hitler and Germany are Amalek.

When the year 5700 drew to a close and the Messiah did not come, the search began for signs regarding the year 5701.

7. It was said, in the name of a certain Hasidic rabbi, "When we begin to blow the shofar,[4] the enemy will be blown away."

8. The Targum Jonathan on the weekly reading "When you mount the lamps . . ." (Num. 8:1–12:16) speaks in [chap. 11] verse 20 of a nation, Magor,[5] that will arise on the eve of the redemption. It will be extremely well armed, organized, and disciplined. This nation will conquer many other nations and will subjugate them. This nation will reach the Land of Israel and wage war on it. At that time, all the soldiers of this nation will perish, the dead will be revived, and the Messiah will appear.

9. Fake signs were also invented. Thus, a report spread that in the book *'Alumah* by the great kabbalist Rabbi Moses, it is written that in the days of the Messiah, there will be a ruler of a certain land who will torture Jews greatly and will conquer many lands. Indeed, this ruler will be an evil spirit named Hitler. In the end, when the evil spirit Hitler will wage war in the year 1940, he will be defeated, and the Messiah will come.

As it turned out, there was no such statement in the entire book of *'Alumah*; the sign was a total fabrication.

10. Following the Passover festival of 1941, handwritten fliers appeared, which were copied from one another. The fliers ostensibly contained a text from the *Sefer Etanim* [The book of Eitanim]. It was allegedly stated in this book that on the twenty-second day of Iyar 5701, the redemption would come. It then emerged that there was no book in existence with the name of *Sefer Etanim*.

4. At the beginning of the month of Elul, i.e., in the late summer.

5. Actually, a scribal error; it should read "Magog."

II. Legends

1. ON THE FALL OF POLAND

The Maggid of Kozhenitz was a great Polish patriot. He was on friendly terms with the Czartoryski family of the Polish nobility. Members of that family came frequently to Kozhenitz to request that the Maggid include them in his prayers and to submit slips, *kvitlekh*, containing various petitions. Not only the Czartoryskis but many other families of Polish nobility were intimately involved and acquainted with the Maggid.

A number of Polish songs and several Polish aphorisms and sayings of the Maggid have survived to this day. Before his demise, the Maggid also spoke, among other things, about the future of Poland.

The Maggid said that Poland was a lion. There would come a time, however, when the lion would be captured and tied to a leash. For close to 150 years, the lion would pull at the leash but would be unable to free itself.[6] Ultimately, however, at the designated time, the lion would tear off its shackles and free itself.

But the lion would not be free for very long, the Maggid continued. It would be free for some twenty-odd years. Then a nation would appear that would recapture it and enslave it anew. But this would not last for long, for when this would occur, the Messiah would appear.

2. THE WOMAN WITH THE SHORN BRAIDS

It happened during the first days after the fall of Poland. Ration cards had not yet been instituted, the ghettos did not exist, and there were still no "badges" to distinguish Jews from Christians.

6. A reference to the partitions of Poland, 1772–95. The Polish Republic existed from 1919 to 1939.

Jews and gentiles stood together in long lines in front of the bakeries to buy bread. Jews who stood in line were primarily women, for the men feared they might be seized for forced labor.

The Germans kept order in the lines. They were unable to recognize which women were Christian and which Jewish. But having it in for the Jews, the Poles would point them out in line to the Germans. The latter would shout at them, "Jews, get the hell out of here!" Hearing such shouts, the Jewish women would leave the line at once. But there were some women who were not identified as Jews from their appearance. They would ignore the shouts of the Germans and remain in line.

That was how a certain legend spread across all of Poland. Each version had it taking place in a different city or town.

A Jewish woman who could pass as a non-Jew was standing in line for a loaf of bread. The German soldier shouted for all Jews to leave the line. All the Jewish women obeyed, except for this woman, who thought she wouldn't be spotted. So she stayed in line. A nearby Pole called over a German soldier and pointed her out.

After removing the woman from the line, he cut off her braids as punishment for failing to follow his order. Seeing this, the Pole who had informed on her burst out laughing.

The Jewish woman turned to the Pole and said, "Why are you rejoicing? My hair will grow back before your state will be restored."

The Pole flew into a horrible rage. He lunged at the woman and wanted to beat her. Not knowing Polish, the German soldier who witnessed the scene didn't understand what was going on. When it was explained to him, he led the Jewish woman to the head of the line and ordered that she be sold two loaves of bread, instead of the one loaf sold to all the others.

Another version: A German cut off a Jew's beard. A passing Pole, seeing this, burst out laughing. Said the Jew, "My beard will grow back before you get back your state." The German, who understood Polish, told the Jew, "You are a wise *Jude*."

3. THE MIRACLE OF THE GHETTO

Outside the ghetto wall there were two German militiamen who tortured Poles in a brutal fashion. So the Poles decided to do away with them. But knowing full well what bloody acts of reprisal this would provoke, they made a plan to do away with the Germans, load them onto a wagon covered with garbage, smuggle the bodies past the guards into the ghetto, and then plant the corpses inside the ghetto.

But the Guardian of Israel neither slumbers nor sleeps! [Ps. 121:4] That night, as soon as the garbage wagon reached the sentry, one militiaman decided to prod through the garbage with his bayonet and felt it pierce the flesh of a corpse. He ordered the Poles to empty all the garbage.

Then the whole story came out, and of course the Poles who drove the wagon were arrested on the spot. Under torture, the whole truth came out. The German revenge against the Poles was ferocious. And the Jewish ghetto was rescued from great peril.

4. ANOTHER VERSION

Poles shot two German militiamen on the other side of the ghetto wall. To avoid bloody acts of revenge, they decided to throw the two corpses over the ghetto wall that night, at a location where there were no guards.

Late at night, just as the Poles were carrying out their plan, a German patrol happened by and noticed the goings-on. The members of the patrol jumped over the ghetto wall and grabbed the murderers, who confessed to the crime. The Jewish ghetto was spared a great calamity.

5. IT'S ALL FOR THE BEST

When the ghetto was suddenly sealed off, on a certain Saturday, a great crowd of women came running with shrieks and tears to the great Hasidic master Rabbi Yehoshua. When they entered the rebbe's study, he was in the midst of wrapping himself in his tallith to begin praying.

"Holy rebbe!" the women cried out. "We all live near the border of the ghetto, next to the sentry station. Until now we all earned a good living. But now that we have been locked up like living corpses inside a casket, we will all starve to death, God forbid." The women cried that all the Jews would die of starvation.

The rebbe stood for a moment, immersed in thought, and then replied, "My dear women, you must know that the Lord our God will not forsake us. Whatever the Almighty does is for the best. Before long, everyone will see that even the sealing off of the ghetto is for the best."

Hearing these words, the women calmed down and left the rebbe's study with relief.

It didn't take long. On a certain day, the artist Igo Sym was murdered on the other side of the ghetto wall.[7] Large-scale arrests were carried out on the "Other Side." Hundreds of Poles were imprisoned and executed but not a single Jew, because the ghetto was sealed and therefore no Jew could have been responsible for his murder.

7. Igo Sym, a well-known prewar Polish film director, was executed by the Polish underground on March 7, 1941, for collaborating with the Germans.

Now everyone recognized the great holiness of Rabbi Yehoshua's words, that whatever the Lord does is for the best, even the sealing of the ghetto.

III. Jokes and Puns

1. A teacher asks his pupil, "Tell me, Moyshe, what would you like to be if you were Hitler's son?" "An orphan," the pupil answers.

2. A child who steals from others is said to be manic. An adult who steals from others is said to be a kleptomaniac. A nation that steals from others is called Germaniac.

3. Winter 1939–40. An enormous line of needy people stood in front of a welfare agency, seeking assistance. It was bitter cold. They remarked to each other while waiting, "Now you know how lucky the rich people are. They'll stand in line when it'll be warm, in the summertime."

4. A Jew had all his worldly possessions taken from him, but he remained jolly and in good spirits. So his neighbor asked him, "All your possessions were taken away. Why are you still in good spirits?" The Jew answered, "My dear neighbor, they took away Czechoslovakia, Poland, Denmark, Belgium, Holland, France, and other countries. Someday they will have to return all these countries. So then they'll have to return my things too."

5. Another version of the same joke: Hitler comes to Nalewki Street in Warsaw.[8] A Jew recognizes him and goes over to him. "What's new with you, Mr. Hitler?"

"Go away," Hitler replies. "You're insane. How could it occur to you that I'm Hitler?"

8. A main street of the Jewish quarter.

The Jew answers, “You know that it’s hard to fool a Jew.”

“All right, let’s say I’m Hitler,” he admits. “So what? What do you want from me?”

“I want you to buy a few things from me,” the Jew says and presents him with a list of items he wants to sell him.

“I’d gladly buy a few things,” says Hitler, “but what can I do? I don’t have any money.”

“Well, if you don’t have any money, I’ll lend you some, Mr. Hitler,” the Jew answers.

“How do you know that I’ll give the money back to you?” Hitler asks.

“Listen here, Mr. Hitler, you’ve conquered so many countries that you’re going to have to give back. Are you going to steal just for my few zlotys?”

6. The Führer appeals to General Franco, “Please give me advice, comrade! Help! Things are so bad!” Franco answers, “I’m sorry, but I can’t help you. I can’t join your pact.” So Hitler says, “Then give me at least some advice.”

Franco: “Stretch out a peaceful hand to England.”

Hitler: “I tried that already, but it didn’t work.”

Franco: “Then stretch out your legs, as well.”

7. During the Italian defeat in Greece and Ethiopia, the Führer calls up Il Duce: “Duce, are you in Athens?”

Il Duce (catching the Führer’s joke): “Ha? What? Where are you calling from? I can’t hear you. Are you calling from London?”

8. The Führer inquires of General Franco, “Comrade, how did you solve the Jewish problem?”

Franco answers, “I instituted the yellow badge.”

“That’s nothing,” says Hitler. “I imposed tributes, instituted ghettos, lessened their food rations, imposed forced labor.” He goes on, enumerating a long list of edicts and persecutions.

Finally, Franco says, "I gave the Jews autonomy and Jewish councils."

"Ah," says Hitler, "that's the solution."

9. Germany is waging a war. England is playing a game. Germany will win the war. England will win the game.

10. The Führer embarked on a journey to visit all the hospitals. Upon arriving in a certain one, the hospital director gave him a tour and showed him everything. The Führer unexpectedly barged into a corridor and found a securely locked room. This seemed very suspicious to the Führer. He insisted on seeing the room.

"If you insist, then I must first explain what is inside," the hospital director said to Hitler. "Locked up inside, there is a madman whose external appearance is similar to yours. His illness expresses itself in his self-delusion that he is the Führer."

"If that is the case," says the Führer, "then I must see him." Hitler entered the room alone. After a short while, he left the room. But no one is certain which one left and which one remained inside—Hitler or the madman.

11. God dispatched an angel from heaven to find out what's new on earth. The angel returned with a report that he simply could not understand the world. "England is unarmed and does not want peace. Germany is armed and wants peace. And the Jews are screaming that everything is fine."

12. During the rumors that the Russians would conquer the General-Government[9] of Poland, it was said that whoever is studying German is a pessimist, whoever is studying English is an optimist, whoever is studying Russian is a dreamer, and whoever is studying Polish is a realist.

9. The area of Poland under German civilian administration, established October 1939.

13. The Jews worshiped other gods and were therefore granted a ghetto.[10]

14. It is forbidden for a Kohen to marry a woman from the ghetto, because she is a *gerusha*.[11]

15. A Jew was arrested. None of his relatives knew that he was in custody. The Jew pleaded that he be allowed to notify his relatives, but he was not granted permission. He asked to be allowed a brief telephone conversation with his family. The prison warden allowed him to speak only for five minutes. The Jew agreed and had lifted the receiver when the warden told him to speak no more than one word. The Jew agreed to this condition as well. He took the receiver to his lips and screamed into it, "Help!"

16. A contemporary Jewish prayer: Oh, Lord, help me become a chairman or vice chairman, so that I can allocate funds to myself.

17. No garbage was permitted to be taken out of the ghetto. A Jewish ghetto administrator appeared before his German commissar to request permission to remove garbage accumulating in his home. When the Jew came into the commissar's office and did not raise his arm in the Hitler salute, the commissar became furious and threw him out of the room. A few days later the Jewish administrator appeared a second time in the commissar's office. The commissar was certain that this time the Jew would salute him by raising his arm. And indeed, the Jew entered his room, raising his arm. So the commissar addressed the Jew, "This time, *Jude*, you acted correctly

10. "Gods" (*geter*) and "ghetto" (*geta*) sound almost identical in Warsaw Yiddish.

11. Hebrew-Yiddish for divorcée; can also mean exiled or deported woman.

by raising your arm in the Hitler salute." "No, Mr. Commissar," the Jew answered, "I just wanted to show you how high the garbage has gotten."

18. Where does Hitler feel best?

In the toilet. There, all the brown masses are behind him.

19. Rubinshteyn[12] says, "I had a *groschen* but lost it; I had a *tsveyer* [two-*groschen* piece] but lost it; I had a *drayer* [three-*groschen* piece] but lost it. Only the *firer*[13] [four-*groschen* piece] I can't seem to lose.

20. God forbid that the war last as long as the Jews are able to endure it.

21. Another version: How long will the hardships last? God forbid that the hardships last as long as the Jews can endure. Because if the hardships last that long, who knows if they will really endure them?

22. If we can endure for twenty-one days, then we'll be saved: namely, eight days of Passover, eight days of Sukkot, two days of Rosh Hashanah, two days of Shavuot, and one day of Yom Kippur.

23. We eat as if it were Yom Kippur [i.e., we fast], sleep in *sukkahs* [i.e., in makeshift quarters], and dress as if it were Purim [i.e., in outlandish clothes].

24. The Jews are now very pious. They observe all the ritual laws: they are stabbed and punched with holes like matzahs and have as much bread as on Passover; they are beaten like *hoshanahs* [willow twigs beaten at the end of the Sukkot festival]; rattled like Haman [during the reading of the Purim Megillah]; they are as green as *esrogim* [citrons used for Sukkot]; they fast as if it were Yom Kippur; they are consumed as if it

12. A popular wit in the Warsaw Ghetto.
13. A pun on "Führer."

were Hanukkah [and they were the candles]; and their moods are as if it were [the day of fasting for the destruction of the Temple on] the Ninth of Av.

ca. 1941
Ringelblum Archive I:1257
Translated from the Yiddish by David E. Fishman

SHIMON HUBERBAND was born into a rabbinic family in 1909 and ordained by his grandfather. A religious Zionist, he founded the Society for Jewish Scholarship in Otwock and published widely on theological and historical topics. After his wife was killed early in World War II, he moved to Warsaw, where he remarried. Huberband became Ringelblum's most valued collaborator in the chronicling of the Warsaw Ghetto. He died in the Great Deportation in the summer of 1942.

PERETZ OPOCZYNSKI

House No. 21

House No. 21 on Wołynska Street was the author's residence both before and during the war. The time: the first months of the German occupation, before the establishment of the ghetto. The building sustained heavy damage during the aerial bombardment of Warsaw in September 1939.

A peasant drives into the courtyard with a cartload of cabbage, bread, and potatoes; he sells the potatoes to one of the tenants, who has been waiting for him by the road from Wola.[1] Nobody knows how much the man pays, but barely five minutes later he is asking a price for the potatoes that makes eyes pop. The other tenants buy the bread—bread and cabbage. There is a rush, a scramble; they pay the peasant whatever he asks—so many gulden[2] for a kilo of pasty black bread and the same for a kilo of cabbage. However, in the midst of the commotion one snatches a small loaf from behind his back, while another carries home a head of cabbage without paying a penny. When the peasant realizes that he is being robbed, he lifts a swingletree from his cart and brandishes it with such fury that the crowd

1. One of the western sections of Warsaw, close to the Jewish quarter.

2. Gulden is used throughout as a synonym for zloty, the basic Polish currency issued by the Germans.

backs away; people quietly make off with what they have. The peasant stands by his cart, eyes flashing like knives, while his wife pours out curses on the Jews, screaming that all they are suffering isn't as much as they deserve.

The Zelechower,[3] who has helped himself to a few heads of cabbage, rubs his hands together gleefully. Even after the fire he hadn't lost heart, and now he is even hopeful. His apartment is being rebuilt; the walls are already up, although the roof is not yet covered. The autumn rains have come, and the rainwater pours down from the damaged apartments onto the heads of the tenants below. It has even reached the bottom story, flooding the egg dealer's floor.

The landlady rises at five o'clock and cleans the courtyard by herself; her husband will sleep until late in the morning, but she cannot rest. After the janitor took leave of her company, she herself was seized by an extraordinary desire to work, to toil. Work gives her pleasure. It reminds her of her younger years. However, she isn't allowed to enjoy it; every moment another tenant runs out of his ruined apartment to inform her that it is her own fault that her property has fallen to shambles, that the entire house will be ruined if she doesn't speed up the restoration.

Hearing these arguments, the landlady becomes very agitated. Not this, anything but this: her house go to ruin, her sweat and blood? She promises to finish building as quickly as possible. As soon as the bricklayers arrive she will get things moving, and while she's at it, she thinks to herself, start demanding rent. . . . Can the building be put up for nothing? She knows that the Zelechower, the shoemaker, and Pearl have stripped the wood from the ceilings and walls of their ruined apartments,

3. A Zelechower means a man from the town of Żelechów, near Warsaw.

every beam, and laid it under the beds in their "shelters" to burn for heat during the winter, yet she doesn't say a word; she understands that if you can't enter by the front door, you have to go through the back, besides which, she is not about to start up with Pearl . . . no need to make trouble—they will be paying rent soon enough. She holds her peace and goes back to work, cleaning, sweeping, dragging the scattered bricks into the yard and sweeping out her big apartment . . . the entire house. . . .

From every direction peasants come with cartloads of produce from the villages, with potatoes, cabbage, wood, and even with coal, for Jews cannot get coal from the trains. Some claim that these aren't peasants at all but people from the city's outskirts who want to make their living by trading with Jews. It's hard to say how they got permission to bring their carts into the city, but probably the authorities in these parts are lenient in such matters. After all, the German commandant in an out-of-the-way place has to live too.

All of Miła Street is filled with the peasants' carts. They also weave through Lubeckiego and Wołynska Streets and, indeed, throughout the entire neighborhood, especially those with wood.

In front of Wedel's shop[4] on Marszalkowska Street and later on Bielanska Street, people are standing in long lines, just like that, each one suspiciously watching the others. If a passerby asks why they are waiting here, he is told that they themselves don't know, they are simply waiting. . . . However, it eventually comes out that for two gulden one can buy a slab of prewar chocolate from Wedel, with a small sack of candy thrown in. People don't buy this for themselves but as merchandise, for there is still a small remnant of Jews who can afford a slab of

4. Wedel's chocolate factory had a chain of shops throughout Warsaw.

good chocolate, even though there are many, many more who are already dropping in the streets from hunger. So let there be chocolate—as long as it helps you stay alive.

In the state-run shops of the Christian section, such as those far down on Marszalkowska, one can obtain milk and even candy to sell. The furrier's wife, the glove maker's daughters, and the shoemaker's wife hear about this and spend entire days waiting in the lines so that they can bring home a few slabs of chocolate and a little cheap milk. The milk, which the peasants have just brought in from the villages, like the butter, cheese, and sweet cream, is expensive.

Suddenly, Jewish men with yellow Stars of David on their sleeves appear all over the city, along with women who have yellow patches sewn onto their shawls.[5] Giant flatcars pass by, carrying Jewish men, women, and children whose noses are red from the damp, cold autumn weather. What's this? Who are these people?

As they pass through the streets, people shout at them, "Where are you from?" And the men, embittered by the endless questions, answer, "From Rózaniec, from Sierpc. . . ."[6] Forty Jews from Sierpc come to No. 21 and settle in the front, in a vacant store. The landlady doesn't emit a word of protest; on the contrary, she talks with the commandant, the head of the tenement committee, about helping them out. Since it's Thursday afternoon, they come up with the idea of providing them with a *cholent*, the traditional dish for the Sabbath, which begins the

5. The refuges from Wartheland, the western part of Poland incorporated into the German Reich, were required to affix a Star of David to their clothing, while in the General-Government, where Warsaw was situated, the Jews wore white arm bands instead.

6. Towns that were absorbed into Wartheland and from which Jews were expelled from February 1939 to February 1940.

next evening. (Later the commandant will brag that this cholent cost a good hundred gulden.) When the Sabbath is over, the commandant runs to all the tenants who wanted to take in subtenants and places the forty newcomers in the building. The landlady hears all about this: tenants are making the Sierpcers pay good money for the kitchen corners, under sinks, where they place them—why then is she forbidden to collect rent?

The four thousand Sierpc Jews and an equal number of Jews from Rózaniec have already been quartered in the city. However, there is news of expulsions from other areas, and all at once Jews stop hoarding supplies. Katz, who has stored a wagonload of coal in his cellar, refuses another; the butcher and the landlady stop buying up potatoes and cabbage for the winter; the sausage maker stops buying salt, and the shoemaker, leather. Why should they, when no one knows what lies ahead?

A peasant stands in the yard with a wagonload of potatoes from early on in the morning. Instead of the eighty gulden a bushel he had demanded yesterday, he is asking only seventy. After a while he lowers his price to fifty, but although he stands there until dusk, asking as little as forty-five gulden a bushel, no one buys. The peasant spends the night in the yard and drives away in the morning, his lips forming a curse on the "kikes"—has some devil suddenly possessed them that they've stopped eating, or what?

This state of confusion lasts a day or two, and then suddenly a rumor spreads from ear to ear: they are coming, the Russians . . . they are already near Praga[7] . . . the border has been opened . . . Jews are passing to the Other Side in broad daylight. . . .

7. In the first weeks of the German-Polish war, rumor had it that the Russians would advance to the Vistula, thus including the Warsaw suburb of Praga on the eastern side of the river.

The tenants crowd the courtyard. Not only the butcher, the Zelechower, and the volatile commandant but all the tenants carry the conversation from the yard into the street. People gather in groups in front of the gate to discuss the news, and the scene is repeated in front of all the other gates on the street. Every courtyard is packed. In the street you can learn the latest developments faster by simply shouting to the passersby, "So what's up? Are they really coming?"

"What a question. You'll see, tomorrow morning they'll be in Warsaw."

As soon as the Zelechower gets back his apartment, he will know what to do. . . . Ah! They can't pry open his mouth. . . . His slanted little Mongolian eyes sparkle shrewdly; his firm, broad, square shoulders straighten out over his low frame like a board as he tightens his belt and chuckles.

The army tailor is also very secretive. He doesn't even tell his own wife, Pearl, that he is planning to take their son, Zalman, with him to the Other Side. However, Pearl soon gets wind of this and leaves no doubt that she won't let Zalman, her only son, out of the apartment—her husband can forget about that. Besides, she doesn't care for the whole business—no, you can make a living here too, and it's a fair chance that you can do better under the Germans than on the Other Side.

The tenement commandant toys with the idea of going to his brother-in-law in Tel Aviv, but he knows very well that this is only talk. Yes, certainly the Germans will let you out of the country for good money, and the Italian Jews issue visas; the Italian consulate in Warsaw won't make things difficult, at least not yet. . . . When Hitler and Il Duce meet at the Brenner Pass, things will be different.[8] However, in the meantime one has to earn the favor

8. Hitler and Mussolini met there for a mutual nonaggression pact.

of the Germans, that is, not so much earn it as buy it. The commandant knows stories about Jews who have fled to the Land of Israel and beyond, but always for a price, say, twenty thousand gulden, and if you have that kind of money, you don't need a visa.[9] People also go to America. How do they manage it? Don't ask questions! There are those who arrange such things. . . . But what does it matter? . . . He, the commandant, is not one of the rich, and besides, he has a revolutionary past . . . 1905. . . . Still, he considers sending his sons to the Other Side—he has another brother-in-law in Małkinia.[10] . . .

The Germans order the Jewish shopkeepers to put up signs in Yiddish, no, in Hebrew. . . . "*Your forefathers . . . lived beyond the Euphrates*" [Josh. 24:2].

This causes no surprise. It is seen simply as a continuation of the Polish ordinance from before the war, under the OZON regime,[11] which ordered all Jewish shopkeepers to hang small placards by their stores, bearing their authentic Jewish forenames: not Hela Wierzbicka or Bernard Leczycki but, in true biblical style, Chana and Boruch. Hebrew sign makers spring up overnight and flood the streets with their inadvertently comic reading material: *Akhilo mezoynes minim* [Hebrew: All kinds of foods for eating], *Barzel yoshon koni* [Hebrew: Secondhand iron buy I], *Khayot bgodim ishim* [Hebrew: A tailor of clothes [for] people], and similar nonsense. Winebaum puts up a sign: *Khonus lekhem mezoynes vekhol akhilo* [Hebrew: A

9. At that time, the Palestine Office in Geneva used the Italian steamship line Adriatica to help individuals reach Israel. That company had a branch office in Warsaw.

10. A town on the new German-Soviet border; as such, it was the last stop for thousands of refugees before they crossed into the Soviet Union.

11. OZON, or the Camp of National Unit, was the Polish political party that came to power in 1937.

store of bread, foods, and everything for eating], and his new wife, his late wife's sister and not at all the stepmother that Rukhtshe the baker's wife had prophesied, argues with the dealer in gauze, the Yiddishist, who makes fun of her because, although she could have made a better sign solely in Yiddish, she has wasted a perfectly good sign board by using both Yiddish and Hebrew. What does he want, that she should provoke the Germans? If they want Hebrew, let it be Hebrew. They can rack their brains over it, so long as they leave her alone!

Already Jews are forbidden to travel by train; however, this ordinance is not yet strictly enforced. Besides, it isn't such a great blow to Warsaw Jewry: only a few individuals take the train to the Soviet side; the majority make the journey by bus, cart, or simply by foot. To travel anywhere else by train is unheard of, except for those who are extremely daring: smugglers and other cunning souls who can talk like demons and pay good money for papers that permit them to travel through almost all of Poland.

There's a big to-do at the entrance to the tenement: the tax collector's daughter, whose fiancé had joined the Children of Warsaw[12] and been killed during the defense of the city, fell in love with a thief and married him. Her father, a Hasid, had run out on his daughter in the middle of the bombardment because she had taken several thieves into the apartment as subtenants. Now she was married to one of them. From heartache her father took sick and passed away. Pearl serves up this story with all the trimmings, crying, "Who would have believed that such things could happen? But naturally she is, of course, the daughter of a Hasid—the trash! Our own children would

12. The Children of Warsaw was a volunteer brigade for civil defense set up in the first month of the war.

never do such a thing; only a Hasidic daughter could fall for a crook." The shoemaker's wife listens to this with deep satisfaction, while the Zelechower strains his patchwork mind for an appropriate illustration of how inferior these Hasidic bunglers are to ourselves . . . yes, even in Żelechów he knew this.

Pearl goes on and on discussing this story in the "provisional" quarters, where she continues to live with the Zelechower and the shoemaker until her own apartment is ready so as not to let the other neighbors see how eagerly she is awaiting the day when she will move her few possessions back into her freshened, refurbished home. The kitchen is already prepared, and she has begun secretly cooking dinners there; after all, the others don't have to know of every single thing she eats. She's already ordered the paint. Meanwhile she stands every day at the Wołowka Flea Market selling jackets, thinking as she smugly pats her belly, "Well, if your head's on straight, you can have it all—a new apartment, all the wood off the walls, and even get out of paying rent."

The baker Brodsky's eldest son has left for the Other Side; he went by bus. On Nalewki Street there are buses that will take you all the way to Białystok for two hundred gulden. Where on Nalewki Street? The commandant knows; he too wanted to send his eldest son on the bus, but he has hit on an even better plan: he himself will take him to Małkinia by train. . . .

Rivkele's son, who makes lightweight shoes called *gandis*, is now also in transit. A few of the subtenants leave to the Russian Zone each day. In every tenement the talk is only of leaving, escaping. The army tailor and the Zelechower, both waiting for their apartments to be made ready, spend entire days dreaming like schoolboys about going to Russia, making it to the big cities—Moscow, Leningrad, Kharkov, where you can get huge loaves of white bread and bowls filled with rice, fish, and meat.

"Listen, neighbor, listen," stammers the Zelechower. "I talked with this kid from No. 10 who came back from there yesterday to fetch his wife and children. He says that if you get a position in the Bolshevik Party, you can make up to five hundred rubles a week, there are all kinds of good things to eat. All you need is a little luck."

"And what if you don't get a position?" asks the army tailor.

"You sleep in the House of Study," answers the Zelechower, "and there will still be food. Three times a day they serve bread and soup, enough to live on."

The army tailor would agree to everything, even though his service in the world war has made him skeptical about easy answers, but he is afraid of his wife, of Pearl; it won't be easy to talk her into letting him go. The two men cannot sit indoors for long; they are constantly running out to listen to those who are gathered in front of the gate. Suddenly a cart with a woven lining, such as one sees in the little towns around Lublin, moves up the street, and this cart is crammed with Jewish men and women who look like they belong to a wedding party. The women, dressed beautifully, hold small valises in their laps, and their faces are flushed. Where are they headed?

"To the Other Side!"

"Really? I don't believe it."

"Then don't believe it, but that's where they're going, to the Other Side."

Now the number of carts that pass through the street, filled with people bound for the Other Side, increases from day to day. None of the tenants can sit home anymore, business and work are at a standstill, the remaining household possessions are sold, and everyone dreams only about going to the Other Side. The army tailor, who has seen something of the world, knows all the routes: through Małkinia by train; through Otwock by the commuter line and then by regular train through Kolbuszowa and Zamość; through Siedlce by train; or through Sokolow and Biala by bus. The bus to Sokolow goes there straight from Bonifraterska Street in Warsaw; however, you have to wait in the ticket line a whole week and then pay double for the ticket.

Rivkele's son, who didn't have money, went to Praga. The sentry at the bridge let him through for five zlotys, which he stuffed into the hand of a Polish policeman while the German guard pretended not to see. And so he walked to Małkinia, and from there it was easy to cross the border. Actually, he was detained at the border, in "no-man's land," for a whole week, but then a good sentry arrived and the soldiers shouted, "Tovarishtshi, perekhadityel!" which means, "Comrades, pass through!" and so he crossed the border. Now he is not in Białystok but in some little town, where he is doing very well. He has work and writes to his mother that he will bring her there.

This letter from Rivkele's son makes the rounds of the tenement; people read it and run their hands over it as though it were some wonderful talisman—a wishing ring. Every moment a different neighbor runs into her apartment:

"Good morning, Rivkele."

"Good morning, good year."

"Rivkele, may I have a look at that letter from your son?"

"The letter? It's not in the apartment. They took it to the cane maker."

Without even bothering to say good-bye, the neighbor slams the door behind him and runs down to the cane maker, in the basement. His home is already packed; in the center the Zelechower is explaining the letter, although there is nothing to explain.

The letter is written in Yiddish, with German characters: "Dear Mamma, I am working and doing very well. I have enough food and can go wherever I please. You can make a living here; people sing in the streets. I have already submitted a request for your papers, and God willing, I will bring you here soon."

"Ah, you understand," says the Zelechower, extending his index finger as though about to open a lock. Exposing the tip of his tongue, he contracts his low, blunt forehead and stammers, "Yes, he has enough f-food and can go wherever he pleases. Just as I said, what m-more do you need? Here, if you step out, they g-grab you for forced l-labor. There, you do just as you please. Neighbor, do you hear, n-neighbor?" His eyes moist, he turns to the army tailor, "Are you with me? Come, let's leave this week."

In the basement all is chaos. Everyone speaks at once, interrupting the others. Only the cane maker remains silent.

"Why should we leave?" asks the shoemaker. "The Russians will soon be in Warsaw anyway."

The day after the war began the shoemaker was already back at work, refurbishing old shoes and looking for a place to sell them until the ruined Wołowka Flea Market should be repaired. He has no desire to venture out into the world. He is perfectly content with the black bread he earns by rising at five in the morning, just as before the war, and hammering on his shoemaker's bench, and therefore he is willing to wait for the Russians to come to Warsaw. However, the cane maker, the Zelechower, and even the army tailor, although they too can eke out livings, are drawn to the world beyond the border. They don't have the patience to wait for the Russians; they want to be free.

The cane maker maintains his silence one day, two days, three. He is constantly going out to listen to the conversation at the gate, and early one morning, not at all a beautiful morning but gray and foggy, he puts his wife and child onto a wagon that has driven up to the tenement and, with other Jews and their wives and children, sets off for the Other Side. The only one left in the basement apartment is his aged mother, who will live by taking in subtenants.

By now this has become the sole topic of conversation in the tenement: in front of the gate, in sitting rooms by day and in beds by night. Wherever one walks or loiters, the question is always the same: "So when are you going? And Zelig? He has already gone? Through Hrubieszow or Małkinia? How, on the commuter line?"

The whole city talks of leaving. Workmen and artisans, merchants and clerks, teachers and writers, doctors and lawyers—there is no type of Jew who does not think of going away. Traveling brotherhoods are created. One man attaches himself to another, and he, in turn, to another; these returned yesterday from Praga, turned back by the border guards, while those will set out tomorrow for a second time. This one is accompanied by a gentile guide, who will take him from Warsaw to the other side of the border, but that one is afraid that a gentile might lead you on only to desert you along the way. Another has hired a reliable gentile, a peasant from near the border who speaks Yiddish. In fact, he is so reliable that he has made a hiding place in his wagon where one can put gold and jewelry, like in a bank. God forbid that one should lose one's few remaining possessions.

Already brokers have appeared to manage the "reliable" gentiles from near the border, and there are also Jews who drive flatcars, buses, and all kinds of carts. From morning to night one sees the carts on Wołynska, Lubeckiego, Niska, and Zamenhofa Streets. Where does one not see them?

A peasant's cart now passes through the alley; a Jew with a short, blond beard sits next to the peasant on the cab. On the only seat for passengers, a sack of straw, sit two boys of six or seven, swaddled in shawls and gazing with sad, dark little eyes from which peers a world of terrible suffering—gazing as if to say, "Look what we've lived to see: destined to wander yet again . . . war in the land, nothing to eat, one's very life hangs by a thread . . . those murderers . . . those brutal decrees. . . ."

In a propitious hour Pearl moves into her renovated apartment. The Zelechower is furious; his apartment still isn't finished. His need is greater than Pearl's. The shoemaker has also moved back into his apartment; only the Zelechower is still shut out. Now the tailor, the former tenant of the "shelter" who had moved out before the bombardment, is giving him trouble, claiming that he needs it again. The Zelechower understands that he wants to rent it out, even if he doesn't say so. He runs to the landlady three times a day, insisting (as if that will help) that he be let back into his old apartment already. But the landlady, unabashed, informs him that first he must pay his back rent.

"What?" The Zelechower doesn't understand. "Rent? What kind of rent can there be now, during the war?"

Right away he runs to Pearl with the news only to discover—alas!—that she, Pearl, who had always joined the others in insisting that nothing could make her pay rent in wartime, when evictions are forbidden, has nevertheless handed over a hundred zlotys down payment. Of course, she would never have done such a thing had she not learned that the newly established Polish courts ordered the payment of rent on pain of eviction.

The Zelechower has no choice; he too must hand the landlady a couple of gulden, his last, if he is to move into his apartment. However, he has barely been in his new home a week when he realizes that with the scarcity increasing, there is no work, business is at a standstill, nothing pays . . . and so he sends his wife and children back to Żelechów. He takes a subtenant into his home, a musician, and the "shelter" is let to a rabbi from whom the former tenant, with the landlady's assent, collects rent.

The Zelechower, alone now, spends entire days contemplating escape to the Other Side. He is constantly trying to persuade the army tailor to join him. It seems, however, that the other has plans of his own, for he vanishes from the house so suddenly that not even the roosters give warning. Pearl swears and curses: What kind of husband is this? Nothing but heartache. But on realizing that he is indeed gone, she gradually calms down and carries all the sewn things he had left behind to sell on the flea market. Her eldest daughter can also stitch a pair of pants or patch a garment, and so Pearl continues climbing the stairwell, carrying loaves of bread and sacks of potatoes with which to feed her family.

Having a rabbi as a neighbor is agreeable to everyone but especially to the landlady, who wants to get rid of the more disreputable tenants and replace them with others who are more respectable. There is general approval, and soon the rabbi is picking up a clientele: the girl from Skerniewice, who subleases from the furrier's wife, has found herself a lad who will accompany her across the border. Since her dowry is to be used for traveling expenses, the young man readily agrees to take her under the bridal canopy before they depart.

Such weddings are now a frequent occurrence throughout the city, and not only in Warsaw, for half of Poland yearns for the Other Side. In Warsaw and everywhere else, girls are meeting young men, and their parents are only too happy to get a daughter out of the house by marrying her off. These weddings provide the rabbi with a tolerable living.

Boys from Wołynska Street cross over to the Other Side and come back in a few weeks in order to earn a few gulden as experienced guides. While they're at it, they take along wrist-watches, which are very expensive there and dirt cheap here, as well as suits and shoes, likewise worth their weight in gold on the Other Side.

Brodsky's son has already returned. He doesn't look well, but he plans to go back someday. He already knows all the routes, gives advice on how to make the journey, and proposes himself as a reliable guide across the border. He has brought regards from the army tailor, but Pearl just laughs: Ha! What did she say? Doesn't she know her husband, the big shot? So he's going to make it on his own, as though he can get along without her for a single day! He was full of talk about how he could find work and make money. So what? He knows nothing about housekeeping, or if he does . . . let him tell it to his grandmother. She, Pearl, will never be convinced, never be fooled. She knows that if he goes a little hungry just once, he'll remember her good cooking, her full pots, and he won't be able to take it anymore. . . . Well, now he wants to come back. Didn't she tell him there's no way around it, that you can live better here, from jackets and from Germans, than there?

Outside the rain pours incessantly; it's foggy and bleak, and the streets are filled with mud and filth, but the carts keep going to the border. Already there are houses with vacant apartments, and elsewhere you can rent a furnished apartment for next to nothing. An apartment that rented for up to two thousand gulden before the war can now be taken for three or four hundred gulden. It's said that the border is closed; people are held up in "no-man's land" for a week, two weeks, three—and nothing can pass over the border. Many become sick from waiting in the cold, rainy, late-autumn days and many more from spending the cold autumn nights under the stars. Children are dropping like flies. It seems that the Germans no longer allow people to cross; they force any wanderers they encounter to hand over not only their last groschen but also their overcoats and boots and in return give them terrible German beatings, merciless blows, and drive them back. It's also rumored that the Russians no longer call the wanderers "comrades" but curse them and beat them and sometimes place them under arrest. The woods are full of bands of Polish thieves who ambush the wanderers, rob and beat them, and even tear the gold teeth from their mouths.

The shipping clerk's young son has come back from Białystok without the jewels that were hidden in the hollow buttons sewn onto his overcoat. The Germans saw through the ruse and cut off the buttons. The hairdresser in the neighboring tenement hid a diamond under the filling of a gold tooth; but the tooth was cut out, and he returned a pale, broken man, full of hatred even more for the Russian "comrades" than for the Germans. However, people continue to leave for the Other Side. The buses to Białystok have stopped, it's true, but still people find dozens of other ways.

The weather gets colder and colder; in "no-man's land" there is already frost. The peasants near the border are making piles of money letting people spend nights in their stables and rooms. All of this is known here, yet people continue to leave.

The Lithuanians have already retaken Vilna,[13] and a new exodus begins. Lithuania is now a "neutral" country—under the German heel but, formally, neutral—and it offers a chance

13. The Soviets signed a mutual-aid agreement with independent Lithuania on October 10, 1939, and returned the city of Vilna as part of the package.

of escape to the free world. People leave from here with the clear goal of smuggling themselves over two borders: the German-Polish-Soviet and the Soviet-Lithuanian. At first the Lithuanians had let themselves be bribed, but now they have become unbending and cruel and allow no exceptions: anyone seen stealing over the border gets a bullet in the head.

Pretty young Khayale Auerbach, married barely six months, sews all her worldly possessions, the dowry that she has exchanged for jewels, into the square, hollowed-out buttons of her overcoat and passes without incident over the border at Małkinia. But when, after joining her husband in Białystok, she tries to cross the Lithuanian border, she falls dead with a bullet in her heart. Her husband goes out of his mind with grief.

This isn't the only tragedy. People know it, but the stream of travelers doesn't stop.

When the army tailor returns, there is snow in the courtyard. His hands and feet are frozen, and he must lie in bed several weeks; but he is relieved to be home again. It's not worth it, he says, to labor for nothing; the Bolsheviks don't let you live. . . .

The landlady stands in the yard but no longer sweeps or cleans—she is once again the mistress of the house. She stops every passing tenant and demands rent. At first she asks rather timidly, with a faint smile and a quiet voice: "Well, Mr. Grauman, someone has to pay for water, for garbage collection. My husband is, after all, only human; he too must make a living!" People respond quietly and politely, so she is contented, satisfied with a promise, with a good word, and it gives her a strange pleasure; she never imagined it would go so smoothly. Only two months ago she would have been stoned for showing such nerve.

The next day she is bolder and less tongue-tied, she speaks a little louder, and each succeeding day she grows more confident. Now she is heard far out in the courtyard, arguing with the "good-for-nothings." The defiant, sharp-tongued women are ready for battle: What is this? They should pay her rent, now, during the war—rent "under the Germans"? She should lie sick for so long!

But the landlady knows her rights: "You won't pay? Then I'll take you to court. You'll pay at the green table. Do you want to eat, to buy bread? You also have to pay for the roof over your head. No free lodgings, not with me!"

"Look at her, the scum, the trash," the broker's wife shouts up from the basement.

"She won't be happy if she doesn't get her money. You can't gorge yourself on our labor now—curses I'll pay you!"

"During the bombing I guarded this house for nothing, stood entire nights by the gate," says the butcher. "Now, you rich bitch, a curse on your years; do you think we don't know you? We all know that your fortune comes from Buenos Aires, not . . . 'from the sweat of your brow.'[14] You should choke on it all. . . . Shove it up your ass!"

The landlady says nothing but, leaving the butcher and the broker's wife, walks quickly into her apartment.

Pearl, who held her breath as she stood in a corner by the hall window and listened to the slanders with delight, now shouts to the furrier's wife, "Did you hear that quarrel? How they gave it to her! I should live so long. It's given me back a little courage; she thinks it's going to be easy, the filthy whore; she actually threatened to take me to court. Well, we'll see if it

14. An allusion to the Jewish white slave trade.

works out so nicely for her, we'll see. If the Germans say no to evictions, just let her try it."

The army tailor, his frozen hands and feet already healed, helps his wife deal with the landlady. He claims that he paid her the hundred zlotys just like that; it wasn't worth fighting over it. But to pay all the rent he owes, no, she can forget about that! When the war is over—then we'll see.

The Zelechower, who has already received a clear, precise, and exhaustive account of the army tailor's journey to the Other Side, runs all over the tenement letting every neighbor in on his secret: had the army tailor not sneaked off alone but crossed together with him, he would not have returned in such a state, for he (the Zelechower) would have shown him the best route, and, of course, he has many relatives in Russia—aunts, uncles, brothers-in-law—who are all doing very well, making a lot of money in good positions. Now he has no choice but to go it alone. Yes, he still intends to go; he's only waiting for a letter that a goy is going to bring over from the Other Side any day now, and people will see who the big shot really is; he doesn't like to boast, but they will see! . . .

And they do indeed see, that is, not so much see as hear that the Zelechower has sold two of his three new sewing machines and quietly taken the third by cart to Żelechów, and he is gone—no more Zelechower.

"Where is the Zelechower? Where is he?" the neighbors ask one another. "Has he really gone to the Other Side?" However, in a week or two he is back. It seems that the Germans confiscated his sewing machine on the way. He no longer wears his heavy winter coat with the sheepskin collar but a rubber summer coat; also his cheeks have grown hollow from the journey. He says he has come back to Warsaw on business and will soon be off again, and he is true to his word—he leaves once and comes back and leaves a second time, until finally he grabs the chance to sell his apartment to the musician, who is playing at Polish weddings again, as he did before the war. And there's an end to it. Now the Zelechower leaves Warsaw for good, to join his wife and children in Żelechów; he would trade all the opportunities of the city for one bowl of Zelechower garlic borscht with potatoes!

Pearl holds open the door to her refurbished, brightly painted apartment, with the polished red floor that she didn't even have before the war. She stands with her hands on her hips and meets each oncoming neighbor with a grim countenance: "What do you say to that lowlife, the landlady? She's taking us to court, a curse on her years, she's sued ten people. Well, we'll see who gets thrown out; may she be thrown from the top of a roof! Father in heaven! . . ."

The furrier's wife is also standing in her doorway. Her red hair again neatly combed, she wears a sporty vest that makes her figure seem even more slender, as if she were getting herself ready again to work out at the Shtern Sports Club.[15] It seems that her husband gave up his wartime business. They no longer go to Otwock for milk, she no longer waits in line for chocolate and candy or sells German papers. Instead, he makes fur collars, and their neighbor the purse maker, who stopped making purses, makes a living by selling the furrier's collars at the flea market.

The furrier's wife, who is among the ten who have been sued, argues Pearl's position in the phraseology of propaganda booklets: "One pays no rent in wartime. Such 'dealings' aren't legal. Sorry, neighbor, if she wants to collect for water and the

15. A Jewish sports club set up by the Left Labor Zionists.

sewage, let her want to. And did she have the right to pocket security deposits before the war? To steal the last morsel from the worker's mouth? We won't pay. Together, we won't capitulate; in unity lies strength!"

Suddenly Khavtshe, the shoemaker's wife, comes in from the street bearing news: a paruvke—a fumigation.

Pearl looks daggers at her. She believes that Khavtshe is responsible for all her problems, because she was the first to deliver rent to the landlady after the war began, when the bombs were already falling. But when she hears Khavtshe pronounce the dreaded word, she ducks into her apartment like a thief, quickly shuts the door behind her, and forgets about court, about the landlady, about curses—a paruvke!

Soon the screeching of closet doors and the scraping of the sofa are heard from inside the apartment; the sewing machine stays put, but benches are tumbling, and there is a stirring from within, all the rushing and sounds of things being bundled up that you hear when someone yells "fire."

A quarter of an hour later Pearl emerges carrying a bundle of clothes wrapped in a shawl, followed by her daughters carrying fabrics and bedding, and before most of the other tenants have even been properly informed, Pearl has returned with her daughters to carry a second load of bundles to her mother on Smocza Street. Now prepared, she can wait for the official decree.

As the news spreads, the tenement is thrown into a panic: Who could have guessed that the smooth-talking little doctor with the black whiskers who had, after all, confessed that in almost all the apartments he had encountered scoured floors, fresh bedding, and scrubbed heads—who could have guessed that he would still call for a paruvke? And where is the tenement commandant, the tenement committee? How is it that just yesterday enough money was collected to pay off everyone?

People run into the yard, the women with kerchiefs on their heads, and the sharp, freezing wind doesn't let them stand in one place. They are waiting for the members of the committee to tell them that the situation isn't so dangerous, that there may still be a good chance of avoiding this threat, for a paruvke, which took place in the neighboring tenement only a few days ago, strikes terror into every heart. But wherever or whoever the members of the committee may be, they seem to have vanished into thin air.

The women return to their homes and try to copy Pearl, carrying whatever they can to neighbors and relatives; there is a great deal of running about, for no one knows when the brutes will come, perhaps today or perhaps tomorrow. Then, suddenly, the angry, threatening voices of the Polish police are heard in the courtyard, calling everyone to the bathhouse.

Ah, now they're in for it. . . . People run to their windows and look out into the yard. The gate is already closed, there is no place to run or hide, they have them in their grasp.

Soon screams are heard in the yard; the Polish police are hitting people with rubber truncheons;[16] they block every exit from the house so that there is no place to go except into the line for the baths. Some of the police stand in the exits, while others run through the apartments, driving people to the bathhouse. From everywhere screams and cries are heard. The stall keeper's wife, who is pregnant, tries to explain to a policeman that she can't go into the bathhouse in her condition; but he

16. Many of the Polish police, known as the Blue Police, helped persecute and murder Jews; others worked for the Polish resistance, and some did both.

brings his stick down on her head, and her agonized cry echoes through all the floors.

In truth, the brutality of the police is a first-rate ploy: the butcher calls in several policeman and, locking the door behind them, takes a flask of whiskey from a cabinet, sets a plate of sliced wurst on the table, and even . . . opens up his wallet. Afterward the police emerge with red mugs, and everything is hush-hush. The butcher stands calmly by the window and looks out at the crowd being driven to the bath.

Pearl goes down with her daughters and little boy and stands for appearance's sake in the line, but the members of her household won't be going into the bath. She has paid off the police brute, who opens the gate and lets both her daughters out. Now the policeman at the gate becomes even more severe, more demanding; the Polish janitor, who has been waiting for this blessed hour a very long time, acts as middleman, and he too receives special bribes from those who want to buy themselves out. Only big money is accepted, not single gulden but five- and ten-gulden pieces, which will be used to buy big flasks of liquor and sausage. The majority of the tenants are led with their wives and children into the bathhouse on Spokojna Street—the "slaughterhouse" they call it. On the way, several try to sneak out of the line; but the police have sharp eyes, and as soon as someone even raises a foot to run, the club comes down on his head.

One resident is allowed to remain in each apartment, until the bedding can be removed for cleaning and the homes fumigated. Meanwhile a mob of Polish riffraff, men and women, enters the yard. These are the disinfectors, the fumigators; they have a list of dwellings that have to be disinfected, that is, wherever the tenants didn't pay them off in cash. The committee members get straight to the point; they direct the doctor and the fumigators to those apartments that require . . . fumigation. It makes no difference if a room is clean or not, if the bedding is spotless or not. The only thing that matters is . . . money.

The fumigators go about their work with perverse joy, with an almost insanely malicious pleasure in destruction. They drag the bundles of clean bedding with the freshly changed sheets and throw them onto the filthy stairwell, then they pile them up in the yard on the wet asphalt. The piles lie there for a long time, until the trucks from the bathhouse come to collect them; sometimes they lie like that for a day or two or even three, and no one cares if it rains or snows. Then they are stacked up high on the bathhouse trucks and trodden down by muddy shoes until the wagon is full. If a sheet should happen to catch on a nail and tear, this bothers the fumigators no more than any of the other little disturbances they endure; they are having a fine time—getting their revenge on the kikes. . . .

The commandant comes in off the street and stealthily crosses the yard, but the few remaining housewives spot him and run after him, shouting, "Mr. Bernholtz, Mr. Bernholtz, so this is how you serve us? Is that what we paid you for?"

The commandant gets angry. His eyes flashing, he shouts, "I warned you to keep your homes clean!"

"Oh yah? But whoever laid out some dirty cash didn't get fumigated, and the committee members' homes weren't fumigated either!" the knitter's wife screams down from the fourth floor. "Wait, just wait, your time will come; you won't always be in charge!"

The commandant, furious, storms out of the yard screaming: he's through with doing favors for everyone; he isn't a Moses that he should take everybody else's problems on his shoulders. . . . But it's readily apparent that this display of anger is really intended to let him slip quickly out of the yard, so that he can show up at last with the other committee members, now that the danger is almost over.

On Spokojna Street the tenants encounter long lines of Jews who have been brought to the bathhouse from other tenements. Placards now hang from these tenements, with yellow letters spelling out in German and Polish, "Spotted Typhus," although no typhus victims have been removed from any of these buildings. The Jews, who stand here pushing and shoving in order to enter the baths more quickly, are very much aware of this and bear their humiliation patiently: What does it matter how one suffers, from blows or from baths? They save their bitterness and impatience only for each other. They argue and curse and do not spare their fists: "Look at the great man, the rag picker, how he shoves, what a hurry he's in. What, you don't have time? Are you so afraid the Germans haven't purified you yet? May your brains rot to hell, you trash!"

In the midst of this jostling an attendant comes out of the bathhouse and starts to smash whatever heads he can reach with his broom or simply rips off the caps of those who've reached the door of the bath and makes them go to the back of the line. All in all, about twenty are admitted to the baths, while the others have to wait outside in a new line. Those who can stuff something into the attendant's hand are let in first. Others enter through a back door or window and with the help of a gift get taken first. Those who don't have money may have to wait outside or in the first or second anteroom for half a day or more before they are let inside. Those lucky enough to get in must immediately strip themselves naked and hand over their clothes for fumigation, but the clothes can lie bundled up for hours because the fumigation machines are so busy. The naked crowd stands on the cement floor, freezing, hungry, and shivering.

And now the shearing ordeal begins. A brutal Pole appears with a dull, blunt shearing device and proceeds to mercilessly shave everyone's head, taking special pleasure in lopping off the hair of young men with finely coiffed locks. The Hasid saves a bit of his full beard with a couple of gulden, while the butcher's son keeps the whole head of hair by placing a substantial coin in the Pole's hand. After the shearing comes the examination by the "doctor"—really only a barber surgeon—a young lout who makes sure that the barber shears have been applied to all the hairy parts of the body and sends back anyone who has not been shaved to his satisfaction. Those who have been shorn and examined are driven naked through the cold corridors that lead from these rooms to the bath, but there they must wait for the water to heat up, since there isn't enough coal. And there they stand from eight until midnight and sometimes even longer, until they are finished bathing. After that they still must wait a few hours for their clothes to be brought from the disinfecting machine, and only then, after enduring an entire day of this, can they go back home carrying cards attesting to their purification.

So it goes in the men's bathhouse; for the women it is even worse. The gentile women who examine their hair know where to land blows—after all, they themselves are women! For good money one can get by with a dirty scalp, but those without money have their heads mercilessly shorn, whether they are young girls or mothers. One hears screams, desperate cries, hysterics; those with shaven heads go home sick, shattered, humiliated, and the next day, wearing kerchiefs on their heads, they will seem like dazed old women. Pearl stands among the women, loudly cursing the tenement committee. She takes the injustice personally; she herself knew what to do, how to buy her own way out as well as her daughters, but her heart aches for the others, only for the others.

The shoemaker's and the furrier's wives were also lucky, because they too took along a few gulden, but everyone else in the tenement goes home broken in spirit. The egg dealer's daughter has almost fainted from weeping; she won't be seen in the courtyard for several days.

The furrier and his wife are both still young, just over thirty, and both suffer from asthma. Still, they laugh off their troubles. It is, after all, only the first winter of the war; one can still make a joke. At two in the morning, enveloped by the frosty, starlit winter night, the people, their stomachs empty, say to one another, "To health . . . We've been koshered and rendered pure. So where are the challah and fish?"[17] The children, after enduring the full day of torment along with their parents, also forget about their hunger and weariness and enjoy the walk: "Look, look Papa, a falling star . . . a star."

A few sinister characters are standing by a street lamp in the distance. Although the war curfew prohibits people from staying out at night, members of the Polish underworld lie in wait for Jews emerging from the baths, from whom they can steal a towel, a jacket, or even snatch a purse. Many return from the baths chilled and half sick, but there is no bedding in their apartments; they have to wait long days, even weeks, until it is returned from the paruvke. Right now there is absolutely nothing to sleep on. When the bundles are returned, they will see that several items are missing, but they will be happy to have escaped with their lives.

The stall keeper's wife was brought back unharmed; she had suffered less than others, and she only hopes to give birth soon, before the next paruvke, because everyone already knows

17. In preparation for the Jewish holidays, men would immerse themselves in the ritual bath.

that when these butchers get hold of the house again, they won't let them off so easy.

The next day those who stayed home are rounded up for the baths, even the aged and the infirm, deaf old people, the mute, the crippled, the mentally impaired. No one is overlooked. As they are driven away, the house heaves a heavy sigh for the paruvke, and heads are lowered.

Also on the next day the members of the tenement committee are reluctant to venture into the courtyard, as though ashamed to show themselves. But they aren't ashamed, no, for how would it have helped matters, argues one member, if they had gone to the baths, if they too had suffered a paruvke? Pearl, however, won't let him off so easily. "If there's a paruvke," she screams, "it's for everyone. No privileges. To the baths—everyone must go to the baths."

"And your children went to the baths?"

"My children, my children," Pearl's eyes begin to flame, "my children weren't in the baths? Didn't my Zalmele go to the bath? Didn't my husband go to the bath? Wasn't I in the bath? How dare you, you brazen lout!"

"And what about your daughters?"

"My daughters also."

"You're lying."

"Oh, look who's talking—the fine man, everyone's toady—he's calling me a liar. And if I sent the girls to another bathhouse, what of it?"

"Oh yeah, another bathhouse?" drawls the committee man. "That's a different story."

Those gathered around understand what this means: Pearl paid Bernholtz for a note from the bathhouse stating that her daughters had been bathed. But still Pearl deafens everyone with her tirade against the injustice she has suffered at the hands of man, and she will go on cursing until the next paruvke, so that the commandant shall know with whom he is dealing and keep her off the list.

Now, after the brutal paruvke, even those who have lagged behind want to flee to the Other Side. What kind of life is this here? There at least you're free—true, you may starve, but you're a human being just the same. But here? Even the purse maker joins the chorus. However, the traffic to the Other Side has already slowed; only the daredevils go now, people with nothing to lose, for the frost burns terribly at the border, and every day a few travelers show up in the alley with frozen arms and legs. In the facing tenement a youth returned with his leg frozen up to the knee, and who knows if it will heal without an operation?

The frost is bad enough, but the news that the Russian border guards are shooting at anyone who tries to cross the border is much worse. This bursts like an icy current on all speculations: How can they, who call everyone "comrade," shoot at people who are escaping from hell? At Jews, victims of Hitler's reign of terror?

The shoemaker, who cannot bear for his basic faith in human justice to be trodden underfoot, tries to explain: "What do you expect them to do? The Jews themselves are to blame, bringing goods to Białystok and speculating, dealing in bread, cigarettes, and all sorts of contraband, sneaking from village to village, smuggling dollars and jewels into Russia—what do you want, that the Russians watch all this and keep quiet? There's a war going on, and the Russians also have to keep an eye on the Germans."

But as soon as the shoemaker mentioned the Russians and the Germans in the same breath, the faces of his listeners turn somber. The furrier's wife especially wants no more fancy talk about justice and humanity: if Russia can make a pact with Germany, well, it's the end of the world—what's left?

The butcher simply laughs at the whole business: why should it matter to him if it's Russians or Germans? If you want to, you can live here as well as there; it's the same world. A sensible man can get along anywhere . . . take, for instance, Hershl the butcher. . . .

Only the army tailor stands apart, listening to this conversation in the furrier's home with his head cocked, smiling. Oy, he has seen these Russian soldiers, how they creep through the woods at night, lying in wait for all who try to steal across the border. He has heard the cries of the captured ring through the frosty nights, although for sixty gulden he himself was allowed to cross the River Bug in a little boat. But no, they won't be able to squeeze any answers out of him. "If freedom is such that it cannot save me, just me, me first of all—understand?—from the claws of the beast, then it's over, no more freedom or justice; then it's live as you can . . . rob, steal, and fill your own belly, because there's nothing better or more beautiful on the face of this earth than a good meal, and there never will be."

Under his whiskers the army tailor breaks out into a shrewd smile. He already knows what he has to do, yes, already knows . . . just now he has begun to live . . . the real life of the war . . . his own life.

1941
Ringelblum Archive I:1228
Translated from the Yiddish by Robert Wolf

PERETZ OPOCZYNSKI, born in Lutomiersk, near Łódź, in 1895, was given a yeshiva education far away from home, which precipitated a break with his Hasidic upbringing. His earliest literary efforts were poems, but he turned to prose to describe his experiences in World War I as a prisoner of war in Hungary. A shoemaker by profession, he also worked as a Yiddish journalist, first in Łódź and then, as of 1935, in Warsaw, where he worked for a Right Labor Zionist newspaper. In the ghetto, he wrote prolifically for the Oyneg Shabes archive and also became an activist in his house committee at 21 Wołynska. Opoczynski was most likely rounded up in the deportation of January 1943.

LEYB GOLDIN

Chronicle of a Single Day

How differently my song would sound
If I could let it all resound.
—*paraphrase of "Monish"*[1]

Tired, pale fingers are setting type somewhere in Kraków:

> "Tik-tak-tak, tik-tak-tak-tak. Rome: the Duce has announced . . . Tokyo: the newspaper *Asahi Shimbun*[2] . . ." Tik-tik-tik-tak . . . Stockholm Tik-tik . . . Washington: Secretary Knox has announced . . . Tik-tik-tik-tak . . . And I am hungry.

It's not yet five o'clock. At the door of the room, a new day awaits you. A quiet breeze. A puppy wants to play with you. Jumps up at your neck, over your body, behind your back, nuzzles up, wants to tease, to get you to go out and play. A discordant orchestra of sleepers breathing. As one begins, another—a child—interrupts right in the middle. And a third—and a fourth. The conversations in one's sleep are over, complaints satisfied. From time to time someone groans in his sleep.

1. A mock-heroic poem by I. L. Peretz, first published in 1888.
2. A major Japanese daily.

And my brain is bursting, my heart is sick, my mouth is dry. I am hungry. Food, food, food!

The last portion of soup: yesterday at twenty to one. The next will be today at the same time. The longest half, already endured. How much longer to go? Eight hours, though you can't count the last hour from noon on. By then you're already in the kitchen, surrounded by the smell of food; you're already prepared. You already see the soup. So there are really only seven hours to go.

"Only" seven hours to go; it's no joke. Seven hours—and the fool says "only." Very well then; how does one get through the seven hours—or the nearest two? Read? Your brain won't take it in. All the same, you pull the book out from under the pillow. German. Arthur Schnitzler. Publisher so-and-so. Year. Printer. "Eva looked into the mirror." You turn the first page and realize you've understood no more than the first sentence: "Eva looked into the mirror."

You've reached the end of the second page. Didn't understand a single word. Yesterday the soup was thin and almost cold. You sprinkled in some salt, which didn't dissolve properly. And yesterday Friedman died . . . of starvation. Definitely of hunger. You could see he wouldn't last long. And there's a gnawing in my stomach. If you only had a quarter of a loaf now! One of the square-shaped quarter loaves, like the ones in that display window, by that table. Oh, brother! You realize that you've jumped up, the idea was so delicious. There's some name or other on page four of the novella: Dionisia. Where she's from, and what she wants, you don't know. There! A quarter of a loaf! There! A bowl of soup! You would make it differently. You would warm it through until it began to boil. So that a spoonful could last five minutes at least. So that you would sweat as you ate. So that you would blow at the spoon, not be able to swallow the soup all at once! Like that!

Maybe it isn't nice to think about oneself in this way—only about oneself, oneself. Remember once, preached a thousand times: the century of the masses, the collective. The individual is nothing. Phrases! It's not me thinking it; it's my stomach. It doesn't think, it yells; it's enough to kill you! It demands, it provokes me. "Intellectual! Where are you, with your theories, your intellectual interests, your dreams, your goals? You educated imbecile! Answer me! Remember: every nuance, every twist of intellectual life used to enchant you, entirely possess you. And now? And now!"

Why are you yelling like that?

"Because I want to. Because I, your stomach, am hungry. Do you realize that by now?"

Who is talking to you in this way? You are two people, Arke. It's a lie. A pose. Don't be so conceited. That kind of split was all right at one time when one was full. *Then* one could say, "Two people are battling in me," and one could make a dramatic, martyred face.

Yes, this kind of thing can be found quite often in literature. But today? Don't talk nonsense—it's you and your stomach. It's your stomach and you. It's 90 percent your stomach and a little bit you. A small remnant, an insignificant remnant of the Arke who once was. The one who thought, read, taught, dreamed. Of the one who looked ironically from the dock directly into the eyes of the prosecutor and smiled directly into his face. Yes, stomach of mine, listen: such an Arke existed once. Once, once, he read a Rolland, lived side by side with a Jean-Christophe, admired an Annette, laughed with a [Colas] Breugnon.[3] Yes, and for a while he was even a Hans Castorp, by some writer . . . Thomas Mann.[4]

3. The last three names are characters in novels by Romain Rolland (1866–1945).

4. In Mann's *The Magic Mountain.*

"I don't understand, wise guy. Haven't you eaten?"

Yes, stomach, sure, I ate, but I didn't know I had eaten. Didn't think I was eating.

"Do you remember, buddy, the first day in jail? You sat in solitary confinement, bewildered, sad; they had just thrown you, like a piece of old clothing, into a pantry. For two days you didn't eat, but didn't feel the least hunger. And suddenly the peephole opened in the door: 'Good evening, Arke! Keep it up! *Grunt się nie przejmować, dobrze się odżywiać!* [Polish: Keep your spirits up and eat well!] Listen, Arke, corner, behind the radiators, there's bread and bacon. The main thing, brother, is to eat—the next installment comes tomorrow, on the walk.' Remember?"

And yesterday Friedman died. Of starvation. Of starvation? When you saw him thrown into the large—the gigantic—mass grave (everyone covered his nose with a handkerchief, except for me and his mother), his throat was cut. Maybe he didn't die of hunger. Maybe he took his own life? Yes . . . no. People don't take their own lives nowadays. Suicide is something from the good old days. At one time, if you loved a girl and she didn't reciprocate, you put a bullet through your head or drained a flowered vial of vinegar essence. At one time, if you were sick with consumption, gallstones, or syphilis, you threw yourself from a fourth-floor window in a back street, leaving behind a stylized note with "It's nobody's fault" and "I'm doing the world a big favor." Why don't we kill ourselves now? The pangs of hunger are far more terrible, more murderous, more choking than any sickness. Well, you see, all sicknesses are human, and some even make a human being of the patient. Make him nobler. But hunger is a bestial, a wild, a rawly primitive—yes, a bestial thing. If you're hungry, you cease to be human; you become a beast. And beasts know nothing of suicide.

"Brilliant, my pet, an excellent theory! So how long is it, wise guy, till twelve o'clock?" Shut up, it'll soon be six o'clock. Another six hours and you'll get your soup. Did you see the burials yesterday? Like dung—that's how they drop the dead into the grave. Turned the box over and flipped them in. The bystanders get such a livid expression of disgust on their faces, as if death were taking revenge for the aura of secrecy. For the various irrelevant, unnecessary things that had been tied onto him, now, out of spite, he let down his pants and, here, look at me, kiss my ass. Like a spoiled child, who's sick of endearments. And do you know, Brother Stomach, how I imagined death when I was a child? I remember when I was four and five, I went to a kindergarten. They played the piano and split their sides laughing and spoke Hebrew. And I remember there was a funeral in the same courtyard. I only saw the hearse entering the courtyard and, soon after, cries and laments. I fancied that the man in the black coat and stiff hat wanted to drag a woman into the hearse, and she didn't want to go, and in fact it was she who was making the noise, and she threw herself on the ground, and he took hold of both her arms, and she was sitting and sliding along, and shouting and screaming. How do you like that, my little stomach? You don't answer—are you asleep? Well, sleep, sleep, the longer the better. At least until twelve o'clock.

Food, food. It isn't my stomach talking now—it's my palate and my temples. Just half a quarter loaf, just a little piece of crust, even if it's burnt, black, like coal. I jump off the bed—a drink of water helps; it provides an interruption. On your way back to bed you fall—your feet are clumsy, swollen. They hurt. But you don't groan. For the last few months you've got used to not groaning, even when you're in pain. At the beginning of the war, when you were lying in bed at night and thinking about the whole thing, or in the morning, when you had to get up, you often emitted a groan. Not now. You're like a robot now. Or maybe, again, like a beast? Perhaps.

Die? So be it. Anything is better than being hungry. Anything is better than suffering. Oh, if only one could use arithmetic to reckon when one would breathe one's last! That woman in the courtyard, from No. 37, who died, had been starving for six weeks. Yes, but she ate nothing, not even soup once a day. And I do eat soup. One can go on suffering for years in this way—and maybe kick the bucket tomorrow. Who knows?

I realize that I'm still holding the book. Page seven. Let's see if I can get through it. I turn the pages. Somewhere, on one of the pages, my eye spots the [German] word *Wonne*. Ecstasy. A piquant, magnificent erotic scene. A few pages earlier they were eating in a restaurant. Schnitzler gives you the menu. No, no, don't read it. Your mouth becomes strangely bitter inside, your head spins. Don't read about what they ate. That's right—just as old people skip descriptions of sex. What's the time? Half past six. Oh, how early it still is!

But it's possible that tomorrow or even today I'll give up the ghost. The heart is a sneak—you never can tell. Maybe I'm lying here for the last time and feeling so sluggish for the last time. So slow to get dressed. And handing in a soup ticket for the last time and taking a new one for tomorrow. And the cashier, and the waitress, and the janitor by the door, they will all look at me with indifference, as they do every day, and not know at all, at all, that tomorrow I won't come here anymore, and not the day after tomorrow and not the day after that. But I will know, and I will feel proud of my secret when I am with them. And perhaps in a few months, or after the war is over, if statistics are made of the diners who died, I'll be there too, and maybe one of the waitresses will say to another, "D'ya know who else died, Zoshe? That redhead who insisted on speaking Yiddish and whom I teased for an hour and, just to fix him good, didn't give him his soup. He's been put in the box too, I bet."

And Zoshe, of course, won't know, as if she would remember such a thing, and then you will have such a high, high [. . .][5] Maybe it will already have been poured; oh, how magnificently Thomas Mann describes it in *The Magic Mountain*. I remember his thoughts, the way he delineated them. Never has their brilliant truth appeared so clear to me as it does now. Time and time. Now it stretches like rubber, and then—it's gone, like a dream, like smoke. Right now, of course, it's stretched out horribly, horribly; it's really enough to kill you. The war has been going on for a full two years, and you've eaten nothing but soup for some four months, and those few months are thousands and thousands of times longer for you than the whole of the previous twenty months—no, longer than your whole life until now. From yesterday's soup to today's is an eternity, and I can't imagine that I'll be able to survive another twenty-four hours of this overpowering hunger. But these four months are no more than a dark, empty nightmare. Try to salvage something from them, remember something in particular—it's impossible. One black, dark mass. I remember, in prison, in solitary confinement. Days that stretch like tar. Each day like another yoke on your neck. And in the evenings, lying in the dark, reviewing the day that had passed, I could hardly believe that I had been in the bathhouse that day—it seemed that it was at least four or five days ago. The days passed with dreadful slowness. But when I went through the gate on that side of the street, all the days

5. In Goldin's contribution, bracketed ellipses signify an indecipherable part of the typescript.

ran together like a pack of dogs on a hunt. Black dogs. Black days. All one black nightmare, like a single black hour.

At the prison gate friends were waiting. I don't remember all of them. But I remember Janek.[6] Yes, Janek. I forgot all about him. Not long ago, last year, I met him. Half naked, in rags, he was tinkering with the gas pipe in a bombed-out house halfway along Marszalkowska Street. He called to me. And out of the blue, as if twelve years hadn't gone by since we met last, he gave me our standard greeting, "Know something?"

"No. And you?"

"Me neither. But it's OK."

Then the supervisor came up and left. So maybe, maybe I should write to Janek. Write to him: Listen, brother, I'm having a hard time. Send me something. Write, then? By all means, write yet more openly: If you could provide me with a quarter of a loaf every day—ah, a little quarter loaf. Yes, when I'm dressed I'll write to him. It may be difficult to send the note, but I'll write to him. A little quarter loaf. And if you can't, then let it be an eighth.

Somewhere in the world people are eating as much as they want. In America sits Hershel eating his supper, and there is bread on the table, and butter, and sugar and a jar of jam. Eat, Hershele, eat! Eat! Hershel, eat a lot, I tell you. Don't leave the crust, it would be a waste, and eat up the crumbs from the table! It tastes good, you become full—true, dear Hershel?

And somewhere in the world there is still something called love. Girls are kissed. And girls kiss in return. And couples go walking for hours in the gardens and the parks and sit by a river, such a cool river, under a spreading tree, and they talk so

6. A Christian Pole.

politely to each other, and laugh together, and gaze in such a friendly way, so lovingly and passionately, into each other's eyes. And they don't think about food. They may be hungry, but they don't think about it. And they are jealous and become angry with each other—again, not eating. And all this is so true, and it is all happening in the world, far away from here, true, but it is happening, and there are people like me over there. . . .

"Sick fantasies!" interrupts the scoundrel, my stomach; he's woken up, the cynic. "What a dreamer! Instead of looking for a practical solution, he lies there deluding himself with nonsensical stories. There are no good or evil stomachs, no educated or simple ones, none in love and none indifferent. In the whole world, if you're hungry, you want to eat. And by the way, it's all nonsense. There are good providers for their stomachs, and there are unlucky wretches like you. You can groan, you idiot, but as far as filling me up—damnation, what's the time?"

Ten past eight. Four hours to go. Not quite four whole hours, but let's say four, and if less, that's certainly to the good. I slowly draw on my pants. I no longer touch my legs. I touched them until, not long ago, I measured them with my fist, to see how far they'd shrunk. No more. What's the point?

And Friedman has died. Tying my shoelaces reminds me of the dozens of dangling genitalia there in the large common grave. And young girls stood around, holding their noses with handkerchiefs, and looked at the islands of hair. Again is it because animals have no shame? Yes, so it seems, at the cemetery—funeral notices of rich men, of doctors, of good citizens . . . there is no end of rickshaws, and an easily recognizable crowd gathers—no poor people there. In other words, this kind of person dies too, though they have enough to eat. One doesn't die of hunger alone. Things even themselves out. They'd better get the message.

"Tell me, friend, are you starting up with your stories again? It's already time to go. Maybe the soup will be earlier today. Move, my dear!"

In the air and heat of early fall the street is full of the smell of sweat and the smell of corpses, just as in front of the ritual cleansing room at the cemetery. Bread, bread everywhere: it costs the same as yesterday. You want to go to a stall, feel, pinch the fresh whole-wheat bread, satiate your fingertips with the soft, baked brown dough. No, better not. It'll only increase your appetite, that's all. No, no just as you didn't want to read what the lovers ate in the restaurant on the quiet Viennese street. And fish roe is cheaper. Cheese—the same price. Sour cream is now in season—but it's expensive. Cucumbers are cheaper, and onions are at the same price. But they're bigger today than yesterday.

Cheerful tomatoes, full of joie de vivre, laugh in front of you, greet you. Trips into the mountains, backpacks, shorts, open shins, wild, joyous songs of earthly happiness rising into space. When, where? Two years ago, altogether two years. Tanned faces, black hands and feet. And hearty laughter, and brooklets of unexpected spring water, and bread-and-butter sandwiches with sweet tea, and no armbands on your sleeves, no mark of being a *Jude*.

Bread, bread, bread. *Razowka. Sitkowka. Vayse sitka. Hele sitka. Tunkele sitka. Walcowka.* First-class bread. *Beknbroyt.*[7]

Bread, bread. The abundance of it dazzles your eyes. In the windows, on the stalls, in hands, in baskets. I won't be able to hold out if I can't grab a bite of breadstuff. "Grab? You don't look suspicious, says he, my murderer. "They'll let you near,

7. There are no English or American equivalents for these breads. They are listed in rough order of desirability.

they'll even put it in your hand. They'll trust you. They can see you aren't one of the grabbers."

Shut up, buddy, you've forgotten that I can't run. Now you're the wise guy, huh?

"You're a goner, you are, my breadwinner," says he. "Just take a look at those two having their identity papers checked at the gate.[8] Look at the color of their faces. You can bet they've eaten today, and they'll damn well eat again, soon. But look over there—they're waiting for the car to pick them up. If you were a mensch, you'd have looked after me earlier on, and you'd be eating like a human being, and not have swollen legs. And you'd also be able to wheedle yourself in and go along for the ride. They give you half a liter of soup and a loaf of bread a week. Too bad you're such a *shlimazel*."

Wrong again, you argue with him, your stomach. To begin with, there isn't soup every day. Often enough they come back without eating. And they're not treated with kid gloves either. Sometimes they get pushed around. You take your chances. But now, you're guaranteed the soup in the kitchen; you have a ticket. And for doing nothing, and without working. Well, where could you be more secure?

The secondhand dealers by the gates look at you, at everybody, according to the value of the jacket you're wearing, and expertly value the pants that will be pried off you tomorrow—whether you're dead or alive. A light breeze carries a torn fragment from the wall: "Four hundred grams of black salt. Chairman of the Judenrat." Go to him, perhaps? Something rises in your memory: a committee, a hall not very large, a bell, a carafe of water. You recognize him: a tall figure, a fleshy Jewish nose, a

8. These were the workers who were reporting for duty to be taken to their workplaces outside the ghetto.

bald head. A small bow tie. Yes, he is now the chairman. Maybe you really should go to him? Write to him: Honored sir, I do not request much of you. I am hungry—you understand?—hungry. So I request of you (and remind him here of your becoming acquainted, in 1935, I think—does he remember?). Therefore, I request of you, Mr. Chairman, that you see to it that I receive a piece of bread every day. I know, much honored sir, that you have a thousand other things to do. What importance at all can it have for you that such a wreck of a person as I am should kick the bucket. All the same, Mr. Chairman of the Judenrat . . .

You stumble over something on the ground. You nearly fall. But no, your two feet keep their balance. On the ground, across the sidewalk, lies a mound of rags with a . . . a green, hairy lump of wet dirt that was once a face with a beard. Now for the first time you realize that the calls, "Hello, hello!" were to you. At first you didn't look around because Jews don't have names anymore—all Jews today are called . . .[9]; but now one of those secondhand dealers is standing by you. Didn't I see that I nearly stepped on a corpse? Philosopher! As if his jacket hadn't been sufficiently creased and disheveled? Must I add insult to injury? The shoes have been pulled off by someone and sold; at least leave the pants! What use is it to tell him that I was just thinking about the chairman of the Judenrat. The gatekeeper walks slowly, lazily, from the gate, carrying bricks and an old, excrement-stained sheet of newspaper, ties it round the dead body and walks slowly away, and that's it.

According to some clocks, old and crippled, it is already eleven o'clock. You get a liking for the ones that tell you it's later. Those big ones are haughty and not in any hurry, and you

9. Expletive deleted by the author.

hate them. Another hour, no, stand around and wait . . . standing is also a way of passing the time. Another hour. A few dozen minutes—they count for something too! It's nothing, indeed, but if you were eating a good old piece of bread, eh? What would you do, for example, if you were now to be given a slice of bread? Would you eat it right away, or would you keep it for the soup to make it more filling? I think you'd keep it. And if the soup was late, and it came out much later, let's say, would you also wait? Enough stories for the time being; don't make a fool of yourself. You'd devour it like a wolf. Oh, how you'd demolish it!

"Just a little bit of bread . . .," the refrain of all, the criers, from the sidewalks, from the cobbles, a little bit of bread. Oh, you jokers! Don't you know that I too want nothing more than a "little bit of bread"?

"My father's dead, my mother's in hospital. My elder brother's missing. A little bit of bread . . ."

You've eaten today, you bastard, haven't you?

"Small children at home—a little bit of bread." And I would so gladly add my voice: I'm hungry, hungry, hungry. Another hour till soup, another hour. You understand? "A little bit of bread!!!!"

The soup was not late today. The steam is already in the air. Plates are already being rattled. The manager is already shouting at the waitresses, the assistant manager is already measuring the length of the hall with his tiny feet and nodding his plump head from side to side as in a puppet show. The second assistant manager is already shouting at some diners. The day of soup giving is already begun. There are more people here than yesterday, just as yesterday there were more than the day before. Poor fellow! They're starting to hand out the soup from that table. So you'll have to sit here until it reaches you. How do you like that, you can eat your heart out.

Time—and more time. You remember the days when the kitchen announced, indifferently, and you thought, vengefully, "There's no meal today." How bitter were the words on the door: "Today's tickets are valid for tomorrow." How hideously long were those days and nights. And yet it seems to you that that pain was nothing compared with the half hour that you still have to wait.

The opposite table is already in a state of grace. Peaceful quietness—they are already eating. And it somehow seems to you that the people at that table feel superior to you, worthier. Someone or other takes from his bosom a quarter sheet of newspaper and unwraps it, uncovering a thin, round piece of bread. Unlike you, they don't gobble the soup directly. First they stir it, wrinkling up their noses in disgust, just as they do every day, because it's thin. Start at the side, where it's shallow, chew for a long time, slowly; pretend to be looking around, as if the soup were of secondary importance and the main thing—the ceiling. After the first few spoonfuls they add salt. They play with the soup as a cat plays with a mouse. And after the soup their faces wear an expression of near-religious bliss.

And it hasn't reached your table yet. And—are you only imagining it?—somehow the people sitting here all have such long faces, not-having-eaten faces, with swollen ghetto spots under their eyes, which give the face a Mongolian look. You think of a master of world literature, a Tolstoy, a Balzac, a Wassermann. How they made a fuss over people; they chiseled every feature, every move. "You seem to be somewhat pale today!" one of these geniuses would write, and the world was enraptured. "You seem to be somewhat pale today," and women dabbed their eyes with handkerchiefs, critics interpreted, and serious, business-like gentlemen, owners of textile factories or partners in large, comfortable manufacturing businesses beneath white marble signs, felt a quiver in their cheeks, reminiscent of the first kiss, fifty years ago. "You seem to be somewhat pale today"—ha, ha! If someone today were to read or write, "You seem somewhat pale today," when the whole world is deathly pale, when everyone, everyone has the same white, chalky, lime-white face. Yes, yes, it was easy for them to write. They ate, and knew that the readers were going to eat and that the critics were going to eat. Let these masters now show their true colors and write!

"Why don't you eat?" What is this? Everyone around you is eating; in front of you, too, there is a bowl of steaming soup, glistening and glittering with delicious splendor. You were looking across at the people and saw nothing. And did she take the ticket? No, you're still holding it in your hand. What's going on? Should you call? Turn it in? You've already finished with the helping, while around you people are smacking their lips, spitting, sipping as a cat sips milk, and grumbling, exactly as if they weren't eating. And that scoundrel over there, who has such a full plate, full of fried onions, sits there sniveling. You could just faint. It's all right, they're hungry; everyone may eat any way he likes. I'm probably comical too when I eat my soup. And there are some who tilt the plate so convulsively and scrape together the last drops . . . and submerge their whole face in the plate and see nothing else, as if it were the entire earth, the world. Can she possibly have given you the soup without a ticket? You steal a glance—the date is right. She simply didn't notice in the confusion. No, don't give it to her. Revenge. And she will realize it maybe; maybe not. It can't be—maybe, maybe to get another helping? And say nothing? But she did it on purpose. You know what, Arke? If a *man* sits down at your table now to eat his soup, you'll take the risk; if a *woman*, it's a bad omen, and you won't give up the ticket.

You stare hard. On one side a mother is now sitting with a child. A waitress hurries past; the mother says to the child, loudly, with a smiling, ingratiating look, "Wait, wait, the lady will soon bring you some thick soup." The bench squeaks; someone has sat down. That person is hidden from view; you see a bit of white toast. A fragment of a second: man or woman?—man or woman? A woman! Apparently—a pair of eyes—a mummy, eyes without expression. A woman, a woman, damn it. This means not turning in the ticket, not taking another bowl of soup? Too late, that's the way you set it up. But now the soup is better and better, thicker, hotter. How do you know? That's the way it always is. The later the better. Though it's not so certain. But this time, yes. And so once again, from the beginning. Man or woman, man or woman?

There is movement around you. People come and go, sit down, speak. Polish, Yiddish, Hebrew, German. First here, now there, like a rocket, a question flutters with an exclamation: "Who, him? I saw him only yesterday! Who, her? She ate here only the day before yesterday! They are talking about those who have died, one of hunger, another from "that" louse and today's sickness. And they whisper so mysteriously in each other's ears: "Don't shout—so, it looks like he died at home, unannounced." But above all other conversations, one theme—we won't be able to survive it. There's such a winter coming. If the war lasts through the winter. Last year we still had something. Parcels were still arriving; it wasn't sealed so shut. What are they splitting hairs about? Whether we will survive or not. What can people do, when they are sentenced to death and know the exact time of the execution? Thus the French aristocrats in the prisons during the great Revolution gambled at cards, acted in plays, until the man in the tricolor came in and called out the names, and "The guillotine is waiting." Yes, you see? But they weren't hungry and weren't threatened with starvation. Yes, indeed, this is really the main point. Well, and during the more recent Russian Revolution? But why am I getting involved in these great stories? Man or woman, man or woman?

At this point she showed up, the waitress, and automatically began taking tickets. Everyone held them out, you as well. It's over. And now you dip your spoon in the bowl, in the second bowl of soup—you understand? It really is thicker than the first. Now you can afford to play with it, to eat graciously, like all the rest, and not gobble. You don't eat in whole spoonfuls. Sometimes you spit out a piece of chaff, like a VIP.

In the street the smell of fresh corpses envelops you. Like an airplane propeller just after it's been started up, which spins and spins, and yet stays in one place; that's what your feet are like. They seem to you to be moving backward. Pieces of wood.

They were looking, weren't they? Involuntarily, you cover your face with your arm. And what if they find out? They can, as a punishment, take away your soups. Somehow it seems to you that they already know. That man who's walking past looks so insolently into your eyes. He knows. He laughs, and so does that man, and another and another. Hee, hee—they choke back their stinging laughter, and somehow you become so small, so cramped up. That's how you get caught, you fool. A thief? Only unlucky. That one soup can cost you all the others.

A burning in your left side. Your arm, your leg, your heart; not for the first time, but this time it's stronger. You must stop moving. You feel someone is watching. It's already too late to respond. A director of social assistance, in a rickshaw,[10] is riding down the street. A former acquaintance. Yes, he looked at you, yes. You notice when someone's looking—it's your nature.

10. The major means of conveyance in the Warsaw Ghetto; a symbol of luxury.

Always, when you see him traveling past, you look at him, wanting to catch his eye, and always in vain. Today it's the other way around: he noticed you. Maybe . . . maybe he already knows.

The director is already far away. Behind him are dozens of rickshaws. But the burning remains. Why the devil did you have to be in the street just now? Others go past, actually touch you and don't recognize you, or pretend not to. And he saw you from up there in his rickshaw and pierced you with a glance. What will happen now?

By a gate, in a narrow crack, a cucumber. A whole one, untouched. It seems that it fell from a housewife's shopping basket. Mechanically, without thinking, you bend down, take it, no disgrace, no joy. You deserve it. Just as a dog deserves a bone. A bittersweet cucumber. From looking at the skin you can already taste the sweetness of the seeds. It's not healthy. Typhus? Dysentery? Nonsense. For thirty centuries, generations of scholars have devoted their brilliant abilities, their youth, their lives to extorting from Nature the secrets of vitamins and calories in order that you, Arke, by a gate in Leszno Street should munch on a cucumber you found, which someone lost, or threw down for you.

What? It's impossible to [. . .]? Oh, if you only tried . . . if you only tried . . . if you only tried to beg. The first housewife that comes along . . . make a piteous face. . . . So what? Better people than you are out begging. Should I list them for you? You don't want to? Then, don't! If you don't want to, you don't have to be stopped at L[. . .].

You feel that today you have fallen a step lower. Oh, yes, that's how it had to begin. All these people around you, apparently, began like that. You're on your way [. . .] The second soup—what will it be tomorrow?

It's getting dark. The darkness thickens; you could cut it with a knife. It would be good to buy some bread now; it's cheaper. It would! A round-bellied prostitute gives irises to two of her friends. On their lime-white faces, all skin and bone, the rouge and color on their spear-sharp eyebrows look ghostly.

A small group of people stand on the sidewalk and look across at the other side, from where a long beam of light falls. It's the children's hospital. Low down, on the first floor, in a wide, high window, a large electric lamp hangs over a table. A short woman in a white mask moves something very quickly with her hands. Around her, other women, also in masks. A calm hurry. And everything—to the table, to the one who lies on the table. An operation. You've never seen one before. At the movies, in a book, in the theater, yes, but in life, no. Strange, isn't it? You've lived some thirty-odd years, seen so much—and now you're seeing an operation for the first time—and it has to be in the ghetto! But why, why? Why save? Why, to whom, to what is the child being brought back?

And suddenly you remember that dead Jew whom you nearly tripped over today. What's more, you now see him more clearly than before, when you were actually looking at him. Somewhere, years ago, there was a mother who fed him and, while cleaning his head, knew that her son was the cleverest, the most talented, the most beautiful. Told her aunt, her neighbors his funny sayings. Sought and delighted in every feature in which he resembled his father, his father. And the word Berishl was not just a name to her but an idea, the content of a life, a philosophy. And now the brightest and most beautiful child in the world lies in a strange street, and his name isn't even known; and there's a stink, and instead of his mother, a brick kisses his head and a drizzling rain soaks the well-known newspaper around his face. And over there, they're operating on a child, just as if this hadn't happened, and they save it, and below, in front of the gate, stands the mother, who knows that her Berishl is the cleverest and the most beautiful and the most talented—Why? For whom? For whom? And suddenly (you, a grown, tall man, a male) you feel a quiver in your cheek, in your hands, all over your body. And your eyes become so rigid, so glassy. Yes, that's how it must be. This is the sign—you understand?—the equation, the eternal Law of Life. Maybe you are destined now, of all times, in your last days, to understand the meaning of this meaninglessness that is called life, the meaning of your hideous, meaninglessly hungry days. An eternal law, an eternal machine: death. Birth, life. Life. Life. Life. An eternal, eternal law. An eternal, eternal process. And a kind of clarity pours over your neck, your heart. And your two propellers no longer spin round in one spot—they walk, they walk! Your legs carry you, just as in the past! Just as in the past!

Somewhere a clock is striking dully: one, two, half past. Four thirty, three thirty, five thirty? I don't know. Here there is no sunrise. The day comes to the door like a beggar. The days are already shorter. But I—I, like the fall, autumnal, foggy dawns. Everything around you becomes so dreamy, lost in thought, longing, serious, blue-eyed, concentrated in itself. Everything—people, the world, clouds—draws away somewhere, prepares for something responsible that carries a yoke, something that connects everything together. The gray patch that stands in the corner of the room with open arms—that's the *new day*. Yesterday I began to write your experiences. From the courtyard came the shouts of the air-raid wardens telling people to turn out the light. There's a smell of cholent. How come? It's Thursday, not the Sabbath [. . .] A forest, a river, the whistle of a train, an endless golden field. Kuzmir, Tatrn [. . .] The Lithuanian border. This longing, this wound will never go away; it will stay forever, even if today, tomorrow should once again [. . .] Let it be in the city itself, go, go—go forever, without stopping, at least see the bank of the Vistula, at least see just the city. The city that you know. The happiness of quickly turning a corner, then [. . .] the hundredth. With an open jacket, with happy, swift steps. *Your* city, your second mother, your great, eternal love. The longing pierces your heart. It remains.

Somewhere they are typing [. . .] They're reporting. It is reported from Brussels . . . Belgrade, Paris. Yes, yes, we're eating grass, yes, we're falling in the streets without a word of protest—we wave our hands like this, and fall [. . .] Each day the profiles of our children, of our wives, acquire the mourning look of foxes, dingoes, kangaroos. Our howls are like the cry of jackals. Our hymn, *papierosy*, *papierosy* [Polish: cigarettes, cigarettes], is like something from a nature reserve, a zoo. But we are not animals. We operate on our infants. It may be pointless or even criminal. But animals do not operate on their young!

Tokyo. Hong Kong. Vichy. Berlin. General number of enemy losses: six thousand eight hundred and forty-nine. Stockholm. Washington. Bangkok. The world's turning upside down. A planet melts in tears. And I—I am hungry, hungry. I am hungry.

Warsaw Ghetto, August 1941
Ringelblum Archive I:1219
Translated from the Yiddish by Elinor Robinson

LEYB GOLDIN, born in 1906 in Warsaw, where he was raised in poverty, early became active in the city's communist youth organizations and joined the Bund in 1936. A translator as well as critic and essayist, Goldin published in the Bundist underground press in World War II and was a member of the Oyneg Shabes staff. He was murdered in the Great Deportation in the summer of 1942.

CHAIM A. KAPLAN

From Scroll of Agony

November 13, 1941

The journal is my life, my companion, and my confidant. Without it I would be lost. In it I pour out all my heart's feelings, until I feel somewhat relieved. When I am angry and irritable and my blood boils; when I am full of reproach and bitterness because I have so little strength and capacity to fight the vicious waves that threaten to engulf me; when my hands tremble with inner feeling—I take refuge in the journal and am immediately enwrapped in the inspiration of the Shekinah[1] of creativity, though I doubt whether the task of documentation with which I am occupied is worthy of being called "creativity." In the future let them evaluate it as they may: the main point is that I find repose for my soul in it, and that is enough for me.

Why am I angry? Typhus has attacked my home too. My wife has contracted that dread disease. Her life is in great danger, and I must save her. Our material means are limited, infinitesimal. Only with great difficulty did I manage to earn a day's sustenance in normal times. In times of danger, when physicians, medics, and all sons of healers frequent your house, and you must spend more than a hundred zlotys a day on them, my

1. Divine presence.

strength is insufficient. And there is no help on the side. The Joint [Distribution Committee] community fund and other social welfare institutions are open to but a few, to those close to them, to bootlickers, to the director's lackeys who submit to his ways. And what am I? I have no foothold there. So, with my meager forces, I bear and suffer the expenses of the illness, which must also be concealed from strangers' eyes, because it's a contagious disease and those who have caught it are forbidden to stay in a private house. In addition to all that, I am alone and bereft in my troubles. My sons are in the Land of Israel, and I am in exile. There is no one to nurse the patient, whose illness is severe and demands care day and night. Therefore, you need a nurse, a "sister of mercy," for whose pains you must pay 120 zlotys a day. The cost of medicines has increased sevenfold, and the Judenrat imposed a surtax of 25 percent on their high price, for its coffers. And the main point is—the patient, who feels, as she says, the approach of death. Her sighs and moans tear at my heart. She is certain that the thread of her life will be severed in just an hour, two hours, that her minutes are numbered, and she will never see her children again. Though the danger to her life is great, and she is close to the portals of death, she is conscious and her mind is clear. Therefore, she realizes and understands that she is about to die. I console and soothe her, but only outwardly. Sometimes suspicion creeps into my heart that the patient knows her condition with more certainty than the doctor. Now the evil tidings of Job are reaching the city. In town it is said that the disease is laying low hundreds of patients daily.

My brain teems with but a single thought: Whence will come my aid? It plots stratagems for finding money. What valuable thing remains in my possession that I can sell and get some decent sum for? During the two years of the war my possessions have become almost completely depleted. One by one I have sold them to evade the disgrace of hunger. With a sinking heart I removed them from my house and accepted mere pennies for them, for woe to man and object when there is need or necessity to bring it out to the marketplace for sale. "Bad, bad!" says the buyer, valuing it seven times less than what you reckoned while you sat at home. With pain in your heart you place the beloved object in a stranger's hands, and in return you receive a few crumpled bills, which bring you slight relief for a few days, for in the meanwhile the prices have soared, and the money melts away between your fingers. But there's no choice. The danger of death lurks at the head of the patient's bed. At moments like that you repress all kinds of sentiments.

But before my weary brain can labor and choose some object, a dark, cloudy autumn night spreads its wings over the ghetto dwellers. With evening comes darkness, and the ghetto then becomes a city of madmen and lunatics. The darkness is double: no light outside for fear of air attack. The gas lamps are not lit. Shop windows are extinguished. Shutters are sealed over doors. Quite simply, as it is written [Exod. 10:21]: *a darkness that can be touched*. Inside the houses there is no spark of light. At midnight the electric current is cut off, and a watery tallow candle that melts and drips replaces it. To go out at night in darkness such as that is to risk mortal danger. People collide and crash into each other, and they are left wounded and bruised. This is no time to settle your affairs, whether buying or selling. You must put everything off till morning light. By the dim light of the candle the night shadows thicken. You are completely sunk in thoughts and shadows. The silence of the ghetto in the darkness increases the fear of night, full of secrets and hints. In my room there is no living being except the patient with her burning fever and death lying in wait for her.

If only it were morning! [Deut. 28:67]

November 18, 1941

Warsaw is depressed and wrapped in deep mourning. But it is no ceremonial mourning with only the outward trappings, lacking heartfelt grief. On the contrary, if we could, we would weep bitterly, and our cry would rise to the high heavens. Were it not for fear of the evil kingdom, our wailing would burst forth in the dark alleys, and we would cry and weep and wail dreadfully for our calamity, as vast as the sea. But because of the sword, drawn and waiting for our plaint to lop off our heads—our grief does not break out. Our hearts are our graves.

Group by group the Jews of the ghetto, shrunken, shriveled, and frozen with frost, shadow Jews whose flesh cries emaciation, and the bones of whose faces jut out like skeletons, deathly ill, worn down, and wretched in their great poverty, the hardships of displacement, wandering, and expulsions—they stand next to a red proclamation signed by the commissioner of the ghetto, [Heinz] Auerswald,[2] in which there is official notice that because of the "sin" of crossing the border of the ghetto illegally, eight Jews were caught and tried, and all were condemned to death. The sentence was carried out yesterday, November 17,1941. [. . .]

See here: simple Jewish women died to sanctify the name of God like heroines of the human spirit. One of them was a young maiden less than eighteen years old. In her innocence she asked a Jewish policeman, who was present when she was murdered, to tell her family that she had been sent to a concentration camp and would not see them again soon. Her companion

2. Auerswald (1908–1970) was the Nazi-appointed commissioner for the Warsaw Ghetto from April 1941 to November 1942.

proclaimed out loud, before her death, that she begged the God of Israel that her death be an atonement for her people, and that she might be the last victim.

While they were being murdered, a representative of the Jewish prison on Zamenhofa Street, Mr. Lejkin,[3] was present, along with a deputation from the Jewish Police. Their task was to bring the condemned people to the gallows, to bind their eyes and tie their hands. The men were unwilling to die with their eyes closed and hands tied. Their wish was not honored. The ones who shot them were Polish policemen, and after committing the act of murder, they wept with great emotion.

Oh earth! Do not hide my blood!! If there is a God to judge the land—may he come and take revenge!!!

December 2, 1941

"The Kingdom of Israel" was the magic slogan for the Revisionists. But if those who used that enchanting rallying cry, "the Kingdom of Israel," could have known how it would be implemented in life by the Jews of Poland, by the *shmendrikes*[4] from the brothels who came to power, they would not have inscribed it on their banner even as a propaganda measure. The Nazis, wishing to bedeck us with shame before the entire world, to show our baseness and the abysmal level of our culture, granted us broad "autonomy," almost a "state," as it were. They granted us that "privilege" with the premeditated intent to prove how incapable we are of being our own masters and to reveal

3. Jacob Lejkin, who became head of the Jewish Police in May 1942 and was shot by the Jewish underground on October 1942.

4. Here meaning social climbers, Jews ashamed of their Jewishness.

our corrupt nature and our desire, stamped in our blood, to do injustice even to our brethren, not only in religion and race but also in grief and disaster.

True, only a caricature of autonomy was granted us, and not out of excessive affection but rather out of excessive hatred, the main point of which is only to separate the Jews from the nations, to undermine our material and spiritual existence, to hem in our steps, to have us perish slowly. In essence it is no more than a stillborn child lacking the power to flourish and grow, a sickly administrative and political creature lacking true vitality. By its principles and foundations it would seem to be only the kind of "self-rule" that prisoners have in a jail, where some will be hanged and others will die a degrading death from exhaustion. That is known to everyone.

Nevertheless, if only we could be brethren not just in race and religion but also in suffering. Were we truly a single national unit, at least during the violent persecution that has come upon us to extirpate us from the land of the living, we could use that tool called "autonomy" (i.e., the ghetto) to ease our sufferings and gain some relief under the unbearably difficult conditions of the ghetto. After all, the entire administration is in our hands, and we have the right to shape its inner form as we wish. It is precisely in that regard that we have gone bankrupt. Without exaggeration I may call it the government of evil, a band of villains, murdering the poor and oppressing the needy; the cronies of unjust wrongdoers, each one of whom has an unsavory past, and as types they are little more than criminals who have not yet been brought to trial. At the very mention of the word *rulers* (i.e., the Judenrat), helpless rage makes our blood boil and our fists tighten of themselves. The rulers have become the symbol of tyrannical injustice; and the leaders, the symbol of bullies and ruffians.

At the first opportunity, not one stone will remain upon another of the building at 26 Grzybowska Street [office of the Judenrat], which has become the headquarters of injustice and tyranny, a den of robbers and evildoers. And if a prophet lived among us to reprimand us, he would raise his voice against them:

—*Why do you oppress My people?!* [Isa. 3:15]

And his voice would be heard from one end of the earth to the other. From the depths of our troubles we would be consoled at once: "Their day shall come too!" They will not be immune forever. Together with the Nazi they will be undone, and the property of strangers that they have swallowed—they will vomit it forth.

Thus the masses console themselves when they are aroused. But the wisest among them know it is merely a vain consolation. At the time they agree, but in their hearts they think differently.

A joke is making the rounds:

> Two degenerates from the Judenrat are talking with each other, and in the midst of their friendly conversation, one starts threatening the other with "What will happen."
>
> "Money won't help on Judgment Day! Zygmunt![5] Think of your end! Beware of the anger of the mob and its rage!"
>
> But Zygmunt has no fear, answering:
>
> "You fool! When the earth is overturned and the order of life changes, then I'll be up on top, not down below."

5. A name typical of highly acculturated Polish Jews.

I suspect he spoke the truth. In the end, not a hair of his head will come to grief. . . .

In my coming notes I shall tell posterity something of the deceptions of the rulers and their abominations.

I'm not an insider; on the contrary, I come from outside.[6] It could be that's my advantage. Their "fine" deeds and straight rules are known to me by rumor, and some facts I was an eyewitness to. I cling to a great general principle: The voice of the people is like the voice of the Lord!

December 3, 1941

—When the Jewish representative body was appointed, we were certain we would find shelter from our troubles in it, that it would extend a brotherly hand, alleviate our suffering, that even in the difficult, bitter times it is subject to, it would do everything in its power to bring balm and healing to our wounds. The huge and dreadful trouble that has befallen us has made everyone equal, without any exception, for nothing makes for common feelings so much as shared trouble. It increases sentiments of mercy, love, and solidarity in times of trouble, even among strangers who are not brothers by blood and origin. So much the more so among those who are brethren, members of a single people, related in flesh and spirit.

However, Polish Jewry did not behave thus. Therefore, eternal shame shall be its lot.

6. In the ghetto, Kaplan stood apart both from the Judenrat, which he excoriated as a den of self-hating Jews, and from Oyneg Shabes, which looked to Yiddish (as opposed to modern, spoken Hebrew) as the unifying language of the ghetto population.

An alien power coming from the outside assembled the *shmendriks* among us and appointed them leaders over us. They are half-, third-, or quarter-assimilated circles. In peacetime they did not wish to know us and confined themselves to their own Jewish-goyish society, insulting and insulted at the same time. They themselves reviled the Jewish *holota* [Polish: mob], and their gentile neighbors also included them in their hatred and contempt. The Jewish community has not yet acknowledged them. They were strangers to their people, its spirit, and its culture. Perhaps even more than strangers; there was hatred in them for everything that could be called by the name of Judaism. Their opposition to the Jewish masses did not derive from an ideological opposition, for they had no ideology at all aside from materialism.

And those "gentlemen," once they were appointed the heads of the Judenrat, began to trample our heads with exceptional brutality. And since the day the ghetto was established a wide-ranging and extensive network of great enterprises has been set up, such as the Jewish Police, the ghetto food-supply department, the housing agency, the post office, the internal administrative body, the representation for external relations, the primary schools, health matters, and in general, all sorts of official functions—they have a vast field for enriching themselves by taking bribes and by favoritism. Those in the know concur, saying that the corruption within the Judenrat has reached a level unprecedented in the entire world. It is beholden to no one except the commandant of the ghetto, who himself is a partner in all the conspiracies formed at the expense of the oppressed masses gripped in a material and spiritual vise like incarcerated prisoners helpless to free themselves. When times improve, certainly trustworthy people will emerge and tell coming generations what must be told on the basis of documentation and exact statistics.

January 7, 1942

"Whatever is on land is also in the sea." That is true of the ghetto on the one hand and of all nature on the other. Everything found in the wide world of nature is found on a small scale in the narrow, confined ghetto. There is penury and poverty and, in contrast, wealth and plenty. The Nazi overlord acts according to this rule: whoever makes the great equal the small misses the mark. The means of destruction do not have a uniform effect throughout all ranks of the ghetto.

There is a certain percentage of ghetto residents who become wealthy and have secured a life of sustenance, perhaps even a life of ease, and that is because they trade on their brothers' distress. There is one great principle of life: no one has a misfortune that does not benefit someone else. The all-embracing restrictions that most of the residents of the ghetto cannot tolerate have produced a full complement of smugglers and practical men who risk their money and lives, amassing fortunes that permit them to enjoy the pleasures of life. Two leeches suck our marrow: the Nazi leech, the elite of the elites and the *primum mobile*, the first "father" in setting up the machinery to make us perish and suck our blood, and its spawn: the Jewish leech, born of contraband and price gouging. Despite draconian measures, smuggling does not cease. Even the danger of death does not restrain it. Rather, as those means become more severe and harsh, they drive up prices. Every price rise increases the extent of the profits. That is in reference to the large-scale smugglers who are in cahoots with the Nazis and share their spoils with them. No eye oversees their misdeeds, and they have permission to set prices as they see fit. Everything depends on their hard hearts and avid greed for wealth.

That is human nature. In a crisis the urge grows stronger: *Eat and drink, for tomorrow we die!* [Isa. 22:13]

The ranks for whom dollars are valued as pennies seek pleasure and pursue the pleasures of life. Therefore, the ghetto is full of luxuries: but only the minority enjoy them. The shop windows are cluttered with all sorts of pastries and delicacies that only a small percentage buys and eats their fill of. Places of entertainment have been established in the ghetto, full to the brim every evening, with every seat taken. Someone who didn't know, for example, that his feet were standing on the earth of the ghetto, if he were to enter the luxurious pastry shops and look at the well-dressed crowd enjoying the sounds of music and, with great pleasure, drinking coffee and other expensive beverages, every sip of which costs several zlotys, could not imagine that those guests were life's outcasts, lacking elementary human rights. He would not notice that until he went outside. Upon leaving, he would trip over a dead body at the entrance, a victim of starvation!

February 2, 1942

One trouble is unlike the next. The latest is the gravest. We have a motto: "If only the present condition would not worsen!" We always reel that the murderous eyes of robbers are staring at us and casting their venom upon us. At all times we are prepared for some new evil decree. Passive preparedness lightens the oppressiveness of the decree once it has come. We are immune to surprise. Occasionally the Jews themselves imagine that some strange, psychopathic decree will be imposed on them. When you first hear of it, you are surprised: "Is it possible?" But after a few moments you say, "It is possible, quite possible." For that reason the decrees no longer terrify us. "Come what may, we shall not be wiped out of this land!"

But in recent days dreadful, horrifying rumors have been oppressing our spirits. Even the ghetto dwellers, inured to suffering, are struck by them. In essence each evil decree only sets difficult living conditions, ordered by unjust laws; nevertheless, it contains some legality, for in the end a hard life is still life, especially for a group that has always lived a life of grief and humiliation.

But the recent rumors are different, for if they have even a bit of truth to them, they are no longer in the category of decrees but have become physical destruction, extinction, bitter death. It is hard to assess their truth. But we are sure of one thing: even if they are exaggerated, there is a little truth to them, and that "little" is sufficient.

The Führer has ceased legislating evil decrees against us, which it irks him to enforce and implement in life, as the adversary discovers subterfuges to negate and annul them. He has condemned an entire nation to death. Not by starvation, not even by contagious diseases, and not even by expulsions and conversion,[7] but simply by shooting. There is no need for legal authorization and all the other illusions that go along with it. Rather you take thousands of people out of the city and shoot them to death—and that's the end of it.

The rumors make our blood freeze:

In Vilna forty thousand Jews were shot to death without any trial or judgment, without even a legal pretext, and the remainder—their number comes to ten thousand four hundred.

In Slonim a Nazi was killed by someone; the living Nazis knew very well that no Jewish hand was involved in that killing.

7. The Hebrew here is unclear.

But it provided them a broad field for blood libel. Thus outside the city eight thousand Jews were shot to death.

In Kleck—the flying rumor continues—of all the Jewish inhabitants of the city, only six families are left. And that is the same in the other cities of Lithuania and the Ukraine. The Nazi comes and holds a massacre, and the Jewish question is solved.

That "solution" hits the target. Those rumors exaggerated their evidence; therefore, we took them to be mere tales up to now, created by popular imagination and therefore excessive and overblown. Disastrously for us, recently we have witnessed dreadful facts such as those in the General-Government too:

Not expulsion, not even epidemic, but physical shooting to death. Any accusation is superfluous. Whole groups are taken to slaughter only because they are Jews. Whole towns have been wiped out by killing and slaughter in a fashion barbaric beyond all the murders and slaughters that have taken place in world history. We have become like sheep to be slaughtered. . . .

Yesterday we read the speech of the Führer commemorating the date of January 30, 1933. In that speech he proudly said that his prophecy has begun to be fulfilled. From the beginning he said that if war broke out in Europe, the Jewish race would be extirpated from it. That process has already begun and will continue until it reaches its conclusion. He has condemned all the Jews of Europe to physical death on the basis of the law of their doctrine: "Eye for an eye!" "Tooth for a tooth," "Arm for an arm," "Leg for a leg." That is a kind of justification before the entire world.

But in particular that gives us an indication that the horrors being reported are not mere rumors but real and true facts. The Judenrat and the Joint have documents indicating the new direction taken by Nazi policy regarding the Jews in conquered areas: death by the sword, the physical murder and destruction of whole groups of Jews.

Till now we were afraid of being deported. Now we are afraid of death. Moreover, the signs of deportation are becoming clearer:

The Judenrat is arranging a census of the Jews in the ghetto. By January 31, 1942, every one of the residents of the ghetto is required to fill in a questionnaire with his name and his parents' names; whether he is the head of a family; his address in Warsaw before the war broke out, his present address; his profession before September 1, 1939, and his present profession—

Is there no catastrophe lurking in that whole census? The refugees from other cities say that in their towns, too, the tortures of deportation began with such a census. In the meanwhile—fear and trembling have seized us.

Here we are: *an anguished heart and eyes that pine and a despondent spirit!* [Deut. 28:65]

March 7, 1942

After the first reduction [in the area of the ghetto] the Gęsia Street Cemetery was removed from the Jewish zone. Legally, therefore, no Jew may set foot there, living or dead. Geographically, it is beyond the wall dividing Jews and Aryans. But in fact it is impossible to forbid the burial of Jewish dead there, because the sanitary situation demands that the cemetery be placed outside the city. The ghetto is completely surrounded by a wall within a wall, and it is against the law to breach them and lay the Aryan Side open to the entry and exit of the Jewish dead and their funeral parties.

Therefore, they [the Germans] chose the lesser evil. They passed an emergency regulation permitting the continuation of Jewish burials outside the area; but the restrictions are well known. Merely entering the cemetery is strictly forbidden; anyone wishing to enter may do so only after buying a ticket for two and a half zlotys, a new source of decent revenue for something so intimate and familial as a funeral. That caused the number of those attending to decrease to the minimum. First, they spare themselves the small expense, and second, you must pass through two sets of guards, German and Jewish, who watch every step you take and give you evil looks, for they suspect you haven't come here for a funeral but rather for smuggling. Even the slightest suspicion will bring down such evil upon you that you won't be able to extricate yourself. If you watch yourself, you'll stay away. And perhaps, retrospectively—it's better that not many people attend funerals. For if they came in multitudes, there would be no possibility of carrying out jobs decently. To bury two hundred corpses a day—that's no small matter!! A long line of wagons extends along Gęsia Street, and each one brings not just a single person to the gates of death but several in one trip. Within the wagon there is barely room to squeeze in four bodies; and if there is a fifth, they place it on top of the flat roof. If there is a coffin—fine: they put him in the coffin, whether it is open or closed; if there's no coffin—they lay him on his back and tie him so he won't slide out; and even if he's lying on his back, tied, they don't take care that he be covered.

Simply a dead man, just as he is, without even a paper shroud, lying on his back on the roof of the wagon, and no one feels the indignity. When the wagons enter the gates of death, they begin to remove the bodies, and anyone who has not seen that with his own eyes has never seen ugliness in his life. Anyone who wishes for a life with some spiritual repose should avoid coming here and looking at all the "*Betrieb*" [German: business] of this slaughterhouse for human beings.

Mostly naked corpses are removed from the wagons, without even a paper loincloth to cover their private parts. I was stunned at that ugly sight, which made me feel that simple human dignity had been insulted, the dignity of man. I was so disgusted that physically I had to vomit. Full of anger, I addressed one of the workers: How can this be? But he actually got furious at me and nearly reviled me: "Have you fallen to earth from the sky? Is there cloth for shrouds for two hundred corpses a day? And if there is, who can afford to buy it? A meter of cloth is worth its weight in gold; the wealthy give white sheets instead of cloth, but not always, because they hide them for sale when bad times come. 'Paper,' you might say. There hardly is any to be found. It went up in price, and the average person can't afford enough to bury even one of the dead members of his family. It's wartime, a hard, bitter time. We are in an emergency! The dead will forgive us! Isn't it the same to them? Just as the dead man's flesh can't feel the scalpel, it can't feel its nakedness."

I was left speechless. . . .

The dead brought to burial are divided into three classes. The highest class are those who die and are brought to the purification room near the cemetery. The crowding and shoving are unimaginable. Sometimes two or three are laid on the same sheet. But in praise of the dead let it be said that they are peaceable and calm, and it has yet to happen that one rose up and said, "This place is too narrow!"

The second highest class is those who were cleansed of their disease at home; and most of them are dressed in shrouds made of white sheets, and the men are wrapped in their prayer shawls. They are laid on litters for the dead standing ready in the courtyard of the cemetery by the dozen, and no place is free of them. By their side stand the mourners, weeping and waiting their turn; by the way, a good watch is kept against theft, for if one doesn't keep a good eye out, the prayer shawl disappears in the wink of an eye. Those two classes are buried in individual graves. Those dead are privileged to receive a decent burial, a great privilege in times like these.

The third class is the dead, victims of hunger and epidemic—the majority gathered up in the streets of the ghetto, who went to their deaths outdoors in the ghetto, who perished in the hospitals, who died of hunger in some attic, in general the children of indigence and poverty, who have no one to labor on their behalf and bring each one to burial in his own individual grave. Dead of that sort are brought to burial in a huge, deep mass grave, just as they are: naked, without purification, without planks. For that "elite" no individual funerals are held for each one. Their burial is, after all, a wholesale business. What were formerly the stables of the cemetery have become chambers for the dead. They're thrown there like the carcasses of animals. Body after body of the departed, laid one on top of the other. In such positions, insulting the humane feelings within you, half breaking your body. The impression crushes your breath from you like a vise. Is that man and his end? A living man is unlike a dead one in his ugliness. Ugliness that has some movement is relative ugliness; still ugliness, with no movement, is absolute ugliness. Then man is revealed in all his nothingness and weakness.

Dead of that sort accumulate during the day by the dozens and dozens. Like dung they pile up in the stables waiting for burial till they reach the grave digger's quota. The dawn is still spread over the new cemetery annexed to the left side of the old one, behind the stables. That is an enormous, square grave, nearly fifty meters by fifty meters in length and breadth; and in depth—ten meters. There they are brought down a wooden ladder leaning on the lip of one end of the pit. Down that ladder they are brought to their eternal rest one by one. A thin layer of dust is spread over them, which does not cover them, so that limbs reach out and protrude. But not for long. The next morning new corpses are lowered, laid down, and "buried" in the same fashion. Row after row: layer upon layer. One need fear no strife among the brethren buried together, perish the thought. They lived in darkness, they went to death in darkness, and in darkness they were "buried."[8] No one knows of their grave.

But the day will come when the Jewish people will raise a permanent memorial upon that very mass grave.—

March 22, 1942

—The light of springtime has come to the world, and our heavens are covered with clouds. Evil hours have come such as never were even under the Nazis. Wonder of wonders, the evil decrees have been silenced, but a dreadful evil awaits us worse than any decree. It has not yet come, but with all our senses and emotions we feel its impending arrival. The echo of its footsteps almost reaches our ears. Is there no illusion here?

Horrible, dreadful rumors are passed on in whispers, taking one form and another, depending on the spirit of the one reporting. We feel that someone alien, tyrannical, and dreadful has unsheathed his sword to decapitate us, but all his preparations are made behind our backs; so we see the movements of the murderer only in our mind's eye, not with eyes of flesh. I wish I were imagining things, but I am not free to refrain from writing them down:

8. Paraphrase of a line from "Bontshe the Silent" (1894) by I. L. Peretz.

The first rumor. The deportation of Lublin has taken place; about a hundred thousand Jews were placed in closed railroad cars sealed with the Nazi seal, and under the supervision of Nazi overseers, they were brought . . . where? No one knows. Thus the Jewish community of Lublin has passed away and been removed from the face of the earth. The proof: they tried to speak with the Lublin Judenrat by telephone, but that request was denied, because "there no longer is such a Jewish institution in Lublin." Once again they tried to telephone a private person, and he answered briefly, "My wife and I are living!"

It is clear that some disaster has befallen our brothers in Lublin. But its character and extent are unknown to us.

A second rumor. In Rovno the entire Jewish community was executed. Not a single living soul is left. Why and wherefore? No one knows. Some advance a theory that has a certain foundation—in obedience to the decree of the Führer to bring destruction upon the Jews of Europe. Once more: there is no smoke without fire! The Jews of Rovno have undergone a dreadful trial. But who will rush in and tell us what it is?

A third rumor. It is strange and inconceivable, though one may count on the Nazis to do even the strangest things. It happened in Zdunska Wola. There the Nazis took revenge upon the Jews for the ten sons of Haman who were hanged.[9] They therefore summoned the Judenrat and ordered it to provide a list of ten Jews of the community to be hanged in revenge for the ten sons of Haman. And if not, the members of the Judenrat would take their places. The list was given, and ten Jews were hanged.

9. Yitzhak Katzenelson's epic poem "The Song about Shloyme Zhelikhovsky" (1942) was written to commemorate this event.

Can it be believed? There are arguments on both sides. But one thing is absolutely certain: It is not impossible! We are dealing with Nazis!

March 23, 1942

From flying rumors I shall pass to facts. Here our torture stands out in its full horror. It is known that Litzmanstadt (formerly Łódź) has been sanctified with extreme "holiness" and now has the same legal status as the "Reich," which Jewish feet are forbidden to tread, and special laws are in force there regarding inferior races of men, that is to say: Poles and Jews. The Poles too are deprived of full and complete civil rights, but their deprivation is secondary; the Nazis acknowledge their second-class citizenship, but not so the Jews! They were deprived of their citizenship and all the rights pertaining to it. Furthermore, not only does the law not defend their lives and property, but it is a national duty to do away with them and divest them of their possessions. And no means is more extreme in depriving and impoverishing the Jew than deportation. This must be known: the Nazi deportations are unlike the historical expulsions we have read about in the pages of our history, not even those executed by cruel tsarism. Then they would tell the Jew who was about to be expelled, "Give me your soul, and keep your property, and if you value your soul—take both your soul and your property and leave here." The Nazi repeatedly says, "Take your soul and give me your property!"

The administration of Łódź decided to abolish the ghetto in two or three days.[10] That is always its way, to surprise

10. The first major deportation, of ten thousand Jews, from the Łódź Ghetto took place from January 16 to 29, 1942.

the wretched deportees and cast confusion in their ranks; and the main point is that they not manage to remove their property in the time of emergency, so that the regime will be the "legal" inheritor. In line with that custom it called upon the chairman of the Judenrat, Chaim Rumkowski, decreeing with the full severity of the law, that he was required to abolish the ghetto in two or three days. Immediately after the announcement it began its thievish work: it stole all the cash from the council treasury (estimated at two million zlotys) and plundered all the food supplies and all the raw material that had been brought in to sustain the ghetto. The hand that had given returned to take away. The deportation began. The details of it are not well known to me, because I am far from the scene of the deed. Now Łódź is tantamount to foreign soil, and there is no contact between it and the other Jewish settlements in the General-Government. The local chroniclers will certainly record them in full detail for coming generations. Here I only emphasize the existence of the signs of that dread decree. Now the post office no longer sends letters from Jews to the inhabitants of the Łódź Ghetto, as if they no longer were living. And letters from there no longer arrive here. All one can do is request information about the relatives of people in Warsaw[11] using a printed form not signed by the one making the request but by the head of the Judenrat, so apparently there is still some slender remnant awaiting sentence. That, then, is the end of the splendid city of Łódź!

And Lwów preceded its condemned sisters.

There a slow but systematic expulsion began. There is no ghetto there because it wasn't worthwhile taking the trouble for

11. The phrase can also read, "All one can do is request help from relatives in Warsaw . . ."

a short time. In a short while the Jewish settlement in that populous city will disappear. Before my eyes I have a letter announcing that every day eleven hundred Jews from Lwów are being deported. Before many weeks pass, the Jewish community of Lwów will pass from the face of the earth. That is the end of Lwów, a thriving Jewish city, which, when it flourished, was a center of Torah study and the Enlightenment for the Jews of Galicia. The end has come to its Jewish existence! The synagogue of Lwów was devoured by fire.

April 6, 1942

—This week, under the supervision of Nazi policemen and gendarmes, a total of twenty-six hundred "Jewish" citizens of Germany were brought to Warsaw to leave them . . . where? Apparently in the ghetto, but for the moment they have been left outside the ghetto. In general, they received a different kind of "escort" than, for example, the deportees from Danzig a year ago. With the Danzig deportees, the full weight of the law was enforced. Weary and worn out, tortured by the trip, and overcome with troubles, they were thrown into the ghetto without any support or sustenance. At first they still resembled human beings. True, they knew their path was strewn with thorns and briars and their future boded ill. However, immediately upon their arrival they were considered to be people who had lost their fortune but not all their property. Some of them, before setting out, had smuggled valuables away beneath the murderers' eyes, managing to put aside something for bad times. But that situation did not last. From week to week they declined further and further. Lacking livelihood and left alone in foreign surroundings, they ate up the remnant of their money and became utter beggars. Hunger brought epidemics, bereavement, and widowhood upon them. Many of them died during the year, and some of them are still living a life of shame and humiliation till death has mercy upon them.

The Führer achieved his goal: he brought havoc and destruction upon an entire Jewish community.

The "Jewish" deportees from Germany got a different reception this week.

It is noteworthy how they behaved: the Gestapo greeted them with flowers; they took the trip in Pullman cars, so no signs of the discomforts of travel were visible on them. Their countenance was that of superior folk—fat and lively. Dressed elegantly. In short, aristocratic exiles. Not only that—it is also said—the Poles, too, expressed warm sympathy for their fate and offered them food and flowers. The main point is, they were not considered by the Nazis as polluted people who must be driven from the camp. They remained in the Aryan quarter; apparently a ghetto within the ghetto will be prepared for them. Miserable exiles and fortunate at the same time. Who are they?

They are "half Jews" according to the racial laws. Many of them were born as Christians, because their parents were apostates. Many of them were born to mixed marriages. Some of them have wives who are German by birth and origin. In short, they lived as complete goyim, true Germans who, before 1933, occupied high and exalted positions in all walks of life. Not only that, but they absolutely hate Jews, and if their birth certificates had not betrayed them, they would observe the commandments of Nazism more scrupulously than true Germans. But there was one thorn in their sides: they all lack one generation of Christianity. As everyone knows, until the third generation no one of Jewish race can enter the congregation of Nazis. Nazi law terms them "half Jews," and thus their formal status is their undoing.

In peacetime no harm was done to them for the sake of tranquility. But we are in an hour of emergency. This is a moment of spiritual turmoil in Germany. Once aroused, the spirit cannot be hemmed in. In the air is political ferment. For the time being, the revolt is inward; if the situation is prolonged—a flame will shoot out. In conditions of life such as these, half Jews must not remain in the heart of the German community. They are deeply ensconced and cannot be prevented from arousing the German public to some active deeds. If they are of the seed of the Jews, they can be depended on for all kinds of treach ery. "Throw a stick in the air—it falls on its root." Their Jewish blood has not yet been eradicated.

For that reason they have been condemned to exile. That is the judgment. The doctrine of Nazism and its severe ramifications are no longer acceptable and are already repulsive to the German people. That doctrine demands reinforcement according to the principle "Let justice take its course!" Wherever there is suspicion of the desecration of Nazism, one must act with the full severity of the law. Therefore—out with them!

But their children—the third generation of Christians—and their wives have remained in Germany. And it is unjust to torment them. Thus they must act in this fashion here: the left hand repels, and the right hands draws in. The Jewish part of the body is driven out. The German part of the body is greeted with honor and affection.

Yes, Heine was right: "Judaism is not a religion but rather a tragedy"—a tragedy for generations.

April 17, 1942

Hearing about Lublin, we were gripped by trembling. In danger of their lives a few refugees fled from that city of murder and came to the Warsaw Ghetto. Their stories freeze the blood in your veins. Terrifying rumors had been common among the masses even before their arrival; but who believed them? We thought they had not been heard from reliable sources. Without newspapers, when everything is passed by word of mouth, every rumor is liable to be exaggerated. Experience has taught us that—but now eyewitnesses have arrived, those who were to be deported from their settlement. In the Warsaw Ghetto there is a Lublin colony. The refugees were its guests and lecturers in a secret meeting held to seek a way of saving the remnant. What they reported was so dreadful and horrible that we nearly suspected that they too were exaggerating and overstating. For human beings created in God's image are incapable of such depravities.

But one way or another, it is a fact that reality has outdone imagination. Jewish Lublin, a city of sages and authors, a center of Torah and piety, was completely and utterly destroyed. An entire community of forty thousand Jews was uprooted and banished. Its institutions, synagogues, and houses of study are gone from the earth. All its wealth has been confiscated, for its sons left it for exile as naked as the day of their birth. When the decree first burst upon them, forty thousand Jews were deported; about ten thousand remained. When the first fury had passed, they were almost certain they had reached a "safe haven." They would not be touched again. But once again Jewish confidence was disappointed. After a few days another decree was passed, that Lublin must be Judenrein, and the remaining Jews drank the poisonous draught. Today not a single Jewish footprint can be found in the city of [*blank in original diary*]. The walls of the house of study have been stained with innocent blood. The Judenrat was dissolved and deprived of all its rights. Five of its members remained to guide the murderers in the process of liquidating the community. "They will be shot last!"

the officer reassured them. Whoever expected such a dreadful calamity as that!

[. . .] The decree of expulsion came as a complete surprise to the Jews of Lublin, for in that city the government was not particularly oppressive toward the Jewish inhabitants. Nazism is not an egalitarian system, whether for evil or good. Its principle is, from everyone according to his ability. The local commander is omnipotent, and his opinion is decisive in every issue. It happened that the commander of Lublin and his advisers were rather easy on the local Jews. Apparently it was profitable to them to turn a blind eye. As much as local conditions permitted, the Jews engaged in commerce and manufacturing, and the Nazi overlords ignored them. Lublin was famous as a "Garden of Eden" for the Jews in comparison with Warsaw and Częstochow.

But the luck of the Lublin Jews turned, and the murderous Himmler came to visit. That visit brought their horrible disaster down upon them—the chief murderer gave the word: "The number of Jews in this border city is too great!" Besides, a typhus epidemic broke out there, taking more victims than usual in places where the Nazi sets foot. Typhus acknowledges no borders, and there is no escaping from it for anyone in its vicinity. The chief murderer envisioned great danger for the Aryan population.

Hence—deportation! Here he also took up the pretext of taking revenge for the German blood shed through the fault of the Jews of Russia and America, who called for war against the Nazis. The word of the chief killer went forth, and a massacre of the Jewish population was planned.

First of all, the killers broke into the hospitals and slaughtered all the dying patients—without them the exiles would find the trip easier. From there they went to the old people's home and butchered the old men and women; they simply stood them up in a row and used them as targets. Not one was left. That too would make the exiles' trip easier. Afterward they murdered the children and babies, the abandoned orphans who had found refuge in the community orphanage, those whose parents had previously been killed by the murderers. Following all those "easements" they commenced great expulsion and slaughter. When the evil broke out, people started to slip away. Then the hunt began. They brought an additional disaster down upon the Jews of Lublin. Those who fled for their lives thought they could follow the prophet's advice [Isa. 26:20], *Hide but a little moment / Until the indignation passes*. Perhaps they will be spared! Perhaps the Guardian of Israel will have pity for them! But the killers discovered those hidden places, and anyone found in them was put to the sword. Some died of suffocation in these airless holes because the doors weren't built to be opened from within and there was no one from without to open them. For all the members of the household had fled for their lives or been arrested to be deported.

When the hunt began, they gathered like dumb sheep led to the slaughter. Herd by herd, thousands of Jews, who were taken . . . where? No living soul knows. That is the Nazi's way: he commits his abominations in darkness. There is no crack through which a ray of light might penetrate. Forty thousand oppressed Jews, weary, consumed, broken, bereft, and abandoned by their families. Naked and penniless they were delivered to the Nazi overlords to be taken to some distant place of slaughter.[12]

One rumor is afoot that they were brought to Rawa-Ruska and there burned to death with electricity. They chose a good death for them. The murderers have the virtue of doing everything wholesale.

12. They were murdered in the Bełżec death camp.

Immediately after the expulsion all possessions were removed from the depopulated houses, and after the valuable objects were set aside, they were burned. That was all done to serve two purposes at the same time: extirpation of the typhus epidemic and of the epidemic of the Jews.

So that is the end of Jewish Lublin!

I wrote the foregoing according to rumors I heard and the testimony of refugees from Lublin. Perhaps that is not carefully sifted historical evidence. But the general picture fits the historical truth.

April 18, 1942

The evening of the holy Sabbath, 1 [*month missing*] 5702, was a night of horror and dread in the miserable ghetto. The Nazis committed a massacre against the Jews, and much innocent blood was shed. Darkness covered the murderers' abominations, and aside from officers of the Jewish police force, no one was present at the time of the murder, though the echo of the shooting reached the ears of all the inhabitants of the ghetto in the silence of the night. Most people didn't know why or wherefore there was shooting. Only with the light of morning, when we found the victims at the gates of our houses, did we know that our calamity was as vast as the sea.

Just a day or two before the slaughter it was felt in the air of the ghetto that some catastrophe was in the offing. We sought confirmation in the events of Lublin. In what way is Warsaw favored over Lublin? The battle cry, "Destroy, murder, wipe out," was the same everywhere. Little Lublin was destroyed in a few days. Warsaw was larger and would be destroyed in a few weeks. Greater confirmation was given by rumors that began to spread, saying that the same battalion that had acted in Lublin was coming to carry out a massacre in Warsaw too.

In addition to what has been said, at this time, on the border between the ghetto and the Aryan quarter, a Jonak [hoodlum] was killed, a type of ruffian and bully who supported himself with theft and strong-arm methods. Some of them are Ukrainians, and some are Germans. This time a German Jonak was killed, put to death by a violent villain like himself because of a smuggling dispute. His murderer was known to the authorities. But that didn't prevent them from concocting the false accusation that a Jewish hand was involved. Therefore, our hearts prophesied some impending evil. A person's heart tells him, and that of a nation, even more so.

The night before the slaughter eighteen Jewish policemen who speak German well were summoned to accompany the murderers on their way. A secret movement arose in the ghetto, and in a whisper various words were passed. The Jewish policemen calmed the angry crowd, saying that not a hair on their heads would be harmed! The killing began at midnight. Small groups of four murderers with lists in their hands started going from door to door, arresting those "condemned" to death, with a Jewish policeman showing them the way. They held pistols in their hands, and machine guns were strapped to their waists. They rang the bell at the gate.

The porter would hurry to open the gate, and the murderers beat him shamefully, until his soul nearly fled. And if, for any reason, the porter tarried a little and didn't hurry to open the door in the wink of an eye, he was the first victim. In that fashion six porters fell on the night of the slaughter, though their names were not on the list prepared the day before. Here's something amazing: unlike their usual ways, they [the Germans] behaved with the requisite courtesy this time, saying "good evening" on their arrival and politely inviting the condemned man to come with them. On their way out to the courtyard a powerful searchlight lit up the darkness. Without any unnecessary delay they stood the condemned man up against the wall and put an end to his life with two or three shots. They left the body in the gate and immediately departed, hurrying on to a new killing.

How many squads of murderers like that dispersed throughout the ghetto to shed innocent blood? It's hard to say. But the total number of murders is known to us: fifty-two dead and twelve wounded! In the morning light their corpses were found splayed out in doorways. There was no trial or judgment. Officially they were not accused of any crime or sin—in darkness the list was prepared, and in darkness the sentences were executed. Not a living Jewish soul knows why, for what reason they were killed. . . .

Translated from the Hebrew by Jeffrey M. Green

CHAIM KAPLAN, Hebrew educator, essayist, and diarist, was born in Belorussia in 1880. In 1902 he settled in Warsaw, where he wrote prolifically on pedagogic subjects and founded a pioneering elementary Hebrew school, which he ran until World War II. In 1933 Kaplan began keeping a diary, first as a personal document but increasingly as an objective historical record of the Warsaw Ghetto. He had the diary smuggled out of the ghetto in late 1942, shortly before he was sent to his death in Treblinka.

GELA SEKSZTAJN

Charcoal and Watercolor Sketches (1939–42)

Gela Seksztajn, *Friends* (1939–42). Charcoal on paper. 220 × 165 mm. *Życie i twórczość Geli Secksztajn*, vol. 4 of *Archiwum Ringelbluma: Konspiracyjne Archiwum Getta Warszawy*, ed. Magdalena Tarnowska (Warsaw: Jewish Historical Institute, 2011), no. 280. From the E. Ringelblum Jewish Historical Institute, Warsaw, Poland.

Gela Seksztajn, *Self-Portrait* (1939–42). Charcoal on paper. 170 × 228 mm. *Życie i twórczość Geli Secksztajn*, vol. 4 of *Archiwum Ringelbluma: Konspiracyjne Archiwum Getta Warszawy*, ed. Magdalena Tarnowska (Warsaw: Jewish Historical Institute, 2011), no. 189. From the E. Ringelblum Jewish Historical Institute, Warsaw, Poland.

Gela Seksztajn, *Portrait of Israel Lichtenstein* (1939–42). Pencil on paper. 170 × 199 mm. *Życie i twórczość Geli Secksztajn*, vol. 4 of *Archiwum Ringelbluma: Konspiracyjne Archiwum Getta Warszawy*, ed. Magdalena Tarnowska (Warsaw: Jewish Historical Institute, 2011), no. 267. From the E. Ringelblum Jewish Historical Institute, Warsaw, Poland.

Gela Seksztajn, *Sleeping Little Girl* [Margolit?] (1939–42). Pencil on paper. 240 × 325 mm. *Życie i twórczość Geli Secksztajn*, vol. 4 of *Archiwum Ringelbluma: Konspiracyjne Archiwum Getta Warszawy*, ed. Magdalena Tarnowska (Warsaw: Jewish Historical Institute, 2011), no. 269. From the E. Ringelblum Jewish Historical Institute, Warsaw, Poland.

Gela Seksztajn, *Apartment Interior* (1939–42). Charcoal on paper. 398 × 510 mm. *Życie i twórczość Geli Secksztajn*, vol. 4 of *Archiwum Ringelbluma: Konspiracyjne Archiwum Getta Warszawy*, ed. Magdalena Tarnowska (Warsaw: Jewish Historical Institute, 2011), no. 265. From the E. Ringelblum Jewish Historical Institute, Warsaw, Poland.

Gela Seksztajn, *A Wounded Boy* (1939–42). Charcoal on paper. 318 × 380 mm. *Życie i twórczość Geli Secksztajn*, vol. 4 of *Archiwum Ringelbluma: Konspiracyjne Archiwum Getta Warszawy*, ed. Magdalena Tarnowska (Warsaw: Jewish Historical Institute, 2011), no. 294. From the E. Ringelblum Jewish Historical Institute, Warsaw, Poland.

Gela Seksztajn, *A Young Girl* (1939–42). Watercolor on paper. 450 × 780 mm. *Życie i twórczość Geli Seckstajn*, vol. 4 of *Archiwum Ringelbluma: Konspiracyjne Archiwum Getta Warszawy*, ed. Magdalena Tarnowska (Warsaw: Jewish Historical Institute, 2011), no. 303. From the E. Ringelblum Jewish Historical Institute, Warsaw, Poland.

HENRYKA ŁAZOWERT

The Little Smuggler

Over the wall, through holes, and past the guard,
Through the wires, ruins, and fences,
Plucky, hungry, and determined
I sneak through, dart like a cat.

At noon, at night, at dawn,
In snowstorm, cold or heat,
A hundred times I risk my life
And put my head on the line.

Under my arm a gunny sack,
Tatters on my back,
On nimble young feet,
With endless fear in my heart.

But one must endure it all,
One must bear it all,
So that tomorrow morning
The fine folk can eat their fill.

Over the wall, through holes and bricks,
At night, at dawn, at noon,

Plucky, hungry, artful,
I move silently like a shadow.

And if the hand of destiny
Should seize me in the game,
That's a common trick of life.
You, mother, do not wait up for me.

I will return no more to you,
My voice will not be heard from afar.
The dust of the street will bury
The lost fate of a child.

And only one request
Will stiffen on my lips:
Who, mother mine, who
Will bring your bread tomorrow?

August 1941
Translated from the Polish by Ted Hudes

Born in Warsaw in 1910, Henryka Łazowert belonged to the new wave of Polish poetry that arose in the immediate aftermath of the First World War. Employed by the Jewish Social Self-Help in the ghetto, she was also an active contributor to the Oyneg Shabes archive. Rather than go into hiding on the Aryan Side with her Christian husband, Łazowert was deported along with her mother to Treblinka, where she was murdered in 1942.

STEFANIA GRODZIEŃSKA

Hershek

He was, oh, so scared to go to work each day,
But he was twelve, shouldn't give in to his dread;
Hersh was a smuggler, had to make his way
Beyond the wire, he had to go for bread.

You wait and wait and then the guard turns round,
You lift barbed wire, you wriggle underneath,
You make a dash and you're on Aryan ground,
Your armband's off and you can hardly breathe.

Another dash to where your partner waits;
"Hi mate!" "Heil Jew-boy!" "Gimme two this time."
The bread inside your coat, look sharp, run straight
Back to the wire, once more you cross the line.

So, several times a day Hersh takes this route
(His sister's job is then to sell the bread);
The Germans, if they notice, always shoot,
And each day by the wire he sees the dead.

Hersh is so scared, he really isn't bold,
He goes because he must, because they're poor,

They have to eat and all their stuff's been sold—
Even the beds; they now sleep on the floor.

So all those nasty, dirty ghetto days,
He goes out, quaking, ashamed to feel this fear,
And whistling as he goes, the scared child prays:
"Dear God, today please help me to get clear."

In war, the Lord has bigger things to do—
The ghetto has no direct line to God—
The sentry at the wire just did his job
And neither bread nor Hersh would ever get back through.

1942

Translated from the Polish by Jolanta Scicińska

STEFANIA GRODZIEŃSKA was a leading actress in the Polish-language theater Femina, run by her husband, Jerzy Jurandot, in the Warsaw Ghetto. Buried in a glass jar on the Aryan Side of Warsaw in 1943, *Ghetto Children* was published six years later under the pen name Stefania Ney. Grodzieńska died in Warsaw, the city of her birth, in 2010, at the age of ninety-six.

YITZHAK KATZENELSON

Song of Hunger and Songs of the Cold

Song of Hunger

Dearest one, come out,
To die on the street,
On the pitiless pavement.
And don't forget the children.

Bring the eldest,
And the middle one too.
Our third is still too young,
But when he's a grownup Jew
He'll die on the street of hunger for sure.

Come onto the street
Come onto Karmelicka.[1]
Here we'll fit right in.
Some walk, some fall, some sit themselves down.
There's a hullabaloo in town.

1. Pronounced Kar-me-LITS-ka. The busiest thoroughfare in the ghetto, connecting Leszno and Gęsia Streets.

Come on, get out of the house!
I'm ashamed to say
It's empty anyway.
No point lying in a living grave.
A starving man mustn't die alone.

It's no disgrace to be out on the street.
Just lay yourself down, like everyone else,
Swollen, bloated, belted tight.
A multitude dying wholesale.

So let's lie down on the thoroughfare.
Or better yet, heart to heart,
Body to body,
Die with those already there.

Come onto the street . . .

Warsaw Ghetto, May 28, 1941
Translated from the Yiddish by David G. Roskies

Songs of the Cold

1
It's cold indoors, a bitter cold.
Wolves run around the room.
Frost-bears beset the window panes.
I, my wife, and children tremble
And don't know what to do.
And no one sees, and no one wants to hear.
Don't cry, please don't cry.

Though your tears are silent
They could freeze in your eyes.

It's cold indoors.
Fear attacked me in my house
and I went out into the empty streets.
I stepped over people who were frozen
Lying like felled trees.
Their arms flung out in a dumb terror,
Like a vain, empty cry.
Stiff ones,
Is it me you greet?

2
It's cold indoors and dark.
Quietly one night I pulled the black paper shades
down from my windows
and the high moon looked in
and poured her cold and misty light on me.
Just as happened long ago,
when innumerable stars
glittered through a crack and said:
"Joy and gladness, joy and gladness."
—Will you stop it!
It's just a trick. You're cheating,
making eyes at me,
as in those nights of long ago.
Stop it!

But the stars pretended not to understand,
and did not tear away from me

their threads of trembling gold.
They did not stop winking at me.
—Go to hell!
Ardently I stretched out cold hands
to my old friends the stars:
—Oh, go to hell!

Warsaw Ghetto, January 10, 1942
Translated from the Yiddish by Elinor Robinson

YITZHAK KATZENELSON, born in Lithuania in 1886, won recognition for the poems and plays he wrote in Hebrew and Yiddish before World War II. A prolific Yiddish poet, translator, and playwright in the Warsaw Ghetto, he is best remembered for his *Vittel Diary,* written in Hebrew, and his jeremiad in Yiddish, *Dos lid fun oysgehargetn yidishn folk* (The song of the murdered Jewish people). He and his eldest son died in Auschwitz in 1944.

RABBI KALONYMUS SHAPIRA

From Holy Fire

Parashat Mishpatim [Exod. 21:1–24:181]

(SHEKALIM [ADDITIONAL READING OF EXOD. 30:11–16])

Now the Jew who is tormented by his afflictions thinks that he alone suffers, as if all his personal afflictions and those of all Israel do not affect [God] above, God forbid. Scripture states, however, *In all their troubles he was troubled* (Isa. 63:9); and the Talmud states [B. Sanhedrin 46a], When a person suffers, what does the Shekinah say? "My head is too heavy for me, my arm is too heavy for me." Our sacred literature tells us that when an Israelite is afflicted, God, blessed be He, suffers as it were much more than the person does. It may be that since He, blessed be He, is not subject to any limitation—for which reason no conception of Him is possible in the world—therefore His suffering from Israel's troubles is also boundless. It is not merely that it would be impossible for a person to endure the experience of such great suffering but that even to conceive of His suffering, blessed be He—to know that He, blessed be He, does suffer, to hear His voice, blessed be He: "Woe to Me for I have destroyed My house and have exiled My children"—is impossible, because He is beyond the confines of the human. It is only when Rabbi Yose entered one of the ruins of Jerusalem so that his selfhood was further[1] annihilated, and the constricted, bounded aspect of his being was further destroyed, that he heard the voice of the Holy One, blessed be He.[2] Even then he only heard a bit of it: he heard a divine voice that merely cooed like a dove, whereas Scripture states, *He surely roars over His habitation* (Jer. 25:30)—like the roar of a lion, as it were, over the destruction of the Temple.[3]

This explains why the world remains standing on its foundation and was not destroyed by God's cry of suffering over the afflictions of His people and the destruction of His house: because His great suffering never penetrated the world. This may be what underlies the passage found in the Proem [24] of Midrash Lamentations Rabba [which speaks of God's weeping at the destruction of the Temple]. [In this passage] the angel said, "Sovereign of the Universe, let me weep, but don't You weep." God replied to him, "If you don't let me weep now, I will go to a place where you have no permission to enter, and weep there," [as Scripture says, *but if you will not hear it*,] *My soul shall weep in secret* (Jer. 13: 17).

Inspect this passage at its source. Furthermore, in *Tanna debe Eliyahu Rabbah* [chap. 17] we find that the angel said, "It is unseemly for a king to weep before his servants."[4] But if the issue was merely that of the unseemliness of a king weeping before his servants, then the *angel* could have gone away; then

1. "Further" may mean that prior to this incident Rabbi Yose had already attained a level of self-annihilation.

2. As the borders of the self recede, the mystic perceives the divine suffering.

3. I.e., if God roars like a lion over the Destruction, then to hear a voice cooing like a dove represents but a partial revelation.

4. Citing the passage from memory, Rabbi Shapira added the attribution to an angel.

[God's weeping] would no longer be "before his servants." In light of what we've stated above, however, the passage suggests the following: What the angel meant to say was that it is unseemly, with respect to the king's servants, for the king to *need* to weep. Now since His suffering, as it were, is boundless and vaster than all the world—for which reason it has never penetrated the world and the world does not shudder from it—therefore the angel said, "Let me weep so that You won't need to weep." In other words, since angels are also messengers of God, for it is through them that He performs His actions, that is why the angel wanted the divine weeping to be manifested in the world; the angel wanted to transmit the weeping into the world. For then God would no longer need to weep; once the sound of divine weeping would be heard in the world, the world would hear it and explode.[5] A spark of His suffering, as it were, would penetrate the world and would consume all His enemies. At the [parting of the] Sea [of Reeds; Exod. 14–15], the Holy One, blessed be He, exclaimed [to the ministering angels who wished to chant their hymns], "My creatures are drowning in the Sea, and you wish to sing hymns!" [B. Megillah 10b]. Now that Israel is drowning in blood, shall the world continue to exist? [So the angel said,] "Let me weep, but don't You weep"—in other words, You will no longer need to weep.[6] But since God wanted to atone for Israel's sins, and that time was not yet a time of salvation, He answered, "I will go to a place where you have no permission to enter and weep there." Now the suffering is so great that the world cannot contain it; it is too sublime for the world. He causes His suffering and pain

5. Here Rabbi Shapira's own voice breaks through the literary convention.

6. I.e., the angel was asking permission to transmit God's pain to the world, thus precipitating a cataclysmic explosion.

to expand, as it were, still more so that they would be too sublime even for the angel, so that even the angel would not see. In the Talmudic tractate Hagigah [5b], we find that this place [where God weeps] is in the inner chambers [of heaven]. There weeping can, as it were, be predicated of Him. In the commentary of Maharsha[7] [ad loc.] we find that the term *inner chambers*, understood kabbalistically, refers to the *sefirah* of *Binah*;[8] inspect this statement at its source. In light of what we've said above, the significance of Maharsha's statement is that Binah is a state in which questioning, but not knowledge, is possible;[9] it is beyond conception. In this state, therefore, His suffering is, as it were, hidden from the angel and from all the world.

February 14, 1942

Parashat Hahodesh [Exod. 12:1–20]

The Talmud states in Hagigah [5b] that, concerning God's outer chambers, we may apply the verse *strength and rejoicing are in His place* (1 Chron. 16:27), but in His inner chambers, He grieves and weeps for the sufferings of Israel. Therefore, there are occasions when, at a time of [Divine] hiddenness—meaning, when He, may He be blessed, secludes Himself in His inner chambers—the Jewish person communes with Him there, each individual in accord with his situation, and [new aspects of] Torah and Divine service are revealed to him there: We have already mentioned how the Oral Torah was revealed in exile;

7. Rabbi Samuel Eliezer ben Judah Edels (1556–1631).
8. "Understanding," the third of the ten divine emanations.
9. See Zohar I:1b, III:193b.

[similarly] the Holy Zohar was revealed to Rabbi Simeon bar Yohai and his son Rabbi Eleazar at a time of acute suffering, caused by the terror of the [Roman] government.

At times the individual is amazed at himself. [He thinks,] "Am I not broken? Am I not always on the verge of tears—and indeed I do weep periodically! How then can I study Torah? How can I find the strength to think creatively in Torah and Hasidism?" At times the person torments himself by thinking, "Can it be anything but inner callousness, that I am able to strengthen myself and study, despite my troubles and those of Israel, which are so numerous." Then again, he will say to himself, "Am I not broken? I have so much to make me cry; my whole life is gloomy and dark." Such a person is perplexed about himself; but, as we've said, God, blessed be He, is to be found in His inner chambers, weeping, so that one who pushes in and comes close to God by means of [studying] Torah weeps together with God and studies Torah with Him. Just that makes the difference: the weeping, the pain that a person undergoes by himself, alone, may have the effect of breaking him, of bringing him down, so that he is incapable of doing anything. But the weeping that the person does together with God—that strengthens him. He weeps—and is strengthened; he is broken—but finds courage to study and teach. It is hard to rise, time and again, above the sufferings, but when one summons the courage, stretching the mind to engage in Torah and Divine service, then he enters the inner chambers where God is to be found. He weeps and wails together with Him, as it were, and even finds the strength to study Torah and serve the Lord.

March 14, 1942

Parashat Mattot [Num. 30:2–32:42]

How can we lift ourselves up at least a little bit in the face of the terrifying reports, both old and new, which tear us to pieces and crush our hearts? With the knowledge that we are not alone in our sufferings, but that He, may He be blessed, endures with us [as Scripture states], *I am with him in trouble* (Ps. 91:15). But more: There are some sufferings that we suffer on our own account—whether for our sins or as sufferings of love in order to purge and purify us—in which case He, may He be blessed, just suffers along with us. There are, however, some sufferings that we just suffer along with Him, as it were. These are the sufferings of *Kiddush Hashem*. [As our liturgy states,] "Our Father, our King, act for the sake of those who are slain for Your holy name." They are killed, as it were, for His sake and for the sake of sanctifying His holy name. [As our liturgy states,] "Save, please, those who bear Your burden." Israel also bears His burden [besides its own]. The sufferings are basically for His sake, on His account; in sufferings such as these, we are made greater, raised higher. As a consequence, we can strengthen ourselves a bit more. [As our liturgy states,] "Save those who study Your Torah whose cheeks are torn of hair, who are given to the floggers, who bear Your burden." . . . How is it possible to study Torah when "our cheeks are torn of hair," when we are "given to the floggers"? Because we know that we "bear Your burden," and we thereby strengthen ourselves a bit.[10]

How can we tell if the sufferings are only on account of our sins, or whether they are to sanctify His name? By [noticing] whether the enemies torment only us, or whether their hatred is basically for the Torah, and as a consequence they torment

10. From Isa. 50:6—the Suffering Servant.

us as well. Regarding Haman's decree, the Talmud asks [B. Megillah 12], "What did the Jews of that generation do to deserve destruction?" whereas regarding the Hellenic decree [against the Jews that resulted] in the miracle of Hanukkah, the Talmud does not raise the question, despite the fact that thousands of Jews were killed, nearly all of the Land of Israel was conquered, and the Temple was invaded. The difference is that Haman's decree was directed only against the Jews [not the religion]; it follows, then, that the decree [against them] was on account of some sin. However, with respect to the Hellenic [persecution], [our liturgy] states, "In the days of Mattathias, when the wicked Hellenic kingdom arose . . . to make them forget Your Torah and transgress the statutes of Your will . . ." So it is not appropriate to ask "for what sin [did the calamity come]," since while they do expiate sins, they are essentially sufferings of *Kiddush Hashem*. . . .

July 11, 1942
Ringelblum Archive II:15
Translated from the Hebrew with commentary by Nehemia Polen

RABBI KALONYMUS SHAPIRA was born into a Hasidic dynasty in 1889. Settling in Piaczesno, near Warsaw, he began to attract a following and became the community's rabbi in 1913. After World War I he moved to Warsaw, founding a yeshiva there in 1923. During the Nazi occupation his home doubled as prayer house and soup kitchen for his followers in the ghetto. There, in the sermons that he delivered until the Great Deportation of July 1942, Shapira developed a theology linking human suffering with the divine. Deported to the Trawniki labor camp in the spring of 1943, he was murdered during the liquidation of the camp on November 3, 1943.

ABRAHAM LEWIN

From the Notebooks and Diary of the Great Deportation

From the Notebooks

SATURDAY NIGHT, 30 MAY [1942]

This day has been among the most difficult, the most nightmarish of all days that we are now living through. Firstly the roundup. Yesterday's roundup brought a rich harvest. I do not know the exact number of those who were seized, but by all accounts their numbers ran into the hundreds. This means that hundreds of Jewish lives are exposed to the gravest danger, the danger of destruction. This morning they were all taken away, in closed trains of course, in freight or cattle trucks. Where they were being sent is not known for sure. I have heard from several sources that they were being sent as far away as Bobruisk to build fortifications. If this is so, it may be that their position will be even more tragic and bitter than that of those who were seized and sent to work camps last year or the year before, because at that time the Warsaw Jewish community organization and also that of the town nearest to the camp tried to do something for the unfortunates. Their position was not greatly alleviated, but a certain protection and small-scale help did reach them, and it was of some slight consolation. Today? If those who have been rounded up are sent to the former Russian territories, there will be no one to take care of them and help them in some way. In Russia proper there are no Jewish community organizations, and the Jews have disappeared from all those areas occupied by the Germans; either they have retreated with the Russian army, or they have been slaughtered by the Germans. Whole Jewish towns have vanished. It is horrific, quite horrific.

And once again we see the sad complicity of the Jewish Police. With great regret they are "obliged" to carry out their duties and round up people. They carry out these duties conscientiously. Thus both large numbers of Jews are seized and the pockets of the Jewish Police are filled with ill-gotten gains. Apparently one could get released with no difficulty for ten zloty.

Last night we had a repetition of the Bartholomew Night action on a smaller scale. It was another Friday night, like the infamous 18 April. The number of those who were brutally murdered is said to be eleven, among them a woman. All the Jews living at 11 Mylna Street were killed, four men from one flat: an elderly Jew, his son, and his son-in-law, Rozycki, as well as his tenant. The elder Wilner was partly paralyzed. In his terror he couldn't speak and was unable to move. The Germans put him on a chair and threw him out of the second-floor window. The old man was killed instantly. The other three men were taken down into the street and shot. There is also talk of a murdered barber from 50 Nowolipie Street and a policeman, who six months ago had been on duty in the hospital on Stawki Street when two Jewish reserve officers in the Polish army escaped, Gomuliński and one other.[1]

1. The organized escape of two Polish reserve officers, Gomuliński and Szymański, occurred in March 1942.

Also a Mrs. [Regina] Judt was shot. She had worked for the Germans and had managed to obtain permits for the Jewish theaters. Altogether, as mentioned above, eleven Jews.

The background to these murders in the night? Hard to say. One opinion I heard was that they were all racketeers. This is, however, not completely accurate. Thus I have heard that the Wilners owned a brick factory in Grodzisk; the son-in-law is supposed to have been a teacher and a very respectable person. The barber from 50 Nowolipie Street is said to have been a member of the Bund [the Jewish socialist party]. In short, we do not have the key to these terrible murders, and none of us has any idea what fate awaits us. All people more or less involved in the running of an organization live each day in terror for their lives.

This morning the gendarmerie drove up with Junaks on Przejazd Street and took away four Jews who were involved in smuggling. They were standing on the ruined wall at number 11, looking over to the Aryan Side. I heard that Auerswald, the Nazi commissioner in charge of the ghetto, was present at the arrest and that on his orders the group was deported immediately, along with those Jews who had already been rounded up. The mother of one of those deported was sobbing pitifully outside my window.

Today a group of community officials [i.e., members of the Oyneg Shabes staff] were sitting together, and for two hours a lawyer from Lwów recited to us the book of lamentations of Lwów and the whole of eastern Galicia. And what he said was so horrific and gruesome that words cannot convey what has happened there. Lwów alone has lost thirty thousand martyrs. The slaughter was carried out in three main stages. As soon as the Germans entered Lwów, they carried out a large-scale roundup, and thousands upon thousands of Jews were murdered in the prisons. The second stage took place later, when

Jews had to move into the ghetto, next to the "bridge of death" that became so tragically notorious, and the third took place in March during the great resettlement of the Lwów Jews, when up to ten thousand Jews died.[2] In the action to dispose of people over sixty, several thousand Jews were killed. The details of these events are so devastating that they are not for the pages of a diary. This must all be told in full. I hope and believe that this will one day happen, that the world's conscience will be taken by storm and that vile beast that is at the throat of the peoples of Europe and choking them to death will be bound and shackled once and for all. The lawyer from Lwów estimates that the number of dead in eastern Galicia is in excess of one hundred thousand. All the Jewish communities along the Hungarian border have been obliterated from the face of the earth. Thus Jaremcze, which had a population of one thousand Jews, has become Judenrein. The same in Tatarow and so on.

When the lawyer had finished his account of these horrors and Mr. G[utkowski] had thanked him, many of us had tears in our eyes.

Those two hours belong to the darkest of my life.

On my way home from this meeting I had the "good fortune" to be stopped and made to work at loading bricks. The Germans were stopping only more respectably dressed Jews. The work lasted an hour. It wasn't so much hard work as humiliating. A soldier stood over us and yelled insults: "Verfluchte Juden!" [Damned Jews] and struck one of us with the back of an iron rod. It is certainly no pleasure to taste

2. From March 14 to April 1, 1942, some fifteen thousand Jews, mostly those without work permits, were deported from Lwów. Those deemed unfit to work perished in the Bełżec death camp.

German barbarity and Jewish servitude, even for just one hour, but I did nonetheless have a certain feeling of satisfaction. I have experienced at first hand, albeit in small measure, that which millions of Jews have been enduring for almost three years now. For this reason it was worthwhile.

Ringelblum Archive I:431
Translated from the Yiddish by Christopher Hutton

From Diary of the Great Deportation

FRIDAY, 28 AUGUST

The acts of terror are continuing. I have heard that yesterday evening a group of workers was returning from work at Oschman's factory, in procession. The SS divided the group in two. Half were allowed to keep walking, and the second group was led away straight to the Umschlagplatz.

The children who were seized yesterday were not rescued. They have perished, perished.

Today we [staff members of Oyneg Shabes] had a long talk with Dowid Nowodworski, who returned from Treblinka.[3] He gave us the complete story of the sufferings that he endured from the first moment that he was seized to the escape from the death camp and up to his return to Warsaw. His words confirm once again and leave no room for doubt that all the deportees, both those who have been seized and those who reported voluntarily, are taken to be killed and that no one

3. One of the adult members and chief organizers of Hashomer Hatsair in the Warsaw Ghetto, who was later company commander of the Jewish Combat Organization. Hashomer Hatsair was a socialist-Zionist youth movement with a pro-Soviet orientation.

is saved. This is the naked truth, and how terrible, when we remember that in the last weeks at least three hundred thousand Jews have been exterminated, from Warsaw and other towns: Radom, Siedlce, and many, many others. From his words we put together a testimony of such stark anguish, so shattering, that it cannot be grasped and put into words. This is without doubt the greatest crime ever committed in the whole of history. Yesterday about four thousand people were driven from Warsaw to their deaths, men, women, and children. The Aktion is continuing today. Workshops are surrounded and besieged, But—I have heard—there are no wagons. They will be held until evening or until tomorrow, and then another large group will be sent away. This is the thirty-eighth day of the great slaughter. From the poison cup have so far drunk—apart from Warsaw—Siedlce, Rembertow, Radom, and many, many more.

Yesterday I heard that the large factory owners, Schultz, Többens, are negotiating with leaders of the murder squads. They are promising them millions in bribes if they leave the rest of the Jews in Warsaw, which they estimate at one hundred thousand, and if they leave the city. In this connection there are rumors going around that the Aktion will continue until Saturday or Sunday, and after that they will leave Warsaw and the town will be quiet. We have so often had our hopes raised of an end to the bloody action, and they have turned out to be false and we have been disappointed. No doubt this time we will also be let down, and blood will continue to be spilled.

God! Are we really to be exterminated down to the very last of us? Now it is certain that all those deported from Warsaw have been killed.—

FRIDAY, 11 SEPTEMBER—THE EVE OF ROSH HASHANAH

Since last Saturday I have had neither the inclination, the time, nor the opportunity to write anything.[4] The human hand and pen are weary of describing all that has happened to the handful of Jews who are for the time being still alive, myself among them. The cup of our sorrows has no parallel in our history.

The horrific and brutal week began on the Saturday night, Sunday morning. A Jewish policeman knocked on the door at three in the morning and gave us the terrible news that all Jews were to be concentrated within the boundary formed by Gęsia, Miła, and Ostrowska Streets, for a new registration. Enough food for two days should be taken and something to hold water. The panic that gripped the Jews of Warsaw on Sunday morning. We all believed that our time had come to depart this life. With tears in my eyes I said good-bye to my whole family: to mother, Frume, Nacia, Jakub, and the children.

The terrible and particular appearance of the streets: Miła, Wołynska, the rectangle that has been transformed into an Umschlagplatz. The crowds of Jews with packs on their backs, streaming from the streets of the ghetto. Everyone is camped out on the street. In this way we spend the whole of Sunday. In the evening the inspections begin by the workshops, and certain groups return back to their factories or to their blocks. On Monday the return to the blocks continues. The inspection brings new victims: children do not pass. The old, women, do not pass However, everything depends on chance. With some

4. During five of the most terrible days of the Great Deportation, known as *dos kesl* (the cauldron), which lasted from September 6 to 10, Lewin did not open his notebook. All Jews left in the ghetto were then forced to leave their homes and assemble in the streets adjacent to the Umschlagplatz. Those not assigned to recognized workplaces were deported in cattle cars to Treblinka.

groups the inspection is not so severe; other groups on the other hand have enormous losses.

Murders in the streets. I saw with my own eyes how a young, strong man and a young, attractive woman were shot. A sight that I will never forget as long as I live: five tiny children, two- and three-year-olds, sit on a camp bed in the open from Monday to Tuesday and cry and cry and scream without stopping—"Mama, mama, chcę jeść!" [Mommy, mommy, I want to eat!] The soldiers are shooting continually, and the shots silence the children for a moment. The children lay there for twenty-four hours, sobbing and screaming: Mommy, Mommy. Tuesday afternoon a middle-aged man, aged about fifty, went up to them, broke down into a continual, choking sobbing, and gave the children a little something to eat. Earlier, women had come up and given them food. Our hearts have turned to stone, and there was no way to save them. What are we saving them for if we are all sentenced to die?

We were waiting for the commissar of the firm, Hensel, to come and take us to the factory. He doesn't come. Our mood becomes more and more despairing. The feeling that death, in the form of the Umschlagplatz, is getting slowly nearer and nearer chokes us and is throttling us to death. A rumor went round that our firm had been closed by the Warsaw SS. The people's mood swings between hope and despair. Meanwhile there are blockades in the nearby streets and in Miła Street.

Several dozen of our people are removed from the buildings at number 61 Miła [where the workers of Landau's factory lived] and from the Werksschutz [factory guard].[5] Rozenowicz and his father, Ryba and his family. This happened on Monday. Our

5. Groups guarding German industrial plants, mostly recruited from among the Jewish Ghetto Police.

despair, and the suffering of the hundreds of people, shut in the alleyway, reaches the ultimate limits of endurance. The shooting that goes on all day and, especially, all night shatters the nerves, bringing a deathly depression. Midday Tuesday a glimmer of hope appears but is immediately extinguished. Hensel arrives for a short visit at ten till eleven in the morning and promises he will soon come to take us away. He leaves, the hours go by, and he doesn't return. Once again our resolve is weakened, and we fall into deep despair that is many times worse. We wait for the end that is inevitable: to be taken to the Umschlagplatz.

It is hard to keep going. I have no food, nothing to sleep on. I am sleeping (a) at 3a Dzielna Street, (b) at [Isaiah] Rabinowicz's, on the floor, (c) with Recymer. People are quarreling with each other. Anyone who has anything left cooks and eats and watches over their property. People steal everything they can lay their hands on, especially food; there is no feeling of common fate, of mutual aid. People wander around aimlessly like shadows.

[My daughter] Ora with the members of [the Zionist youth movement] Hashomer Hatsair. These young people are more mature, more united. Tuesday night was bitterly sad for me. I tried very hard to acknowledge the idea that death is inevitable and to prepare myself. I thought: The whole thing will only last ten to fifteen minutes, the execution, that is, and it will all be over. The lack of news from my sisters and my mother weighs heavily.

There is also an oppressive plague of fleas. Hunger forces us to beg, to ask for a little food. Even in such terrible hours as these a hungry person wants to still the hunger. Wednesday morning: once again a rumor that brings hope. Hensel is coming to get us. He really has come. Joy grips all those who are shut in the street. Straight away most of those who work in the workshop come down, men and women. Left behind in their homes, that is, in their hiding places, old women and children.

We stand and sit in the street from ten in the morning until six in the evening. The mood is almost joyful. A crowd of women, like some unit, is standing in front of us. The hours pass. But still everyone waits patiently. They want to get to the factory. Suddenly four or five SS officers appear and . . . a pogrom begins, the like of which I have never seen. Even the marauding of the Cossacks in the first revolution of 1905–6 bore no resemblance to what the Germans did. They beat men and women with whips, sticks, and strips of wood. They took all the women away to the Umschlagplatz (except for a few with metal numbers) [that is, those exempt from deportation] and large numbers of the men, who had by chance not obtained a metal number, thinking them to be worthless.[6] The best looking and the most elegant women perished. Whole families were cut down. A young officer hit out with murderous blows and shouting wildly, "*Über euch, verfluchte, verdammte, kräzige Juden habe ich 3 Jahren Lebens verloren. Schon 3 Jahren plaget ihr uns, ihr Hunde* . . ." [Because of you, accursed, damned, leprous Jews I have already lost three years of my life. For three years we have been plagued, you dogs . . .] and so on. I have never before seen such bestial hatred. There was also killing.

We go toward 30 Gęsia Street, and there is a roundup going on there that is still continuing today. Yesterday and today there were blockades on our blocks; people have been taken again. The Swieca family has perished. He gave himself up after seeing how his wife and two children were taken. Initially he went with us to Gęsia Street; later he went back, gave himself up, and was sent away. I feel a great compassion and admiration for this straightforward person. Strong in mind as well as strong

6. See Yehoshue Perle's "4580," in this volume.

in body. I think that [my wife] Luba would have done the same, but I didn't have enough strength to die together with her, with the one that I loved so much.

Apart from the hunt for people, the Germans are looting openly, as something quite legal. They take away everything from the buildings that appeals to them. The Ukrainians are common bandits. They break into the buildings at night and steal everything they find, with revolvers and rifles in their hands. The Jews are also in the grip of a frenzied looting and thieving. They loot and steal everything that they can lay their hands on.

Since the day before yesterday we have been shut in the factory. We tremble at every noise and shot that comes from the street. Yesterday the SS visited us for the purpose of looting. Today is the eve of Rosh Hashanah. May the coming year bring salvation for those who have survived. Today is the fifty-second day in the greatest and most terrible slaughter in history. We are the tiny remnants of the greatest Jewish community in the world.

Ringelblum Archive II:202
Translated from the Hebrew by Christopher Hutton

Born in Warsaw in 1893, Abraham Lewin was a popular historian and Hebrew pedagogue who taught at the Yehudia Gymnasium for Girls. One of the cofounders of the Oyneg Shabes archive, he is best known for his ghetto diary, which he kept in Yiddish and Hebrew. He was killed in January 1943 during the first fighting in the ghetto.

ISRAEL LICHTENSTEIN

Last Testament

With zeal and zest I threw myself into the work to help assemble archive materials. I was entrusted to be the custodian, I hid the material. Besides me, no one knew. I confided only in my friend Hersh Wasser, my superior.

It is well hidden. Please God that it be preserved. That will be the finest and best that we achieved in the present gruesome time.

I know that we will not endure. To survive and remain alive [after] such horrible murders and massacres is impossible. Therefore I write this testament of mine. Perhaps I am not worthy of being remembered, but just for my grit in working with the society Oyneg Shabes and for being the most endangered because I hid the entire material. It would be a small thing to give my own head. I risk the head of my dear wife, Gela Seksztajn, and my treasure, my little daughter, Margolit.

I don't want any gratitude, any monument, any praise. I want only a remembrance, so that my family, brother and sister abroad, may know what has become of my remains. I want my wife to be remembered. Gela Seksztajn, artist, dozens of works, talented, didn't manage to exhibit, did not show in public. During the three years of war worked among children as educator, teacher, made stage sets, costumes for the children's productions, received awards. Now together with me, we are preparing to receive death.

I want my little daughter to be remembered. Margolit, twenty months old today. Has mastered Yiddish perfectly, speaks a pure Yiddish. At nine months began to speak Yiddish clearly. In intelligence she is on a par with three- or four-year-old children. I don't want to brag about her. Witnesses to this, who tell me about it, are the teaching staff of the school at 68 Nowolipki 68. . . .

I am not sorry about my life and that of my wife. But I am sorry for the gifted little girl. She deserves to be remembered also.

May we be the redeemers for all the rest of the Jews in the whole world. I believe in the survival of our people. Jews will not be annihilated. We, the Jews of Poland, Czechoslovakia, Lithuania, Latvia, are the scapegoat for all Israel in all the other lands.

July 31, 1942
The eleventh day of the so-called "resettlement action"
In reality, an annihilation action
Ringelblum Archive I:1450 (3)
Translated from the Yiddish by Lucy S. Dawidowicz

ISRAEL LICHTENSTEIN (Lichtensztejn), a pedagogue, journalist, children's author, and Zionist activist, was born in 1904 near Warsaw, where he served on the editorial board of the *Literarishe bleter*. As a key member of Oyneg Shabes, Lichtenstein was chiefly responsible for the burial of the first part of the archive in the cellar of the communal kitchen at 68 Nowolipki, the site of his prior employment. He perished in April 1943, during the ghetto uprising.

GELA SEKSZTAJN

What Can I Possibly Say and Ask For at This Moment?

Poised on the border between life and death, more certain that I won't live than that I shall, I wish to take leave of my friends and works.

Work of ten years put together, torn up and resumed, I endeavored to exhibit my pictures, particularly the exhibition *Portrait of a Jewish Child*. Now, insofar as possible, I am trying to rescue whatever I can and as much as will fit in[to the tin boxes that are about to be buried]. Apart from these, I am abandoning to God's mercy dozens of oil works, portraits of Jewish writers, sketches, and charcoal works.

I seek no praise; I merely wish that some trace remain of my name and the name of my daughter, the talented little girl Margolit Lichtenstein (called by my husband's name, Israel Lichtenstein), who, at twenty months, shows some painting talent. A Jewish child, speaks fine Yiddish and is mentally and physically well developed.

I bequeath my works to the Jewish Museum that will be established in the future in order to re-create prewar Jewish cultural life up to the year 1939 and study the terrible tragedy of the Jewish community in Poland during the war.

It is beyond my ability to relate details of our horrifying fate, of the great tragedy of our people; I leave this to my colleagues, the Jewish writers. I ask the person or the community that finds my works to bear in mind that I had to cut down in size and adapt them to the conditions.

I ask that (the following) be informed of my fate, the fate of my husband and daughter: my dear sister-in-law, Yentke Lichtenstein, and her husband, Abraham Puterman, in Buenos Aires (I don't know them personally), my brother-in-law, Shlomo Lichtenstein, and his wife, Naomi Friedman, in Palestine, Tel Aviv (nor do I know my brother-in-law personally). My friend B[en] Z[ion] Haritan in New York, beloved friend, teacher, community worker, and writer. My fellow artists in Warsaw, who left for the Soviet Union. The great Jewish author I[srael] J[oshua] Singer, the first person to discover my talent.

In addition, all the friends, comrades, writers who knew me.

Now I am calm. I must perish, but I have done my share. I am trying to preserve some trace of my works.

Farewell, friends and comrades, farewell Jewish people. Don't allow such catastrophes to recur.

August 1, 1942
Ringelblum Archive I:1456
Anonymous translation from the Yiddish

Born in Warsaw in 1907, Gela Seksztajn (Sekszteyn) studied at the Academy of Fine Arts in Kraków and in March 1937 returned home, where she met and married Israel Lichtenstein and gave birth to their only daughter, Margolit, in 1940. During the war, she worked in various educational settings run by the Jewish Self-Help. She perished in April 1943, during the ghetto uprising. Unearthed in the first part of the Oyneg Shabes archive were 311 of her watercolors, drawings, sketches, and portraits, produced in the years 1930–42.

YEHOSHUE PERLE

4580

A round number. At first glance it looks silly and seems to have no specific meaning.

A detached number such as this can be likened to those gray people who go through life alone and die without confession.

But if an arithmetician or a stargazer were to take a good look at this number, he might arrive at some ingenious conjecture or discover some esoteric numerological computation, from which fools would later infer either the Apocalypse or the Coming of the Messiah.

Sober minds, if they consider it, will probably take it to be the Identity Number of a policeman, a railroad porter, a prisoner, or—pardon the proximity—a dog, or the devil knows what else. But that this foolish number should be a substitute for the name of a living person, who was never a policeman, a railroad porter, a prisoner, or even a dog—that will be difficult to believe.

People will also not believe that great suffering and pain cry out from the number, and so does the disaster of the people from whom it is my lot to be descended.

And yet the impossible has become possible. It happened in the year 1942, in the month of Tishrei,[1] in the land of Poland,

1. The first month of the Jewish civil calendar, which begins with the two-day celebration of Rosh Hashanah.

in the city of Warsaw. Under the savage rule of Amalek—may his name and memory be blotted out; with the consent of the Jewish kehillah—may its good deeds stand it in good stead in this world and in the next.

May it merit eternal life, the Warsaw Jewish kehillah. For it was the kehillah that favored me with the number: *four thousand five hundred and eighty.*[2] It was the kehillah that cut off my head—my name—and set a number in its place. I go around with it and live; it has become "me."

It may be worth recounting how I, a Jew, on a rainy day in Tishrei, turned into a number. I won't brag. Like everyone else I entered the world headfirst and fell into it without a name. For eight whole days, in accordance with Jewish law, I lived not only without a name but also without a number. Someone living in the year 1942 won't want to believe that, although I possessed no number, my dear mother was not afraid to hold me nor to give me warm milk from her beautiful breast. She was not afraid to warm me with her young body, to caress me, to worry over me, as a mother—and Jewish into the bargain—can worry over her firstborn son, the one who will recite the Kaddish.[3]

Eight days later,[4] as is the custom among Jews, they made a blessing over me and said, "May his name in Israel be, etc."

2. Upon arrival in the Warsaw Ghetto in 1941, Perle secured a job in the clothing department of the Judenrat run by Shmuel Winter. In 1942, again with Winter's help, Perle was joined to a shop of ersatz honey and candies, which exempted him from immediate deportation.

3. The firstborn son, who will recite the Kaddish, the mourning prayer, for his parents is especially prized for this reason.

4. A newborn Jewish male receives his name during the circumcision ceremony.

A person's name is like a living organism; it has flesh and blood. You can't feel it or see it, but you can't live without it. I wore it, this name of mine, as a lovely woman wears a still lovelier string of pearls. It was mine, entirely mine. I had, after all, inherited it from my grandfathers and great-grandfathers. I absorbed it, together with my mother's blood, together with the sweat of my overworked father.

My name lived in the same house with me. Under the same roof, in the same bed. It was I, and I was it. It learned to walk with me, learned to speak, just as I did. If I was called, it pricked up both ears. If I suffered, it suffered too. It rejoiced with my joy, wept with my tears, laughed with my laughter, and dreamed with my dreams.

But don't think that my name was a slave to me, that it didn't have a say and a will of its own. On the contrary, when I fell into a melancholy mood and started thinking about the world to come, my name asked to have this world. And just as my mother wished that I should survive her, so my name wanted to survive me.

I don't know and wouldn't swear that my life was rich with good deeds; I also don't know whether I was virtuous. I do know that when a wicked moment came upon me (for we are all but human) and I wanted to injure myself, my neighbor and my enemy—my name stood up and sternly warned me not to do it.

"You must not put me to shame," it said. "If people point their finger at you, their finger will reach me first. I am the phylactery on your forehead. Without me you may shout 'I am Solomon,'[5] and nobody will believe you. And if you want to know, I'll whisper a secret to you: I no longer belong only to

5. Based on a rabbinic legend about King Solomon, who tried to reclaim his throne from Ashmedai, king of the devils.

you. Your life wanted me to be in the public domain. And if indeed I am in the public domain, no blemish may appear on me." That's how my name spoke out. And I wouldn't be honest if I convinced myself that my name had no blemish at all. I lived with it for fifty-three years, kept pace with it for over fifty-three years. How could it be possible, in the course of half a century, for a person not to make one false step? My name was present. I saw it exposed to humiliation. I suffered with it and was silent. Not until later, when I realized that it wanted to survive me, did I make an effort for it to rise up.[6] And it rose and shone, just as my first new little gabardine once shone, the coat that my father had sewn for me for Passover.

And let people interpret it as they wish. Let them say it is pride, self-delusion: my name also shone from *her*.[7] She loved both me and my name. Just as she bore with proud pleasure her majestic head of hair, so did she bear my name with proud pleasure. To her it was the loveliest, the cleverest. She caressed and drew it out. I often didn't recognize it, so strange did it sound. But when I heard it issuing from her pure lips, with all the delight she put into it, I heard it anew, fresh, bathed in her young laughter.

Cruel fortune willed that in her youth she should carry it with her to the grave. It lies there, together with my letters to her, which accompanied her as she had instructed. The name has turned to stone in the tablet that guards her grave. And I believe with absolute faith that, just as I cannot forget her name here, so she cannot forget my name there.

And can one forget one's own name? For fifty-three years it has grown with me, for fifty-three years it has lived with me,

6. Attacked for writing pulp fiction, Perle rededicated himself to realistic prose and published his masterpiece, *Everyday Jews*, in 1937.

7. A reference to his wife, Sarah, who committed suicide in 1926.

for fifty-three years it has blossomed, put down roots, branched out into a child and a child's child. Whosoever looks at times into a holy book knows that one name can destroy a world. And one name can also create a world. The Torah is called the Law of Moses—is named after Moses. Homer's name is written on the *Iliad*.

It is true that there are names that must be cursed, obliterated from the human stock. But there are names that the human race blesses and will bless as long as it exists.

My name is not great; humanity has no reason to bless it. It also has no reason to curse it. But unimportant as this name of mine may be, I did not give the Warsaw kehillah any right to take it away and set a paper number in its place. Amalek, may his name and memory be blotted out, gave the order; and the head of the kehillah, whose learning and wisdom are known throughout the Jewish Diaspora, carried it out—to the letter.[8]

Instead of me, there roams about beneath the desolate walls of the ghetto which that same head of the kehillah has had built a big number, printed in black and white: an arrogant creature, an aristocrat among numbers.

This number—is the former "I." This number is my former name. I have no idea what they will do in 120 years, when I'm given a Jewish burial (I believe that may happen). The Angel of Death will take a trip down and knock on my tombstone: "Mah shimkho?" "What is your name?" . . . How will I answer him then?[9]

8. The Germans appointed Marek Lichtenbaum to head the Judenrat following Czerniakow's suicide. The Judenrat had no influence on the Nazi policies.

9. Based on the folk belief that when you die, you must report your name to the angel of the grave.

That my name is Four Thousand Five Hundred and Eighty? But won't he look at me as if I'm crazy? I also don't know what they'll do about the people who come after me. They'll read in chronicles about the city of Warsaw in the year nineteen hundred and forty-two and will certainly be surprised that it was possible for a living number to be transformed into a dead number. I would like to tell them, the people of the future, that we—who are not reading history on paper but making it with our blood—are not surprised in the least. What is there in it that could surprise us? Our soul has been torn out, our body raped, our Holy Ark spat into, our Torah of Moses trampled by soldiers' boots.

Amalek,[10] may his stock be obliterated from human memory, gave the order; and the Warsaw kehillah carried it out. Of three times a hundred thousand living Jewish souls it was granted that some thirty thousand ciphers of the Chosen People be left, stamped and sealed with the seal of the head of the kehillah himself, whose name will one day be used to frighten children in their cradles.

My name and all that is me also found favor in the eyes of the VIPs and were metamorphosed into a number. And just as Sholem Aleichem's Motl, the son of Peyse the cantor, runs around barefoot and happily proclaims, "Lucky me, I'm an orphan," so I walk around in the tenement courtyard on Franciszkanska Street, which has become the great wide world, and proclaim, "Lucky me, I'm a number."

I'm leading a life of luxury. The aristocratic number gives me dignity, importance. It elevates me above the rubbish heap where the other thirty thousand or so are swarming—and

10. Since the Exodus from Egypt, when the Amalekites launched an unprovoked attack on the Israelites, Amalek signifies the intractable, sworn enemy of the Jews.

persuading themselves that they alone are worthy to remain members of the Chosen People Club. My number receives a quarter of a loaf of bread a day with the consistency of clay and some very tasty grits consisting mostly of boiled water, a potato that someone has already stolen from the pot, and a few grains of cereal that chase about and can never, poor things, catch up with one another. What's more, from time to time they dole out to my number a stale egg with a drop of blood on it,[11] a lick of honey, and, once in a blue moon, a scrap of aging meat that—even if you were to hack it into pieces—would by no means have the flavor of old wine.

Lucky me: I'm a number. I'm inscribed in the Communal Register of the Holy Congregation of Warsaw. The clever head of the kehillah likes turning the pages of the Register. Someone else, in his place, would perhaps read out the Mosaic Curses. He would perhaps hear the weeping of the children who have died, even before they began to live. He would perhaps take cognizance of the roaring of three times a hundred thousand souls, slaughtered on the altar of Amalek, who rush around and do not allow a single one of these classified, happy ciphers of the Chosen People to rest.

But he only sees numbers, the clever head of the Holy Congregation of Warsaw. And, as he is the ruler of the numbers, and as he is not obliged to feed numbers for nothing, he issues edicts every other day and sends out polite notices:

"Thus-and-thus, dear number, I decree that you shall present yourself at six o'clock tomorrow, to help build the bleak wall that confines you as with a chain and wants to strangle and choke you. You must wall yourself up. You must also come and

11. The blood would render the egg unkosher.

wash away the blood of your mother and your father, whom Amalek deigned to slaughter, gladly assisted by the loyal crew. And if there is still something left in your father's house, or in your own house, you must help Amalek to steal it and bring it to him as a precious gift.

"If you are recalcitrant, if you will not come forward—" warns my good head of the kehillah—"if you do not wall yourself up with your own hands, if you do not bring Amalek the candlesticks that your dead mother used when she blessed the Sabbath candles, if you do not bring him the diamond brooch with which your mother adorned herself for the blessing of the new moon; if you do not offer him the pillow on which your child slept, I shall erase you from the Register, and you will cease to be a number."

That's how my head of the kehillah warns me every day. To tell the truth, I'm delighted by these fearsome warnings that I'll stop being a number: I'll become "I" again! I'll get my name back! To put it simply—I'll rise from the dead. Since the world began, not a single Jew has risen from the dead; the Messiah hasn't arrived yet. I'll be the first resurrected Jew. So why shouldn't my heart rejoice? On the other hand, I remember that if I stop being a number, there's an executioner's ax waiting for me. No longer being a number means good-bye to the clay-like quarter loaf each day, good-bye to the smell of the year-old egg, good-bye to the little room they allotted me to live in, good-bye to the potato that other people steal from my plate of grits, good-bye to honor; no longer an aristocrat, no longer of the Club of the Chosen.

Without a number I'll be like my neighbor, who was once as clever as I and as learned as I, as polite as I—maybe more polite. But evil fortune willed that he should not find favor, not be metamorphosed into a number; he kept his name. His beautiful human name. But a beautiful human name has the same value today as a beautiful human heart or a beautiful human virtue. Today the beautiful human hearts, the beautiful human virtues lie bleeding among the scraps that lie scattered in the desolate Jewish courtyards.

My neighbor's honest name doesn't get the quarter of a loaf, doesn't taste the flavor of a little grits, has nowhere to lay its head, hides itself in holes together with cats and stray dogs. My neighbor's name has been erased from the Communal Register. The friends of yesterday, who have numbers, no longer say good morning to him, no longer sit with him at the same table, no longer pray with him in the same house of prayer. He has become a leper, this neighbor of mine, with the honest name and without the paper number.

And how should I not value my number? How should I not worry about it? I do indeed worry about it, as a mother worries about her only child. I guard it as one guards the apple of one's eye. I have a little velvet bag, embroidered with a Star of David, and I carry my number next to my heart. I sleep with it, I eat with it. My dreams are woven around it, with it, of it.

And if I were young today and my number was also under thirty, a woman would surely appear and say tenderly, "Dear little number!"

And she would pamper it: "Darling number, my crown!"

And would use affectionate diminutives: "My numberkin!" Because I was born under a lucky star. Lucky me—I'm a number.

But in order to become a number, my fifty-three years had to be jabbed at until they bled. Jabbed at, mocked, raped. In order for me to become a number, they had to destroy my house first. Destroy it, tear it up by the roots. Under my number lie three times a hundred thousand Jewish martyrs. Three times a hundred thousand Jewish lives, that Amalek slaughtered with the consent of the head of the kehillah and his servants. From under my fortunate number leaps out the cry of tens of thousands of poisoned, strangled Jewish children. In the dark nights I hear the great weeping of the mother of all mothers, our Mother Rachel. She walks across the desolate fields and wraps her dead children in burial sheets.[12] With her beautiful, delicate hands she washes the blood off her sons and daughters. But can she wrap all of them in burial sheets? Can she wash them all? Blood cries out; and the earth, in all its length and breadth, is dissolved in lamentation.

They lie, the slaughtered creatures, naked and shamed, scattered and spread, never purified for burial, without a Kaddish, without a gravestone, violated by the murderous hands of Amalek, with the consent of the Holy Congregation of Warsaw.

Lucky me, I'm a number.

Warsaw Ghetto, end of 1942
Ringelblum Archive II:254
Translated from the Yiddish by Elinor Robinson

YEHOSHUE PERLE, Yiddish prose writer, was born in Radom, Poland, in 1888. In 1905 he moved to Warsaw, where his faithful portrayal of Jewish life won him a large audience, especially his bildungsroman *Everyday Jews* (1937). Perle fled to Soviet-occupied Lemberg-Lwów in 1939 but in 1941 made his way back to Warsaw. There he worked for the Judenrat and contributed to Ringelblum's Oyneg Shabes detailed accounts of Nazi atrocities, which contrasted

12. Based on Jer. 31:15.

sharply with the bright, frank lyricism of his earlier work. A victim of the Hotel Polski deception, while in hiding on the Aryan side, he and his only son were interned in Bergen-Belsen. Transported to Auschwitz in a sealed train with eighteen hundred other Polish Jews, they were gassed on arrival, on October 1, 1943.

WŁADYSŁAW SZLENGEL

Things and Counterattack

Things

From Hoza Street and Marszałkowska
carts were moving, Jewish carts:
    furniture, tables and chairs,
    suitcases, bundles
    and chests, boxes and bedding,
    suits and portraits,
    pots, linen and wall hangings,
    cherry brandy, big jars and little jars,
    glasses, tea pots and silver,
    books, knickknacks and everything
    go from Hoza Street to Śliska.
    A bottle of vodka in a coat pocket
    and a chunk of sausage,
    on carts and wagons and rickshaws
    the gloomy band is going.
And from Śliska Street to Niska everything
all over again went moving:
    Furniture, tables and chairs,
    suitcases and bundles,
    and pots—gents that's it.
    Now there is no carpet,

  of silverware not a sign,
  no cherry brandy this time.
  No suits or boots
  or jars or portraits.
  Already all these trifles
  were left behind on Śliska.
  In the pocket a bottle of vodka
  and a chunk of sausage,
  on carts and rickshaws and wagons
  the gloomy band is going.
They left Niska again and everything
headed for the apartment blocks.
  No furniture or stools,
  no jugs or bundles.
  Teapots have vanished,
  books, boots, little jars.
  Suits and silverware
  dumped together in a pushcart,
  all went to the devil.
  There is still a suitcase, a coat,
  a bottle of tea
  and piece of candy.
  On foot, without any wagon
  goes the gloomy procession.
Then, from the apartment blocks to Ostrowska,
moving along a Jewish road
  with no big bundles or little bundles,
  no furniture or chairs,
  no teapots and no carpet,
  no silverware or jars,
  in the hand one suitcase,
  a warm scarf and that's it.

Still a bottle of water
and a knapsack with straps.
Trampling objects underfoot like a herd
they walked down the streets at night.
And on a cloudy day, at dusk, they walked
from Ostrowska to the Blockhouses.
A small suitcase and a knapsack,
no need for anything else,
evenly . . . evenly by fives
they marched down the streets.
Nights cooler, days shorter,
tomorrow . . . maybe day after tomorrow . . .
to a whistle, a shout or command
on the Jewish road again
hands free and only
water—with a strong pill.
From the Umschlagplatz across the city
all the way to Marszałkowska,
life, Jewish life, is growing
in houses that are empty.
In abandoned apartments
abandoned bundles,
suits and down covers
and plates and chairs.
A wood fire still smolders,
spoons lie there idly,
there are family photographs
scattered in a hurry.
A book lies still open,
a letter in midsentence: "bad . . ."
a glass not drunk
and playing cards, half a hand of bridge.

Through a window the wind stirs
the sleeve of a cold shirt,
an eiderdown cover indented
as if someone nestled there.
Ownerless things lie around,
a dead apartment stands waiting
until new people
populate the rooms: Aryans they
will close the open windows,
begin a carefree life
and make these beds,
these Jewish eiderdowns
and wash the shirt,
put the books on a shelf and empty
the coffee from the glass,
together they will finish the hand of bridge.
While in a wagon
only this will remain:
a bottle half empty
with a strong pill . . .
And in the night of fear that will come,
after days of bullets and swords
all the Jewish things will come out
from chests and houses.
And they will run out through the windows,
walk down the streets
until they meet on the roads,
on the black rails.
All the tables and chairs
and suitcases, bundles
the suits and jars
and silverware and teapots

will leave, and disappear,
and no will guess what it means
that the things have departed,
no one will see them.

But on the judge's table

(if *veritas victi*)
a pill will remain
as a *corpus delecti*.

1942
Ringelblum Archive II:400
Translated from the Polish by John and Bogdana Carpenter

Counterattack

They walked quietly to the trains
As if they were sick of everything,
Dazed, looking into the face of the SS
Cattle!
The splendid officers were happy
That the hordes marched with muffled steps,
Nothing grated on the nerves
And only for fun
Slashed them with whips:
In the face!
The silenced crowd fell on the ground,
Sobs reverberated in the cattle cars,
Blood and tears oozing into sandy soil
As "the lords"
Casually tossed

On the bodies
Empty cigarette boxes,
  "*Warum sind Juno rund*"[1]
On that day,
At dawn in early mist, when they fell like hyenas
On a city still sleepy with *Stimmung*.[2]
The cattle awoke
And
Bared their teeth.
The first shot was heard on Miła Street.
A policeman staggered in a gateway,
Stared in surprise, for a moment stood still
Touched his shattered shoulder
Didn't believe it.
Something here isn't in order,
Everything was so easy, so smooth.
As a favor from friends in high places
He was recalled from the Eastern Front,
Had a few satisfying days
Of rest and relaxation in Warsaw,
Driving this cattle in an Aktion
And cleaning up the pigsty.
But here
On Miła Street, BLOOD . . .
The policeman stepped back from the gateway
And swore: I'm really bleeding.
But already Brownings barked
On Niska Street,

1. "Why Junos are round," an advertising jingle. The translation preserves the original German as it appears in Szlengel's poem.
2. German for "mood."

On Dzika,
On Pawia.
In a winding stairwell where someone's old mother
Was dragged down by the hair
Lies SS-man Handtke.
He is strangely swollen
As if he couldn't digest death,
As if he was choking on this revolt—
He belched up bloody saliva
Onto the little box, *Juno sind rund,*
Rund, rund.
Everything spins in circles,
The sky-blue uniform lying
On the spittle-covered stairs
Of Jewish Pawia Street
And he doesn't know
That at the Schultz and Többens factories[3]
Bullets are dancing in a joyous burst of song:
Revolt of the meat,
Revolt of the meat,
Revolt of the meat!
Meat spits grenades out the windows,
Meat coughs out streams of scarlet flame
And clings to the edges of life!
Here is the front, young masters!
The front—young shirkers!
Hier
Trinkt man mehr kein Bier
Hier

3. In point of fact, there was no fighting in Schultz and Többens shops. This was to happen only in the April uprising.

Hat man mehr kein Mut,
Blut,
Blut,
Blut.[4]
Peel off your gloves of shining leather,
Put aside your riding whips—put a helmet on your head—
Tomorrow issue a press release:
"Penetrated the lines of the Többens Block."
Revolt of the meat,
Revolt of the meat,
Song of the meat!
Listen, O German God,
How the Jews pray in their "wild" houses[5]
Clenching a bar, a pole in their fists.
We beg You, Lord, for a bloody battle,
We implore You for a violent death.
Before the end let our eyes
Not see the rails dragging away
But give the hand unerring aim, Lord,
To stain the blue uniform with blood,
Let us see before the last
Noiseless shout rises in the throat
Our ordinary human fear
In their haughty hands, their paws with whips.
Like crimson flowers of blood
The flames of our gun barrels bloom
From Niska Street, from Miła and Muranow.

4. "Here one drinks no more beer / Here one has no more courage / Blood / Blood / Blood."

5. Houses that were emptied of inhabitants during the Great Deportation. See "The Ghetto in Flames," in this volume.

This is our spring, our counterattack!
The wine of battle mounts to the head!
These are our partisan forests—
The alleys of Dzika Street and Ostrowska.
Numbers of Blockhouses tear at our hearts,
Our medals of the Jewish war.
Like a battering ram the shout
Of six letters flashes in red: REVOLT.

. . . .

And plastered to the street
A trampled package bleeds:
"*Juno sind rund.*"

1943
Ringelblum Archive AŻIH RG 226/273, p. 2
Translated from the Polish by John and Bogdana Carpenter

“MAOR”

The Ghetto in Flames

On April 19, 1943, armed units entered the ghetto to begin its final liquidation. This was the signal for the uprising to begin. Most of the fighting took place in the central ghetto, which had been turned into an underground network of bunkers. In the northern ghetto, where the large German factories (called “shops”) were located, the hiding places were neither widespread nor particularly sophisticated, so that opportunities to go into hiding for a long period were far more limited. Most of the shop workers, moreover, were convinced that as “productive labor,” they would be spared. On April 21, Többens, the owner of the largest factory, issued the deportation order to the managers of the sixteen major shops. Three days later, Himmler ordered the entire ghetto burned to the ground, even if it meant destroying all the factories and machinery.

We had already been hiding for a week—in cellars, between walls, vanished so as never to be found. The German blockades had had only limited success. Of our group, the block of Hermann Brauer,[1] only thirty people had been flushed out of hiding, and the Nazis were having a hard time finding more, even though they searched our cellars and ransacked our dwellings every day. It was as if the earth had swallowed us up. The

1. Located at 30 Nalewki Street, the firm of Hermann Brauer employed six hundred Jewish workers.

forty-five hundred people who had occupied this area seemed to have disappeared by magic, without a trace. Still, we weren't allowed to breathe, unlike previous Aktions, when the nights had been ours and one could cautiously cross the area between one blockade and another. This time they had brought in a group of sharpshooters who were on the lookout night and day and opened fire at even the slightest rustling sound. They were terrified, because in the first days dozens of them had fallen in combat against our armed units.

Just the same, before daybreak a neighbor from another cellar managed to reach us by cautiously stealing through the intervening cellars and quietly uncovering our trapdoor. After asking if we had heard anything, he shared some news with us. He said that in the first days of the uprising about three hundred of the enemy fell.[2] We held good defense positions. They [the Germans] brought two tanks into the ghetto, and we succeeded in destroying one of them. We hung out a Polish flag, and the Germans were unable to shoot it down. Now things were quieter; they could find hardly any of our people, since most were so well hidden. It was impossible to tell how long things would go on this way, but if no one were found in the next few days, the Germans would have to either cut the operation short or bring in Aryan workers for the shops; then everyone would be forced to adapt to new circumstances. On this note, our conversation ended. Our comrade covered up the trapdoor again, pouring dirt over it and hiding it behind a pile of old things; then he discreetly made off.

How little we understood what the Germans were capable of! We simply could not imagine that all of this property, all the

2. These numbers are greatly exaggerated.

warehouses filled with merchandise, all the workshops, factories, and machines worth tens, worth hundreds of millions—that all this would be set on fire because of us, because of all of us who had burrowed underground or hidden between the walls and who possessed nothing more than our lives and our determination, the powerful determination not to give it up. No, we simply could not imagine it.

In our hideout, life went on as in the first days. We still had electricity, we had water in the water closet; we cooked dinner on the electric stove and lay on the plank beds reading pamphlets. The hideout was not large: three small rooms under the front of the house by the gate (8 Nalewki), two of which were taken up by iron cots, and the third containing a kitchen. There were twelve of us: three children, five women, and four men. We were comfortable, for the place had been intended for more people, but the others, fearing that its frontal location and proximity to the street made it unsafe, hid elsewhere; their crowded hideout was less comfortable but more secure.

We were already running low on air; the ventilation was sparse. We couldn't move around or talk to each other because the gate was so near; we had to suppress every cough, every loud noise.

The day passed into afternoon like all the previous days. Twice we heard the sounds of troops marching into and out of the ghetto. Apparently, they hadn't found any victims, because all we heard were the soldiers' retreating footsteps, and then it was quiet again. Around five in the evening we sensed a muffled movement and the frequent coming and going of trucks. Something was being loaded onto the trucks, something was happening, but what? It was possible that they were moving the firm out, but so many goods, workshops, and machines would take them weeks, perhaps months, so what was the meaning of all the shouting and hurry? By seven everything had become quiet once more. Even quieter than before, it seemed. Then, shortly after seven, I smelled fumes in the room. I became a little uneasy and started to look for their source. I found smoke seeping through a wall; perhaps someone in an adjoining cellar had made a fire and the smoke had gotten into ours. We had cement and sand, which we mixed with water and used to quickly seal the opening that had let in the suffocating smoke. When the job was done, we rested, relieved that we had had the cement and sand on hand. It never occurred to us that we were already caught in the fire, which was spreading rapidly around us.

It was eight o'clock. The noise of movement on the street had intensified, while the smoke in our rooms did not thin out at all; we would have to let in more air. There were little windows along the front wall, openings of ten to fifteen centimeters such as you find under every storefront, but they were masked and sealed so that only a couple of holes of not more than a centimeter each remained. Now we had to uncover these. I forced open a small window in the front room and saw a house burning on the other side of the street—from the ground to the roof, the whole house in flames. Suddenly the door to a second-story balcony burst open, and a man of about fifty ran out, his wild face and bulging eyes illuminated by the fire; he had just emerged from a hiding place in the house, crying, "Fire! Fire!" He threw his legs over the balcony and got ready to jump. A few shots cut short his attempt, and he fell motionless, like a block of wood. From nearby, the sound of laughter cut into the roar of the flames—the laughter of the guards who were there to ensure that the fire spread nicely, so that no living thing could escape.

A group of people, mostly women, ran out of another house. I heard their cries for help. They didn't know where to run. Their last cries were silenced by a burst of machine-gun fire.

I turned away from the little window and looked at those who were around me, thinking to myself that this could never happen to us; those were wildcat houses[3] over there, but we were, after all, part of the German Reich firm of Hermann Brauer, a former German spy in Poland, an army man and loyal follower of Hitler. They wouldn't set fire to this. It was their own property.

But things had changed in the territory of Hermann Brauer.

Three days before, Brauer had called in several of his managers, whomever he could reach since all were in hiding, and informed them that his firm would stay open and that in the coming days there would be a reregistration; those who presented themselves would immediately return to work. The first four to respond were given special numbers cut from big pieces of white linen, and with these they were able to move freely over the territory of the firm.

Over the next three days twenty-five managers donned the white numbers; Hermann Brauer pocketed 150,000 zlotys, and his assistant, the invalid Klaus, 50,000 zlotys.

Even after Brauer had learned that his firm would be burned down with all its stock, both living and dead, he said nothing to the managers, just had them carry out small details for his own benefit. At five o'clock in the afternoon of the last day, the SS came up to the office, called together the managers, and led them to the first courtyard. Taken unawares, the managers held their arms up and didn't dare move from their places.

3. Half of the sixty thousand Jews who remained in Warsaw after the Great Deportation were not registered shop workers. These illegals hid in houses abandoned by the deportees. See also Szlengel's "Things," in this volume

Soldiers faced them with rifles poised. They were searched and all their possessions confiscated, not only money, watches, and rings but also documents, every trifle, even scrawled-on scraps of paper. After this came an hour of torture, of punitive exercises. The SS were having a fine time. The German directors stood by the office window watching these SS, with whom they had just shared a drink to celebrate the ransom money they had collected from the managers (the drink serving to keep the SS in a festive and compliant mood). After the exercises the managers were forced to help load helmets, for in the past few hours the evacuation of equipment had begun; a few trucks had brought prisoners of war to the task, and the managers were forced with blows to assist them. However, the enormous warehouses filled with woolen sweaters and socks, the storerooms for leather goods, the paper mills, the huge reserves of field packs and other equipment—all these could not be cleared out so quickly. Only a few flatcars loaded with steel helmets were let out, followed by one other flatcar carrying the managers.

At a quarter to seven (the precise details and exact time were given to me later by one whose hiding place provided a view of the first courtyard) Brauer came down from his office, remained standing at the gate, took a last look around him, smoked a cigarette, and climbed into a car.

Five minutes after his departure German troops and sharpshooters entered and threw incendiary bombs into the firm's living quarters and cellars, onto the stairwells, and into the attics. Then they turned to other details.

And so the German Reich's firm of Hermann Brauer burned from the corner of Franciszkanska and Nalewki Streets to Muranowska Street.

The first to notice this from their hideouts in the houses ran at once to the courtyard. But most of those who had been in hiding didn't make it out, for the wooden stairwells were usually the first things to burn, and by the time the smoke and fire had driven everyone from the hideouts, the whole house would already be in flames and its occupants trapped.

The few who managed to get out alive went knocking on the entrances to bunkers where they knew people were hiding. That is how they remembered me. Around nine o'clock some friends missed me, and the cry went up to find M., to break open the shelter in which I was hiding and save me and my companions. A group entered the first courtyard with irons and crowbars and approached the bunker. But it was already impossible to go down. The corridor that led to our bunker was already in flames, and our hideout was very far away. With lowered heads they turned back. A pity about M. and those who were with him, but were their own lives safe yet? They still faced the enormous task of saving themselves.

In our shelter we still knew nothing. Around nine we sat down to our evening meal. How tragicomic was our situation! How like a scene from a Chaplin film! Our home had been set on fire, the neighboring bunkers were burning, the fire was getting closer and closer to us, the people on the outside who had come to save us couldn't get to us—and we, as though none of this concerned us at all, we sat down to eat.

Around ten I went to wash my hands and felt hot water coming from the faucet. A shudder passed through me; I turned hot and cold as the truth suddenly dawned on me: we were surrounded by fire.

Without a word I went to the opening, crawled out under the wall, and lifted the trapdoor. The small cellar through which one entered our hideout was extremely hot and brightly lit. A fire from an incendiary bomb had spread through the little window. Fortunately, a few days before, I had moved all the things in the cellar to the doorway, so nothing had caught fire by our hideout. I leaped into the corridor that led to the exit; this long corridor and all the cellars on both sides were completely engulfed by flames. I ran back to the shelter, where everyone was waiting for me by the entrance; they had seen me run out and knew that only a serious matter could have compelled me to uncover the trapdoor.

"Listen," I said to the frightened group around me. "If you keep calm, we'll all get out. Everything around us is burning. The corridor that leads out of here is in flames. After a week in this bunker our clothes are soaked through, so they won't catch so easily when we run through the fire, but you must all cover your heads with something damp because hair can ignite very quickly. The children will go first, then the women, and finally the men."

I got them into a line with myself leading the way and the children behind me. We ran through the fire. I couldn't breathe. I thought, "Just don't fall, just don't fall. If you fall, everyone dies in the fire." My face was burning; I pulled the damp rag over my eyes. We reached the exit stairwell and in a few bounds were standing in the open. I turned around and counted twelve heads; no one was missing.

But where were we? All around was the heat of the fire, which was climbing from the houses to the sky. Flames were shooting from the cellars to the high heavens.

I remembered the man on the balcony and his cry: "Fire! Fire!" It was deserted out here, not a living thing in sight. Only burning roofs caving into the courtyard from crumbling walls.

Where could we run? On the street—I knew already—men would be standing on corners with machine guns, waiting for those who had fled the fire. We had to shield our heads quickly, because bricks and burning debris were coming down, entire walls collapsing. We ran to another gate, knowing from previous bombardments that the ceilings of gateways are the strongest. But the wind carried sparks and smoke from every direction; we were suffocating and our eyes burning; we couldn't stay there. Where could we run for refuge?

Suddenly we noticed in the left corner of the last courtyard a black island removed from the fire, and people were moving inside it. We ran to it and found ourselves among friends; we embraced, we kissed. They told how they had tried to save us but couldn't get inside, how they had given us up for dead.

But there was no time for talk. The building, which had formerly housed the printing and editorial offices of *Moment*,[4] had to be saved. Its two stories had already been burned down once before, at the beginning of the war, but half of the building had been rebuilt; now we had to save this refuge from the fire in order to save ourselves. There was water in the cellar, so we formed two columns: one to pass the water in tin cans from the cellar to the roof and the other to pass the emptied tins back down to the cellar.

I was handed a pair of goggles and took my place on the roof. Facing me was my former home, where I had once had a bed and a pillow on which to lay my head and which was now bursting with flames that were swallowing everything inside. The two of us on the roof had to make sure that every spark that landed there was put out immediately, for the tarred surface was extremely flammable. Because the smoke was heavy, we had to relieve each other frequently.

We were surrounded by a sea of fire. The greatest film directors have not yet succeeded in capturing such a scene; it roared and crackled and shot flames; it deafened us so that we

4. A major Yiddish daily in prewar Poland.

couldn't hear a thing, not even the others shouting to us. We were working with our last measure of strength; we were fighting with superhuman endurance. And we were winning.

After laboring a whole night, we succeeded in saving the building. By morning the danger of being engulfed by the fire had passed.

We looked around us. Of the five hundred who had escaped to this place from neighboring houses, many had died in the fire, suffocated by smoke in the cellars. And we who survived—were we really saved? For the moment, we didn't think about this. Everyone was hard at work, removing flammable material from the house, especially from the paper storeroom. An entire warehouse full of paper had to be thrown into the courtyard and burned. We were all exhausted, our eyes smarting.

And then a bright, sunny day dawned and revealed to us the incinerated houses of the ghetto of the murdered city.

And let this remain for a memory.

Sunday, the twenty-fifth of April, 1943. In the evening, the Jewish ghetto in Warsaw was set on fire, and tens of thousands of men, women, and children perished in the flames; those who tried to escape the fire were shot on the streets, and those who miraculously did escape were hunted and tormented for weeks, for months, until they too were annihilated.

And when later, searching through one of the cellars full of suffocated people, I came upon children whose mouths gaped like black, scorched holes and women whose closed fists clutched hair torn from their heads, I wept and clenched my own fists and remembered the millions of clenched fists all over the world, raised against Hitlerism and fascism.

1943

Translated from the Yiddish by Robert Wolf

This document, no. 3177 in the Berman Collection, Beit Lohamei Hagettaot, Israel, is identified as the work of "Maor," a member of the Jewish Labor Bund, who apparently took this manuscript with him to the Aryan Side, where he passed it on to a Christian Polish family for safekeeping. It was not part of the Oyneg Shabes archive.

RACHEL AUERBACH

Yizkor, 1943

Until there came that Day of Curses—a day that was entirely night.

I saw a flood once in the mountains. Wooden huts, torn from their foundations, were carried above the raging waters. One could still see lighted lamps in them; and men, women and children were tied to the ceiling beams. Other huts were empty inside, but one could see a tangle of arms waving from the roof, like branches blowing in the wind waving desperately toward heaven, toward the river banks for help. At a distance, one could see mouths gaping, but one could not hear the cries because the roar of the waters drowned out everything. And that's how the Jewish masses flowed to their destruction at the time of the deportations. Sinking as helplessly into the deluge of destruction.

And if, for even one of the days of my life, I should forget how I saw you then, my people,[1] desperate and confused, delivered over to extinction, may all knowledge of me be forgotten and my name be cursed like that of those traitors who are unworthy to share your pain.[2]

Every instinct in the mass is revealed, entangled, exposed. All feelings churning, feverish to the core. Lashed by hundreds

1. Cf. Ps. 137, "By the Rivers of the Babylon."
2. A veiled reference to the Jewish Police.

of whips of unreasoning activity. Hundreds of deceptive or ridiculous schemes of rescue. And at the other pole, a yielding to the inevitable, a gravitation toward mass death that is no less substantial than the gravitation toward life. Sometimes the two antipodes followed each other in the same being.

Who can render the stages of the dying of a people? Only the shudder of pity for one's self and for others. And again illusion: waiting for the chance miracle. The insane smile of hope in the eyes of the incurable patient. Ghastly reflections of color on the yellowed face of one who is condemned to death.

Condemned to death. Who could—who wished to understand such a thing? And who could have expected such a decree against the mass? Against such low branches, such simple Jews. The lowly plants of the world. The sorts of people who would have lived out their lives without ever picking a quarrel with the righteous—or even the unrighteous—of this world.

How could such people have been prepared to die in a gas chamber? The sorts of people who were terrified of a dentist's chair, who turned pale at the pulling of a tooth.

And what of them . . . the little children?

The little ones, and those smaller still who not long ago were to be seen in the arms of their mothers, smiling at a bird or at a sunbeam. Prattling at strangers in the streetcar. Who still played "patty-cake" or cried "giddyup" waving their tiny hands in the air. Or called, "Papa." O, unrecognizable world in which these children and their mothers are gone. "Giddyup."

Even the sweetest ones: the two- and three-year-olds who seemed like newly hatched chicks tottering about on their weak legs. And even the slightly larger ones who could already talk. Who endlessly asked about the meanings of words. For whom whatever they learned was always brand new. Five-year-olds. And six-year-olds. And those who were older still—their eyes wide with curiosity about the whole world. And those older still whose eyes were already veiled by the mists of their approaching ripeness. Boys who, in their games, were readying themselves for achievements yet to come.

Girls who still nursed their dolls off in corners. Who wore ribbons in their hair; girls, like sparrows, leaping about in courtyards and on garden paths. And those who looked like buds more than half opened. The kind to whose cheeks the very first wind of summer seems to have given its first glowing caress. Girls of eleven, twelve, thirteen with the faces of angels. Playful as kittens. Smiling May blossoms. And those who have nearly bloomed: the fifteen- and sixteen-year-olds. The Sarahs, the Rebeccahs, the Leahs of the Bible, their names recast into Polish. Their eyes blue and gray and green under brows such as one sees on the frescoes unearthed in Babylon and Egypt. Slender young *frauleins* from the wells of Hebron. *Jungfraus* from Evangelia. Foreign concubines of Jewish patriarchs; desert maidens with flaring nostrils, their hair in ringlets, dark complected but turned pale by passion. Spanish daughters, friends of Hebrew poets of the Middle Ages. Dreamy flowers bent over mirroring pools. And opposite them? Delicate blondes in whom Hebrew passion is interwoven with Slavic cheerfulness. And the even-brighter flaxen-haired peasants, broad-hipped women, as simple as black bread, or as a shirt on the body of the folk.

It was an uncanny abundance of beauty of that generation growing up under the gray flag of ghetto poverty and mass hunger. Why was it that we were not struck by this as a portent of evil? Why was it that we did not understand that this blossoming implied its own end?

It was these, and such as these, who went into the abyss—our beautiful daughters. These were the ones who were plucked and torn to bits.

And where are the Jewish young men? Earnest and serious; passionate as high-bred horses, chomping at the bit, eager to race. The young workers, the *halutsim*, Jewish students avid for study, for sports, for politics. World improvers and flag bearers of every revolution. Youths whose passion made them ready to fill the prison cells of all the world. And many were tortured in camps even before the mass murder began. And where are the other youths, simpler than they—the earthen roots of a scattered people, the very essence of sobriety countering the decay of idealism at the trunk. Young men with ebullient spirits, their heads lowered like those of bulls against the decree spoken against our people.

And pious Jews in black gabardines, looking like priests in their medieval garb. Jews who were rabbis, teachers who wanted to transform our earthly life into a long study of Torah and prayer to God. They were the first to feel the scorn of the butcher. Their constant talk of martyrdom turned out not to be mere empty words.

And still other Jews. Broad shouldered, deep voiced, with powerful hands and hearts. Artisans, workers. Wagon drivers, porters. Jews who, with a blow of their fists, could floor any hooligan who dared enter into their neighborhoods.

Where were you when your wives and children, when your old fathers and mothers were taken away? What happened to make you run off like cattle stampeded by fire? Was there no one to give you some purpose in the confusion? You were swept away in the flood, together with those who were weak.

And you sly and cunning merchants, philanthropists in your short fur coats and caps. How was it that you didn't catch on to the murderous swindle? Fathers and mothers of families; you, in Warsaw. Stout women merchants with proud faces radiating intelligence above your three chins, standing in your shops behind counters heaped with mountains of goods.

And you other mothers. Overworked peddler women and market stall keepers. Disheveled and as anxious about your children as irritable setting hens when they flap their wings. And other fathers, already unhorsed, as it were. Selling sweets from their wobbling tables in the days of the ghetto.

What madness is it that drives one to list the various kinds of Jews who were destroyed?

Grandfathers and grandmothers with an abundance of grandchildren. With hands like withered leaves, their heads white. Who already trembled at the latter end of their days. They were not destined simply to decline wearily into their graves like rest-seeking souls, like the sun sinking wearily into the ocean's waves. No. It was decreed that before they died they would get to see the destruction of all that they had begotten, of all that they had built.

The decree against the children and the aged was more complete and more terrible than any.

Those who counted and those who counted for less. Those with aptitudes developed carefully over countless generations. Incomparable talents, richly endowed with wisdom and professional skill: doctors, professors, musicians, painters, architects. And Jewish craftsmen, tailors—famous and sought after; Jewish watchmakers in whom gentiles had confidence. Jewish cabinet-makers, printers, bakers. The great proletariat of Warsaw. Or shall I console myself with the fact that, for the most part, you managed to die of hunger and need in the ghetto before the expulsion?

Ah, the ways of Warsaw—the black soil of Jewish Warsaw.

My heart weeps even for the pettiest thief on Krochmalna Street, even for the worst of the knife wielders of narrow Miła, because even they were killed for being Jewish. Anointed and purified in the brotherhood of death.

Ah, where are you, petty thieves of Warsaw, you illegal street vendors[3] and sellers of rotten apples? And you, the more harmful folk—members of great gangs who held their own courts, who supported their own synagogues in the Days of Awe, who conducted festive funerals, and who gave alms like the most prosperous burghers.

Ah, the mad folk of the Jewish street! Disordered soothsayers in a time of war.

Ah, bagel sellers on winter evenings.

Ah, poverty-stricken children of the ghetto. Ghetto peddlers, ghetto smugglers supporting their families, loyal and courageous to the end. Ah, the poor barefoot boys moving through the autumn mire with their boxes of cigarettes: "Cigarettes! Cigarettes! Matches! Matches!" The voice of the tiny cigarette seller crying his wares on the corner of Leszno and Karmelicka Streets still rings in my ears.

Where are you, my boy? What have they done to you? Reels from the unfinished and still-unplayed preexpulsion film *The Singing Ghetto* wind and rewind in my memory.[4] Even the dead sang in that film. They drummed with their swollen feet as they begged: "Money, ah money, Money is the best thing there is."

There was no power on earth, no calamity that could interfere with their quarrelsome presence in that Jewish street. Until there came that Day of Curses[5]—a day that was entirely night.

3. Called *khesedlekh* in Warsaw slang.
4. A Nazi propaganda film made in the ghetto in May 1942.
5. A reference to Deut. 28:15–69.

Hitler finally achieved his greatest ambition of the war. And finally, his dreadful enemy was defeated and fell: that little boy on the comer of Leszno and Karmelicka Streets, of Smocza and Nowolipie, of Dzika Street. The weapons of the women peddlers reached to every market square.

What luxury! They stopped tearing at their own throats from morning until night. They stopped snatching the morsels of clay-colored, clay-adulterated bread from each other.

The first to be rounded up were the beggars. All the unemployed and the homeless were gathered up off the streets. They were loaded into wagons on the first morning of the Deportation and driven through the town. They cried bitterly and stretched their hands out or wrung them in despair or covered their faces. The youngest of them cried, "Mother, mother." And indeed, there were women to be seen running along both sides of the wagons, their head shawls slipping from their heads as they stretched their hands out toward their children, those young smugglers who had been rounded up along the walls. In other of the wagons, the captives looked like people condemned to death who, in the old copperplate engravings, are shown being driven to the scaffold in tumbrils.

The outcries died down in the town, and there was silence. Later on, there were no cries heard. Except when women were caught and loaded onto the wagons and one could hear an occasional indrawn hiss, such as fowl make as they are carried to the slaughter.

Men, for the most part, were silent. Even the children were so petrified that they seldom cried.

The beggars were rounded up, and there was no further singing in the ghetto. I heard singing only once more after the deportations began. A monotonous melody from the steppes sung by a thirteen-year-old beggar girl. Over a period of two weeks she used to creep out of her hiding place in the evening, when the day's roundups were over. Each day, looking thinner and paler and with an increasingly brighter aureole of grief about her head, she took her place at her usual spot behind a house on Leszno Street and began the warbling by whose means she earned her bit of bread. . . .

Enough, enough . . . I have to stop writing.

No. No. I can't stop. I remember another girl of fourteen. My own brother's orphan daughter in Lemberg whom I carried about in my arms as if she were my own child. Lussye! And another Lussye, older than she, one of my cousins who was studying in Lemberg and who was like a sister to me. And Lonye, my brother's widow, the mother of the first Lussye, and Mundek, an older child of hers whom I thought of as my own son from the time that he was orphaned. And another girl in the family, a pianist of thirteen, my talented little cousin Yossima.

And all of my mother's relatives in their distant village in Podolia: Auntie Beyle, Auntie Tsirl, Uncle Yassye, Auntie Dortsye, my childhood's ideal of beauty.

I have so many names to recall, how can I leave any of them out, since nearly all of them went off to Bełżec and Treblinka or were killed on the spot in Lanowce and Ozieran in Czortkow and in Mielnica. In Krzywicze and elsewhere.

Absurd! I will utter no more names. They are all mine, all related. All who were killed. Who are no more. Those whom I knew and loved press on my memory, which I compare now to a cemetery. The only cemetery in which there are still indications that they once lived in this world.

I feel—and I know—that they want it that way. Each day I recall another one of those who are gone.

And when I come to the end of the list, segment by segment added to the segments of my present life in the town,[6] I start over again from the beginning, and always in pain. Each of them hurts me individually, the way one feels pain when parts of the body have been surgically removed. When the nerves surviving in the nervous system signal the presence of every finger on amputated hands or feet.

Not long ago, I saw a woman in the streetcar, her head thrown back, talking to herself. I thought that she was either drunk or out of her mind. It turned out that she was a mother who had just received the news that her son, who had been rounded up in the street, had been shot.

"My child," she stammered, paying no attention to the other people in the streetcar, "my son. My beautiful, beloved son."

I too would like to talk to myself like one mad or drunk, the way that woman did in the book of Judges[7] who poured out her heart unto the Lord and whom Eli drove from the Temple.

I may neither groan nor weep. I may not draw attention to myself in the street. And I need to groan; I need to weep. Not four times a year. I feel the need to say Yizkor four times a day.

Yizkor elohim es nishmas avi mori ve'imi morasi[8] . . . Remember, Oh Lord, the souls of those who passed from this world horribly, dying strange deaths before their time.

6. I.e., on the so-called Aryan Side of Warsaw.

7. A reference to Hannah's prayer in 1 Sam. 1, not in Judges.

8. "May God remember the soul of my father-and-teacher and of my mother-and-teacher . . ."

And now, suddenly I seem to see myself as a child standing on a bench behind my mother who, along with my grandmother and my aunts, is praying before the east wall of the woman's section of the synagogue in Lanowce. I stand on tiptoe peering down through panes of glass at the congregation in the synagogue that my grandfather built. And just then the Torah reader, Hersh's son, Meyer-Itsik, strikes the podium three times and cries out with a mighty voice so that he will be heard by men and women on both sides of the partition and by the community's orphans, boys and girls, who are already standing, waiting for just this announcement: "We recite Yizkor."

The solemn moment has arrived when we remember those who are no longer with us. Even those who have finished their prayers come in at this time to be with everyone else as they wait for the words, "We recite Yizkor."

And he who has survived and lives and who approaches this place, let him bow his head and, with anguished heart, let him hear those words and remember his names as I have remembered mine—the names of those who were destroyed.

At the end of the prayer in which everyone inserts the names of members of his family there is a passage recited for those who have no one to remember them and who, at various times, have died violent deaths because they were Jews. And it is people like those who are now in the majority.

Aryan Side of Warsaw
August–November 1943
Translated from the Yiddish by Leonard Wolf

RACHEL AUERBACH, Yiddish essayist and historian, was born in Lanowce, Galicia, in 1899. After receiving her secondary and university training in Lemberg-Lwów, in 1933 she moved to Warsaw, where she briefly attended the University of Warsaw and was active in Zionist and modernist literary circles. During the war she ran the soup kitchen at 40 Leszno Street, worked closely with Ringelblum, and wrote prolifically while in hiding on the Aryan Side of Warsaw. In 1950 she settled in Israel, where she died in 1976. The Holocaust dominated her postwar writings and activities, the highlights of which were her memoirs of Jewish cultural life in the ghetto; her role in establishing Yad Vashem, where she organized the collection of Holocaust testimonies; her role in planning the Eichmann trial, and her public dispute with Jean-François Steiner in 1967 over his fictional account of the uprising in Treblinka.

Sources and Acknowledgments

Rachel Auerbach, "Yizkor, 1943," trans. Leonard Wolf, from *The Literature of Destruction: Jewish Responses to Catastrophe*, ed. David G. Roskies (Philadelphia: Jewish Publication Society, 1989), pp. 460–64. Copyright 1989 by the Jewish Publication Society, Philadelphia. Published in Yiddish in *Di goldene keyt* 46 (1963): 29–35. Reprinted by permission of the University of Nebraska Press and Yad Vashem. This is translated from a Yiddish translation and revision that Auerbach probably did in 1963 for the twentieth anniversary of the Great Deportation, at the request of Abraham Sutzkever, the editor of *Di goldene keyt*. For the Polish original and its text history, see Rachela Auerbach, *Pisma z Getta Warszawskiego*, ed. Karolina Szymaniak (Warsaw: Jewish Historical Society, 2015), pp. 45–47, 242–57.

Leyb Goldin, "Chronicle of a Single Day," trans. Elinor Robinson, from *The Literature of Destruction: Jewish Responses to Catastrophe*, ed. David G. Roskies (Philadelphia: Jewish Publication Society, 1989), pp. 424–34. Copyright 1989 by the Jewish Publication Society, Philadelphia. Published in Yiddish in *Tsvishn lebn un toyt*, ed. Ber Mark (Warsaw: Yidish-bukh, 1955), pp. 49–65. Reprinted by permission of the University of Nebraska Press.

Stefania Grodzieńska, "Hershek," from *City of the Damned: Two Years in the Warsaw Ghetto*, by Jerzy Jurandot, ed. Dominika Gajewska, trans. Jolanta Scicińska (Warsaw: Museum of the History of the Polish Jews, 2015), pp. 204–5. © 2015. Used with permission of Agnieszka Arnold and Jolanta Scicińska.

Shimon Huberband, "Ghetto Folklore," from *Kiddush Hashem: Jewish Religious and Cultural Life in Poland during the Holocaust*, trans. David E. Fishman, ed. Jeffrey S. Gurock and Robert S. Hirt (Hoboken, NJ, and New York: KTAV and Yeshiva University Press, 1987), pp. 113–29. Used with permission of KTAV Publishing House.

Chaim A. Kaplan, "Pages from the Diary," from *Scroll of Agony*, trans. Jeffrey M. Green, from *The Literature of Destruction: Jewish Responses to Catastrophe*, ed. David G. Roskies (Philadelphia: Jewish Publication Society, 1989), pp. 435–49. Copyright 1989 by the Jewish Publication Society, Philadelphia. Published in Hebrew in *Moreshet* 2 (December 1964): 8–22. Reprinted by permission of the University of Nebraska Press.

Yitzhak Katzenelson, "Song of Hunger," trans. David G. Roskies, "Songs of the Cold," trans. Elinor Robinson, from *The Literature of Destruction: Jewish Responses to Catastrophe*, ed. David G. Roskies (Philadelphia: Jewish Publication Society, 1989), pp. 473–74. Copyright 1989 by the Jewish Publication Society, Philadelphia. Published in Yiddish in Yitzhak Katzenelson, *Yidishe geto-ksovim: Varshe 1940–1943*, ed. Yechiel Szeintuch (Tel Aviv: Ghetto Fighters' House and Hakibbutz Hameuchad, 1984), pp. 493, 620–21. Reprinted by permission of the University of Nebraska Press.

Josef Kirman, "I Speak to You Openly, Child," trans. Jacob Sonntag, *Jewish Quarterly* 7, no. 3 (1960): 17–18. Copyright © Jewish Quarterly. Reprinted by permission of the translator's estate and Taylor & Francis Ltd., www.tandfonline.com, on behalf of *Jewish Quarterly*.

Henryka Lazertowna, "The Little Smuggler," trans. Ted Hudes, from *A Holocaust Reader*, ed. Lucy Dawidowicz (New York: Behrman House, 1976), pp. 207–8. Copyright © Behrman House, Inc., included with permission. www.behrmanhouse.com.

Abraham Lewin, from *A Cup of Tears: A Diary of the Warsaw Ghetto*, ed. Antony Polonsky, trans. Christopher Hutton (New York: Basil Blackwell; Oxford, UK: Institute for Polish-Jewish Studies, 1988), pp. 106–8, 170–71, 176–79. Copyright 1988. Republished with permission of John Wiley and Sons, Inc.; permission conveyed through Copyright Clearance Center, Inc.

Israel Lichtenstein, "Last Testament," trans. Lucy S. Dawidowicz, from *A Holocaust Reader*, ed. Lucy S. Dawidowicz (New York: Behrman House, 1976), pp. 296–97. Copyright © Behrman House, Inc., included with permission. www.behrmanhouse.com.

"Maor," "The Ghetto in Flames," trans. Robert Wolf, from *The Literature of Destruction: Jewish Responses to Catastrophe*, ed. David G. Roskies (Philadelphia: Jewish Publication Society, 1989), pp. 455–59. Copyright 1989 by the Jewish Publication Society, Philadelphia. Published in Yiddish in *Di goldene keyt* 15 (1953): 10–15. Reprinted by permission of the University of Nebraska Press.

Peretz Opoczynski, "House No. 21," trans. Robert Wolf, from *The Literature of Destruction: Jewish Responses to Catastrophe*, ed. David G. Roskies (Philadelphia: Jewish Publication Society, 1989), pp. 408–24. Copyright 1989 by the Jewish Publication Society, Philadelphia. Published in an original Yiddish typescript housed in Beit Lohamei Hagettaot (Ghetto Fighters' House), Israel. The annotations are based on Peretz Opoczynski, *Reshimot*, ed. Zvi Shner and translated into Hebrew by Avraham Yeivin (Tel Aviv: Ghetto Fighters' House and Hakibbutz Hameuchad, 1970). An abridged and censored version of the Yiddish original appears in Peretz Opoczynski, *Reportazhn fun varshever geto*, ed. Ber Mark (Warsaw: Yidish bukh, 1954), pp. 9–48. Reprinted by permission of the University of Nebraska Press.

Yeshoshue Perle, "4580," trans. Elinor Robinson, from *The Literature of Destruction: Jewish Responses to Catastrophe*, ed. David G. Roskies (Philadelphia: Jewish Publication Society, 1989), pp. 450–54. Copyright 1989 by the Jewish Publication Society, Philadelphia. Published in Yiddish in *Tsvishn lebn un toyt*, ed. Ber Mark (Warsaw: Yidish-bukh, 1955), pp. 142–49. Reprinted by permission of the University of Nebraska Press.

Emanuel Ringelblum, "Oyneg Shabes," trans. Elinor Robinson, from *The Literature of Destruction: Jewish Responses to Catastrophe*, ed. David G. Roskies (Philadelphia: Jewish Publication Society, 1989), pp. 386–98. Copyright 1989 by the Jewish Publication Society, Philadelphia. Published in Yiddish in *Ksovim fun geto*, vol. 2, *Notitsn un ophandlungen (1942–1943)*, 2nd ed. (Tel Aviv: I. L. Peretz, 1985), pp. 76–102, abridged. Reprinted by permission of the University of Nebraska Press.

Gela Seksztajn, "What Can I Possibly Say and Ask For at This Moment?," from *To Live with Honor and Die with Honor: Selected Documents from the Warsaw Ghetto Underground Archives "O.S." (Oneg Shabbath)*, ed. Joseph Kermish (Jerusalem: Yad Vashem, 1986), pp. 672–73. Used with permission of the publisher.

Kalonymus Kalman Shapira, "The Holy Fire," from *The Holy Fire: The Teachings of Rabbi Kalonymus Kalman Shapira, the Rebbe of the Warsaw Ghetto*, ed. and trans. Nehemia Polen (Northvale, NJ: Jason Aronson, 1994), pp. 116–20. Used with permission of the publisher.

Władysław Szlengel, "Telephone," "Things," and "Counterattack," trans. John and Bogdana Carpenter, *Chicago Review* 52, no. 2/4 (2006): 282–91. Used with permission of the publisher and the translators.